# GODDESSES OF SELF-CARE

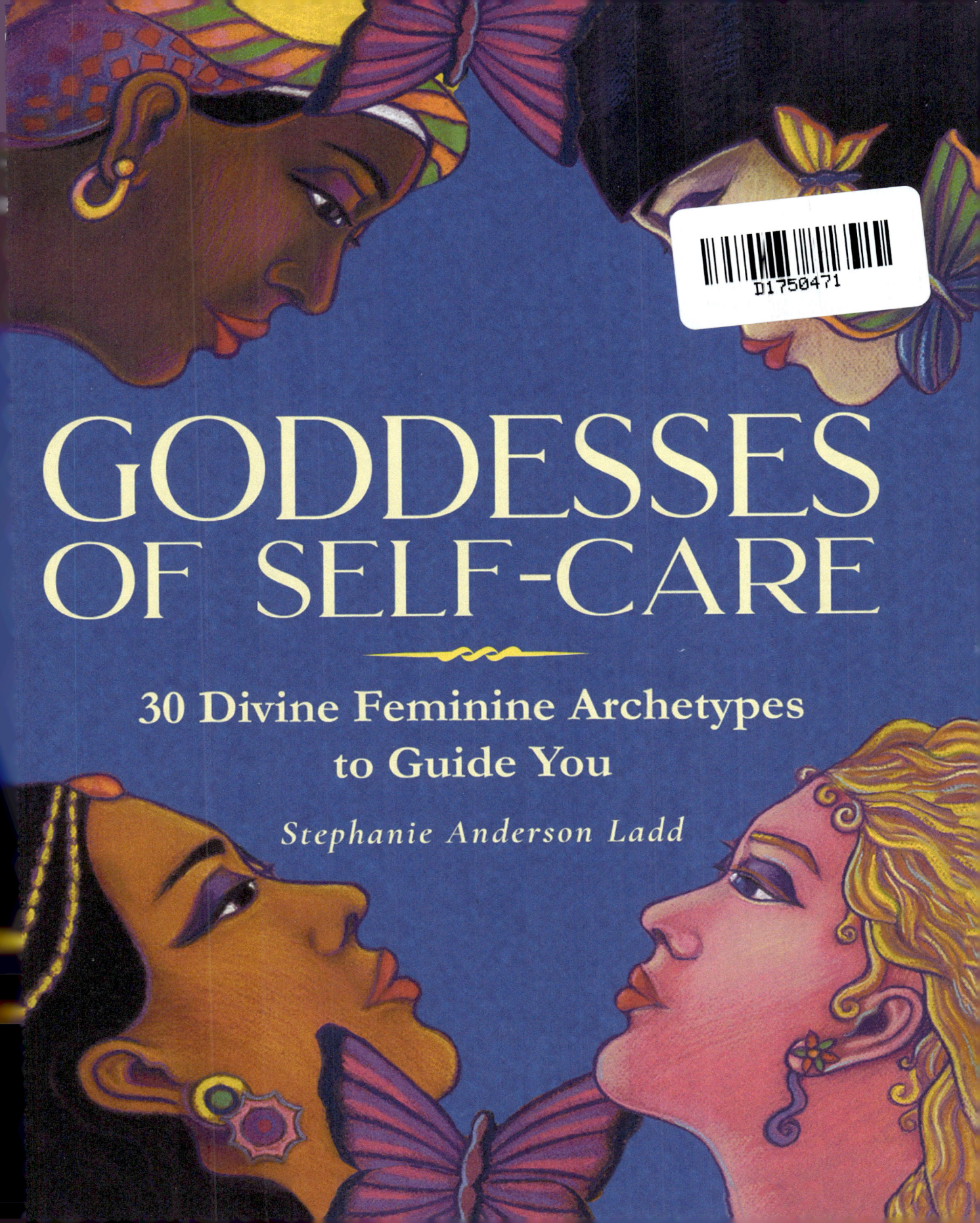

30 Divine Feminine Archetypes to Guide You

Stephanie Anderson Ladd

© 2022 Stephanie Anderson Ladd

All rights reserved. No part of this book may be reproduced in any form without permission in writing from the author.

Printed in the USA

11 10 9 8 7 6 5 4 3 2

ISBN: 978-1-955346-18-4

Cover and Layout Design by Heather Dakota
Cover Illustration © Tracy Turner

© 2022 Stephanie Anderson Ladd Images pages 10, 15, 28, 33, 38, 46, 50, 58, 64, 68, 75, 85, 90, 93, 94, 102, 110, 122, 132, 135, 154, 158, 172, 175, 192, 195, 204, 212, 219, 220, 225, 226, 230, 239, 243, 256, 258, 265, 267, 280

P12 ©Whpics | Dreamstime.com; P17 ©Walter Crane; P21©Liudmila Horvath | Dreamstime.com; P30 Janus/Jana Sculpture © MACM Musée d'Art Classique de Mougins, France; P30 peacock feather ©missisya - stock.adobe.com; P31 ©Edward Burne-Jones rawpixel; P35 ©volkovslava - stock.adobe.com; P54 ©jozefklopacka - stock.adobe.com; P60 ©Elihu Vedder Shutterstock; P66 ©R2d2v1 | Dreamstime.com; P70 ©mens_divinior - stock.adobe.com; P72 ©Saydung89; P77 ©Helen O'Sullivan; P78 ©Shamanska Kate - stock.adobe.com; P79 ©Erika Kavali | Dreamstime.com; P82 ©o-che istockphoto; P83 © Humberto Arellano | unsplash.com; P97 ©Jules LeFebvre; P101 Frederic Leighton; P104 Evelyn de Morgan; P106 William Blake; P107 ©Kate Shamanska - stock.adobe.com; P113 ©gors4730 - stock.adobe.com; P114 R.F. Jehanne; P118 ©agsandrew - stock.adobe.com; P119 Gustav Klimt; P123 ©Olga Che - stock.adobe.com; P125 ©got - stock.adobe.com; P136 Herbert James Draper; P139 ©Annette Schindler - stock.adobe.com; P140 Dante Gabriel Rossetti; P143 Arthur Rackham; P144 ©James Doyle Penrose Picryl; P146 Ludwig-Pietsch; P161©Joshua Laxson | Dreamstime.com; P164 ©Neil Harrison | Dreamstime.com; P166 ©panaceaart - stock.adobe.com; P169 ©sarymsakov.com - stock.adobe.com; P177 ©djahan - stock.adobe.com; P181 ©Malgorzata Kistryn | Dreamstime.com; P182 John Syam Liston Shaw; P187 Anton Raphael Mengs; P189 Piero della Francesca; P201 ©Benjavisa Ruangvaree | Dreamstime.com; P207 ©Varvara - stock.adobe.com; P208 ©Zzvet | Dreamstime.com; P210 ©Juliengrondin | Dreamstime.com; P215 ©Julia – stock.adobe.com; P216 ©Jarvis Cook, sculptor; courtesy of Ann Barron; P217 © Jasenka Arbanas | Dreamstime.com; P218 ©Elegant Solution – stock.adobe.com; P223 Paul Gauguin; P232 Mary Cassatt; P234 ©Agsandrew | Dreamstime.com; P240 Leonardo da Vinci; P246 ©carlos 401- shutterstock.com; P247 ©bernardojbp - stock.adobe.com; P250 ©mpols istockphoto.com; P252 ©iphotothailand – stock.adobe.com; P261©Matias Del Carmine | Dreamstime.com; P262 Giorgione; P269 ©Shiloh Sophia McCloud; P270 ©savcoco - stock.adobe.com; P273 Edward Burne-Jones; P275 ©Shiloh Sophia McCloud

Learn more at www.stephanieandersonladd.com

*This book is dedicated to Chloe Anderson Ladd,
the goddess I gave birth to.*

# GODDESSES
## OF SELF-CARE

Stephanie Anderson Ladd

# Table of Contents

**Introduction** ............................................................................................................... **8**

**Chapter One: New Year, New Beginnings** ........................................................... **28**
Jana .................................................................................................................................. 30
Usha ................................................................................................................................. 38

**Chapter Two: Dreaming and Planning** ................................................................ **46**
Bear Woman ................................................................................................................... 49
Athena ............................................................................................................................. 58

**Chapter Three: Creativity and Play** ....................................................................... **64**
Brigid ............................................................................................................................... 68
Bast .................................................................................................................................. 78
Grandmother Spider ..................................................................................................... 84

**Chapter Four: Depression and Grief** .................................................................... **90**
Inanna .............................................................................................................................. 93
The Triple Goddess of Persephone, Demeter, and Hecate .................................... 100

**Chapter Five: Healthy Relationships** ................................................................... **110**
Hera ................................................................................................................................ 113
Isis ................................................................................................................................... 122

**Chapter Six: Body and Sexuality** .......................................................................... **132**
Aphrodite (Venus) ....................................................................................................... 136
Freya and Frigga .......................................................................................................... 143

**Chapter Seven: Hurt and Anger** ...................................................................................**154**
Kali ...........................................................................................................157
Sekhmet ...................................................................................................161
Black Madonna .......................................................................................167

**Chapter Eight: Abundance and Work/Life Purpose** ...............................**172**
Lakshmi ...................................................................................................174
Artemis ....................................................................................................182

**Chapter Nine: Health and Healing** ..........................................................**192**
Akhilandeshwari .....................................................................................195
Tara ..........................................................................................................204

**Chapter Ten: Anxiety and Fear** ................................................................**212**
Butterfly Maiden .....................................................................................216
Yemaya ....................................................................................................220

**Chapter Eleven: Reparenting: Learning to Mother Yourself** ................**230**
The Virgin Mary .....................................................................................240
Our Lady of Guadalupe .........................................................................246
Kwan Yin .................................................................................................250

**Chapter Twelve: Resting and Being Present** ...........................................**256**
Hestia ......................................................................................................259
Sophia .....................................................................................................266

**Resources** .....................................................................................................**278**
**Acknowledgments** ......................................................................................**279**
**About the Author** .......................................................................................**280**

# INTRODUCTION

YOU HAVE NO DOUBT heard the term *self-care*. It is bandied about quite a bit these days. It is often used in superficial contexts to mean giving yourself the gift of a massage or mani-pedi. It is a popular catch-phrase in many women's magazines and blogs, but what does it actually mean? How do you practice it? As a psychotherapist, I work primarily with women on their particular journey through life, and so I am concerned with helping women answer the questions...

*Who am I on a deeper level than the persona I present to the world?*

*What do I truly need and want, and how do I get it?*

*How do I take care of myself?*

*Who am I on a soul level?*

In a deeper sense, self-care means *soul-care*. It is about knowing who you are and making deliberate choices for yourself, whether taking time to journal or cook a good meal, or pausing from your busy schedule to just breathe and contemplate what you really want and need in the moment. If you are someone who struggles with anxiety and worry, it may be learning to self-soothe and replace fearful thoughts with calming

*Note: While I use the word woman/women and she/her pronouns throughout the book, the concepts and methods presented are meant to be inclusive of genderqueer, transgender, and nonconforming individuals, as well as men who want to explore their inner feminine or better understand divine feminine archetypes from a psychospiritual perspective.*

thoughts. It may mean allowing yourself to feel sad or grieve so that you can find the source of it and work through to the other side. Self-care takes myriad forms depending upon what current struggles you are dealing with or which desires you wish to fulfill. This book is designed with these challenges in mind: anxiety, depression, grief, fear, anger, as well as creativity, play, health, rest, reparenting the inner child, being present, sexuality, body image, and healthy relationships.

Practicing self-care may seem unfeasible, if not impossible, with so much pulling at you from *out there*. How do you care for yourself and your soul in a world where consumerism is rampant? Where the noise of politics and extremism is loud and overwhelming? Where systemic racism requires a long-overdue reckoning, individually and collectively? Where making a living wage is increasingly challenging? Where political division creates upheaval on so many levels? Where celebrity is valued over character? Where social media and technology encourage dependence, false comparisons, and a non-stop state of distraction? Where women are still marginalized, objectified, oppressed, and silenced in a patriarchal society?

It is easy to get caught in the trap of comparing yourself with others, trying to live up to impossible standards of *the perfect woman*, never feeling you are enough. How do you find your way in this chaotic world—how do you go from living with constant external pressure to perform and conform to living with care for yourself and your soul?

Women know how to care for others. Women are taught to be caregivers from the moment they come out of the womb. "It's a girl!" can translate to "She will take care of me" or she will take care of someone. And there is nothing wrong with caring. Being a woman who cares about others—man, woman, child, animal—is a good thing, but what often goes missing from that equation is *Woman caring for herself*. Who is going to teach women to do that?

Not necessarily our mothers, many of whom were squeezed into the old-fashioned box labeled "what it means to be female": mother to all, self-sacrificing, people-pleasing, "good girl" or good daughter/wife/mother/employee, who typically puts everyone else's needs ahead of her own as she waits for approval. Only in this way is she seen and valued by a society that has long looked to women to be the caregivers of the world. But the truth is you can only effectively care for others to the degree that you care for yourself.

Unfortunately, women have been told it is not okay to care for themselves, that it is *selfish*. A woman is not being a "good girl" if she does not put others' needs first—the implication being that it is *unwomanly to take care of herself*. But you can change that message for yourself, and by extension, for other women by practicing self-care, by thinking about your needs and acting on them, by putting your needs first instead of last, and modeling what it means to be true to yourself. That does not mean you stop caring about others; it just means you start caring about yourself. As they say on every flight, "Put your oxygen mask on first before helping others."

Too often women have come to believe it is only good to give, not receive. As a psychotherapist, one of the things I urge women to get used to and do more is ask for what they need and want—whether from a significant other, family member, friend, or co-worker—and most women find this hard to do. Why? Because it requires vulnerability. To do so might lead to rejection. You might not get what you ask for. And that is possible, but you are much less likely to get what you need and want if you don't even ask. And when you don't get what you need and want from others, you have to learn to give it to yourself.

So who can help women with this self-care mission? As I have learned from healing my own *mother wound*—meaning an emotional injury that comes from a mother not being attuned and available to her child—you can heal yourself and learn to love and care for yourself by identifying and working with *The Goddess*, an archetype of the Divine Feminine. The Divine Feminine refers to the feminine godhead as opposed to the traditional idea of god being male or a father. Original religious conceptions saw God as genderless and containing both masculine and feminine or father and mother. But the patriarchal religions cut out the feminine and the mother god, leaving us with a lopsided and incomplete sense of what is sacred and godlike.

Forming a relationship with the Divine Feminine means getting in touch with your own divinity or Goddess Within. Getting to know the archetypes of the *Great Mother* or *Great Goddess*, which represent the feminine power of creation, destruction, and regeneration as well as the nurturing, loving qualities associated with the mother—helps you develop your own Inner Mother or Goddess Within. By aligning or identifying with a particular goddess and the qualities she imbues, you learn to embrace these same qualities for yourself. In doing so, you learn to care for yourself in a way that is unique to you and your needs.

The word *Goddess* may be unfamiliar to you or perhaps one that you recoil from or do not understand. This is likely because you, like most people, have grown up only exposed to the patriarchal religious teachings of Christianity, Judaism, or Islam, which venerate one male God the Father, and in the case of Christianity, the son of God. Even if you don't have a religious affiliation or don't consider yourself a religious person, Western society and its structures are saturated with Judeo-Christian philosophy, ideology, and iconography.

These religious traditions don't recognize a female godhead or Goddess, a counterpart to the male deity, or a feminine manifestation of God, although she is often there, just beneath the surface. And she was there before these religions became dominant some 2,000 years ago. Many who understand God to be a genderless construct, still think of *him* and see *him* as a father rather than as a divine father and mother. However, just as we humans contain both masculine and feminine energies regardless of gender, so does the godhead. *She* is there and has been since time immemorial. When you research religious history, you find that in the beginning, for many thousands of years before religions were organized around God as a man, God was a woman or an androgynous deity.

The Western religions were largely formed and codified for the sake of power, empire, and control. Sacred texts were written by men and reflected the male-dominated societies of the first centuries AD. Before the patriarchal religions took hold, the sacred feminine was highly-valued and venerated—the Mother was seen as the life-giving creative force, for it was through her body that life was born. Early people equated women with the round, fertile Earth, the wise Mother upon which we lived and found sustenance. But over time, warrior invaders supplanted the peaceful hunter-gatherers who paid homage to the earthy feminine, and the patriarchal power structure of male supremacy and control became the standard.

Icons and concepts of masculine power, dominance, and might replaced the feminine images of love, life, and interconnectedness. The dualistic functions of the psyche—feminine and masculine—began to grow in increasing opposition, both internally and externally, leading to a patriarchal power structure that put women in their place—beneath men.

The new story Western religions promulgated was of *Him*—an all powerful Father God and, in Christianity, his son, the Christ. This creation story ghosted The Mother, the feminine, regarded by some as the Holy Ghost in the trinity (see the goddess, Sophia, in CH. 12, page 266). The idea that the Holy Spirit is the feminine part of the godhead has been lost to modern patriarchal Christianity. Never mind that it would follow logically that this third aspect is meant to be a *Her*—thus making the father, mother, and divine child a sacred whole. That was the belief of the early Gnostic Christians as revealed in the hidden Gnostic gospels discovered in Egypt in 1945 as part of the Nag Hammadi cache. A number of literary scholars suggest that this lost feminine is, in fact, the Holy Grail. Thus the search for the symbolic chalice—the feminine vessel—in myth and story reminds us of what has gone sorely missing for centuries, since the advent of patriarchal religions.

In this book, I invite you to reclaim the sacred feminine that lives deep in your bones, in your DNA, in the earth itself. Here you will find spiritual concepts of divine feminine wisdom blended with psychological constructs to provide practical and inventive means for growth and healing—all swirling together in a creative cauldron of possibilities. The purpose of this book is to provide a self-help, self-care manual to show you how to tap into your own divinity— your own internal *Goddess Self* as a way to love and care for yourself unconditionally.

It is important to note that this book is not intended to provide *spiritual bypass*, a term that means using spiritual ideas and practices to avoid the very real work of self-inquiry, individuation, and psychological self-development. Spiritual bypass is often about using a "positive thinking" override. It precludes the hard work of first acknowledging and then transforming old habits and patterns—learned behaviors from dysfunctional family systems or just not being taught self-care skills! Spiritual bypass may involve denial of feelings, avoidance of your *shadow* (discussed below), or refusing to love and take care of yourself because you think the needs of others always matter more.

My goal with *Goddesses of Self-Care* is to provide a practical and helpful way of understanding yourself through the lens of the sacred feminine and goddess archetypes. These figures hold both positive and negative attributes, just as we all do. You have to be willing to see into the darkness of your own psyche as well as work towards a greater lightness of being. This requires you to see your imperfect self with love and compassion, as one who has the ability to transform, and ultimately to achieve individuation.

As a psychotherapist, teacher, artist, feminist, and archetypal explorer, I bring my experience with these various modalities to this work. I borrow from cognitive-behavioral as well as transpersonal psychology, specifically aligning with a Jungian perspective. This includes an appreciation of inner feminine and masculine energies, the shadow, as well as ways of exploring myth and story using active imagination to bring about transformation and integration.

Learning about historic characters such as goddesses helps you understand and see your own story in a mythic context. These stories were originally told to give people an understanding of the human psyche and the world. Myths are rife with psychological meaning, metaphor, and symbolism. My intention is to approach the subjects of this book from both a psychological and spiritual perspective. These concepts are discussed in more detail below.

## What is the Self?

It is helpful to consider the idea of the Self as multi-dimensional. The **Personal Self** contains your functioning ego where you experience life in relationship to the world and others in it. It is the control center, the part that gets things done. You also have a **Higher Self**, which comprises your Wise Mind or God/dess Self that has the gift of overview and knows what is best for you, as well as a **Lower Self**, which contains your sub-personalities and shadow.

The sub-personalities can be seen as the many parts that make up your being, such as The Artist Self, The Cook, The Student, The Hurt Child, The Wise Woman—parts of your psyche that can be a help or a hindrance. They reflect a part of who you are, but not all of who you are. This includes your shadow parts such as The Inner Critic, The Saboteur, The Perfectionist, The Jealous One, or any others that you might identify as unhelpful or distorted human qualities. These facets of your shadow, which make themselves known at various times, reside in the Unconscious. Once brought to consciousness, the task is to reconcile and integrate them. These parts all work together to form the **Whole Self** that is constantly in development, learning, and evolving.

It is also useful to consider the self as containing both feminine and masculine energies that combine to make you whole. Remember that these internal feminine and masculine constructs are not meant to be specific to sex or gender identity, as all genders can be said to have an Inner Feminine or *anima* and an Inner Masculine or *animus*. This is a Jungian concept that helps you see beyond the duality of male and female gender and to think of yourself as more internally androgynous, with both energies at play.

Masculine energy is described as left-brained, characterized by logic, action, and manifestation; feminine energy is right-brained, comprising emotion, intuition, and inspiration. Head and heart; activity and receptivity; yin and yang. One is not better than the other. You need both working together to live in balance and function at your highest potential. You could say you need a harmonious wedding of these two parts—an *Inner Marriage* of equals—to live a fulfilling life.

The goal is *individuation*, a term coined by the psychoanalyst Carl Jung to mean the lifelong process by which the unconscious is made conscious, the many parts of the self are integrated, and you achieve transformation and healing on the continuous journey to wholeness. Jung was careful to say the individuation process, which involves an acceptance of suffering and a willingness to meet life's challenges and learn from them, is not for everyone. It is, however, an exciting adventure for those seekers who want to know more about themselves and who are willing to explore the heights and depths of their soul. The rewards are many: self-discovery, self-awareness, and the coalescence of the many selves, including the *shadow*—that which is hard to see, much less own. This understanding allows you to perceive the Self as containing the *One* and the *Many* that make up the Whole Self.

The **True Self** is also a concept discussed in this book, which is meant to describe the Self that came into this world as a reflection of your *Soul Essence*. It is aligned with the Inner Child, the innocent part of you that was born into this world with a set of inherent qualities, talents, traits, and an impetus to be uniquely you. This is often obscured over time through no fault of your own by the family and over-culture into which you were born. It is then your mission to rediscover and reconnect with this core Self and realize it in the way you live your life.

# What Is an Archetype?

Archetypes are two-dimensional models, universally recognized figures, characters, themes, and patterns familiar to all from myths, fairy tales, and dreams. They live in your imagination. You understand them intrinsically, as they are part of what Jung termed the *collective unconscious*—that vast storehouse of knowledge and images to which all have access; indeed, it is part of your DNA. The myths and figures, like the goddesses of old, according to Jung, "are first and foremost psychic phenomena that reveal the nature of the soul . . . ." So you can access these archetypes and think of them as metaphors reflecting aspects of your Soul—the quintessence of who you are.

Archetypes may be activated within you either intentionally or unintentionally. For example, when you fall in love, you might find the archetype of Aphrodite/Venus, goddess of love, light up within you on a deep, feeling level, without you making a conscious effort to align with her. Or you may be gripped by a goddess archetype when you learn about her and feel a deep resonance with her. And finally, you may make a conscious choice to work with a goddess's energy to help you claim latent abilities and potentialities within you. This book is designed to help you make such choices as you connect with yourself and discover ways to expand your self-care practice.

## What Is the Shadow?

Each and every human being has what Carl Jung termed the shadow—a repressed or hidden aspect of their being that is not fully embodied or seen, but which makes its presence known, often when least expected or wanted. These might be challenging, unhelpful qualities like jealousy, racism, arrogance, judgment, criticism, control, perfectionism, subservience—characteristics with which you do not wish to identify and often feel embarrassed or ashamed of when they reveal themselves. Typically, they are qualities you don't like in others but which you also contain and don't like to admit to.

A shadow could also be some part of yourself that is not inherently bad or troublesome that you have neglected or denied, such as an Inner Artist or Creator that you wish to develop. The Shadow is made up of both over-developed and under-developed features of the self that need to be examined, made conscious, and integrated. By doing so, these shadow qualities are less likely to lie dormant and unexplored or to leak out, subvert your intentions, run your life, or pop up when you least expect it. Shining light on the shadow helps you see and own your own darkness and dispel it, not with shame but with love and self-care. To quote the poet Rumi, "The shadow that follows us is the way in."

Archetypes have shadows, too. While we tend to think of goddesses as positive, beneficent, and helpful, each has a shadow. It is helpful to consider those shadow qualities as you work with an archetype as they can arise just as personal shadow aspects do. Many goddesses of power and wisdom in mythology also show sides of being vengeful, jealous and arrogant. By being mindful of these tendencies, you can better see, learn from, and incorporate them.

## What Is the Goddess?

The Goddess, for our purposes, is not just one entity, but includes the many archetypes of the feminine divine—goddesses from various cultures and corners of the world. In their myriad guises and ethnicities, goddesses symbolize what it means to be a woman—fierce, strong, sexual, sensual, intelligent, determined, powerful, strong, courageous, resilient, healthy, strategic, creative, bold, and yes—helpful, nurturing, compassionate, and loving. It also means facing the shadow aspects of these archetypes and traits within you as a human being on a spiritual path, so as to reconcile them within your own psyche. The goal in working with these multi-cultural goddesses and their traditions is to learn from and honor them, not worship them and not appropriate them. This book is meant to be inclusive of goddesses of various skin colors, cultures, and parts of the world.

The goddesses serve as archetypal role models as well as aspects of the Self. They are reflections of the transformative and healing power of the divine feminine that resides within. It is your task, then, to listen and learn from the goddess archetypes and integrate them into one wholly (Holy) realized woman—Your Self—who knows how to take care of *Herself*. Thus you embark upon a journey of self-care, guided by the goddesses who will step in and advise you, show you, and tell you how to practice caring for yourself according to their expertise and inherent wisdom of a psychological, spiritual, practical, and humanistic nature.

Once upon a time, the ancients regarded their feminine goddesses as equal to the masculine gods. The goddesses held power in their own right, seen as mothers of the earth, creators, whole unto themselves before patriarchy became the rule. When the patriarchal power structure usurped the goddess-loving culture between 2,000 and 5,000 years ago, the men in power rewrote history, burying the feminine myths and stories. They pushed aside the goddesses, weakened and subverted them, often giving them superficial and one-sided feminine attributes based on the predominant male point of view at the time. The archetypes of the Divine Feminine went underground. But their wisdom and potency are still there to be uncovered, mined, and celebrated. Today, women are beginning to see themselves again as empowered and equal to men—not better or less than—and better able to care for themselves than any man.

**The archetype of The Goddess can be seen as representing four stages of a woman's life:**

**The Maiden**, the little girl and young adult before marriage and/or motherhood; a naive and innocent period of life, a time of learning, exploration, and free-spiritedness

**The Mother**, the time in a woman's life when she is occupied with mothering someone or something, be it a child, pet, garden, project, job, or some other occupation that takes up a good part of her life; tending and nurturing something for herself and possibly her loved ones; a busy and productive period of life

**The Queen**, the maturing, peri-, or post-menopausal woman who is fully in her power and sovereignty; both an accomplished and transitional period of life

**The Crone**, the elder who is retired from the busyness of life, who is less concerned with outer approval, and who has earned her wisdom; a restful and enlightened period of life

Most of the goddesses you will meet inhabit one of these developmental stages of life. Each stage of life has its own intrinsic knowledge and sagacity. You do not have to be in the same stage of life as a goddess who represents a particular phase to learn from her. It may be that you are in the "mother" years of life but need to enjoy play, like the maiden; or you may be a "maiden" who seeks the perspective of the sage crone. Wisdom flows in all directions.

# Active Imagination

You may already have come to realize that your imagination is a key element to working with the Goddesses of Self-Care. *Active Imagination* is a term coined by Carl Jung to mean the way we actively engage with our imagination to bring about understanding, enlightenment, and intuitive wisdom. Through creative self-expression, in whatever form it takes—writing, producing art, dancing, etc—you make unconscious processes conscious and discover their meaning. It is a way to comprehend and connect with your dreams, fantasies, and visions, which may feel disorganized, perplexing, and confounding until you work to understand and integrate them. No less a genius than Albert Einstein assures that "Imagination is the highest form of research."

The imagination is integral to your healing and self-care. It allows you to conjure up all kinds of stories, characters, and adventures and to see yourself being and doing in all sorts of ways you may not have dared permit yourself. By imagining possibilities, as well as calling in helpers and inner guides, you better realize your hopes and dreams.

Your imagination is a great resource for practicing self-care. If you see yourself doing something in your mind's eye, if you imagine the goddess within, if you find ways to create stories and art and play with the products of your imagination, you will find that life is more fulfilling and interesting. Developing a rich inner life helps you live a more meaningful and purposeful existence. In this way you forge a deeper connection with yourself. When you interact deeply with your imagination, your soul thrives and you more readily achieve self-actualization. As the artist Pablo Picasso noted, "Everything you can imagine is real."

Neuroscientific studies by Dr. Bessel van der Kolk and others have revealed that traumatic experiences affect the imagination, veiling and blocking it from being fully connected to the Self. By doing the healing work and active imagination exercises suggested in this book—from answering journal prompts, to creating art and altars, to listening to, envisioning, and working with these goddess archetypes—you create the potential to free your imagination from the bonds of past hurts. You can forge new neural pathways and connections that are transformative and liberating. Through creative imaginings and self-care practices, you can heal old wounds and see yourself as the embodiment of *The Goddess* who lives within your imagination. She is a reflection of your Higher Self—the part that knows and wants what is best for you. All religious and spiritual beliefs rely on the imagination, as the concepts of God and Goddess originate within the human psyche.

## Art and Altars

To help you fully experience the goddesses you will meet here, I encourage you to make art and altars to further imagine and bring them into form as you work with them. Each chapter has two or more goddesses to guide you through the given topics. Choosing one or two to work with (or perhaps she will choose you) and envisioning her brings her energy into your inner and outer living space.

At the end of each chapter, you will find a list of suggested items to place on an altar that correlates with the goddess archetype you are working with. This altar can be made on a shelf, a table, a dresser, or any surface that works for you. It is a way to bring yourself in alignment with the energy of the archetype and the self-care you are practicing. You may want to put a picture of yourself now or as a young girl on your altar, reminding you of your Inner Child, your True Self. She is always with you.

Let this altar become your resting place, a sanctuary that reflects *You* in your many facets, where you can check in, meditate, and journal. As you work with a chosen archetype, begin thinking about and collecting gemstones, figurines, pictures, herbs, flowers, and other objects related to the featured goddess to put on your altar, to bring her to life. Or you can discover and create your own images, tokens, and symbols that reflect the goddess you wish to honor, embody, and learn from.

I encourage you to draw, paint, color, craft, sculpt, or collage images of the goddess archetypes and the guidance you receive in an art journal, sketch book, or on cards, canvas, or clay. Each chapter contains exercises, journal prompts, and creative projects to inspire you. You may want to start an art journal as you work your way through these chapters where you can write, draw, paint, and collage, expressing yourself and the goddess energies you are playing with. This allows you to watch these feminine avatars come alive on the page and helps you stay open to their messages. There are suggestions for utilizing various art forms to bring these goddesses into realization throughout the book. You are encouraged to play and create and use your imagination to the fullest as you get to know your Self in all its many aspects. See Resources at the back of the book for tutorials and more information about how to make art journals, SoulCollage® cards, etc.

**As you create images of the goddess archetypes you meet, answer these questions to help you further get to know them and yourself:**

How do I most relate to this goddess archetype?

What kind of self-care do I need now?

How can this goddess help me practice self-care?

What do I need to know to activate this archetype in my life right now?

What personal message does this goddess have for me?

The goddess archetypes are compatible with different *chakras*, a Sanskrit word for wheels, or energy centers of the body, based on Hindu and yogic tradition and teachings. Imagine the chakras as wheels of power within your body that correspond to your mental, emotional, physical, and spiritual well-being. Starting from the bottom of your spine at the Root Chakra and ascending to the top of the head or Crown Chakra, this pathway of seven energy points represents the journey of healing and spiritual enlightenment.

When you are looking to heal or fine-tune some aspect of your Self, look to the chakras for where energy might be either sluggish and deficient or overworked and excessive. The idea is to achieve balance. The following section describes the chakras, their associated colors, and distinct energies. Each goddess archetype corresponds to a chakra center, as noted at the end of each chapter, and by tuning into her, she will help you find the balance you seek.

## The Seven Chakras — Their Light and Shadow Energy

### 1st Chakra – Red
*Root*: survival (fight, flight, or freeze response), security, trust in the world, stability, safety, money, protection, groundedness
*Shadow*: fear, anxiety, mistrust, paranoia, worry, insecurity, envy, miserliness, catastrophizing, over-protectiveness

### 2nd Chakra – Orange
*Sacral*: creativity, emotions and feelings, passion, sexuality, sensuality, pleasure-loving, regeneration, birth/rebirth
*Shadow*: guilt, trauma bond, shame, fear of intimacy, emotional and creative blockage, over-reaction, sexual addiction or loss of sexual desire

### 3rd Chakra – Yellow

*Solar Plexus*: personal power, ego strength, self-esteem, control, confidence, competency, achievement, ability to take action in the world, courage

*Shadow*: egocentricity, arrogance, meanness, spite, dominance, weakness, over- control, unwillingness to take risks, resistance, inertia

### 4th Chakra – Green

*Heart*: love for self and others, compassion, empathy, trust, vulnerability, devotion, loyalty, generosity, friendliness, warmth, openness, nurturance

*Shadow*: hate, bitterness, jealousy, envy, hardness, closed-off, despair, feeling unworthy and unlovable, defensiveness, depression, cynicism

### 5th Chakra – Blue/Turquoise
*Throat*: communication, speaking your truth, will, receptivity, expression of feelings, decisiveness
*Shadow*: shutdown, codependence, meek voice, feeling undeserving, lack of authority, being overly-opinionated, defensiveness, mindless, willfulness, repressed anger

### 6th Chakra – Indigo
*Third Eye or Brow*: intuition, vision, psychic ability, discernment, emotional intelligence, understanding, sense of magic, seeing the bigger picture
*Shadow*: black and white thinking, argumentativeness, confusion, narrow-mindedness, rigidity, closure to new ideas and experiences

### 7th Chakra – Violet/White
*Crown*: spirituality, trust in the universe or higher power, faith, enlightenment, bliss, joy, inspiration, connection to God/Goddess/Universe, awe, a sense of unity and oneness with all that is
*Shadow*: lack of meaning or purpose, feeling adrift, spiritual disconnection, blindness to beauty, numbness to joy, ennui

---

At the beginning of each chapter, you are introduced to a modern woman who is grappling with an issue related to the theme of the chapter. Her story gives you an idea as to how the goddess's wisdom might help her and you in a similar situation. However, these goddesses and their particular strengths and guidance can be applied to any number of life challenges you might face. Elsewhere in the chapter you will find an example of how the woman you met at the beginning of the chapter was able to implement some skill, knowledge, or creative suggestion offered to help her through her dilemma.

You will find journal prompts at the end of each chapter to guide you through the material and help you reflect on the subject, your own self-care practice, and any barriers you have, within and without. It may help to start by assessing your own thoughts and feelings about the goddess, divine feminine archetypes, the topic of self-care, and how your family and religious upbringing have influenced you by answering these initial questions to get started.

# Journal Prompts

What thoughts and feelings come up for you when you hear the word "goddess"?

In what ways is it challenging to accept the idea that you are a goddess or can see and accept the goddess (Divine Feminine) within you?

Which goddess archetype(s) have most resonated with you in life up till now and why?

Who was the nurturing figure in your life growing up? What qualities did this person have that helped you feel cared for or mothered?

What was your relationship like with your mother? Grandmother? Sister? Father? What did you learn from them about being female?

How did the religion you practiced or that you were exposed to growing up make it possible for you to accept the idea of the Divine Feminine (if at all)?

What is the most challenging aspect of your religious upbringing when it comes to the idea of the sacred feminine or imagining a powerful feminine deity or counterpart to a masculine god?

Where in your life can you use the most help in forming a relationship with the Divine Feminine?

Did anyone model self-care for you growing up? What do you remember and take to heart?

What is most challenging about self-care for you?

Next, we will meet the goddesses and explore how to provide self-care in the many domains of a fully-lived life—their helpful qualities and their shadow qualities. It is important to remember that not all shadow qualities are "negative." It helps to think of them as energies that are either in excess or deficient—characteristics that need to be fine-tuned—dialed up or dialed down—and incorporated. As mirrors of the many parts of our Self, you want to pay attention to those qualities of the goddess that you already relate to, those that you wish to embody, and those that still need development, and embrace them all with love and care.

# The Chapters

## Chapter One: New Beginnings

*Jana* — Roman goddess of January, the New Year, doorways, openings, vision
*Shadow*: being stuck, unwilling to see, to move forward or to try something new

*Usha* — Hindu/Vedic goddess of the dawn, new beginnings, who ushers in the light
*Shadow*: resistance, wallowing in a dark place for too long, fear of the dark or unknown

## Chapter Two: Dreaming and Planning

*Bear Woman* — Native American goddess of rest, hibernation, dreams and interpreting dreams, inner journeys, seasons of power, beingness
*Shadow*: lost in daydreams instead of moving, stuck in inner world, inertia

*Athena* — Greek goddess of wisdom, creativity, strategy, planning, warrior spirit, manifestation of dreams, achievement of goals, decisiveness, taking action
*Shadow*: too caught up in details, all-planning-no-action, too much in your head

## Chapter Three: Creativity and Play

*Brigid* — Celtic goddess of smithing (forging and transformation), creativity (writing), healing, new life and energy
*Shadow*: boredom, inadequacy, believing oneself not creative, unwillingness to try new things, repression as artist or writer

*Bast* — Egyptian goddess of maiden energy, playfulness, inner child, lightness, joy, adventure, curiosity, music, dance
*Shadow*: all-play-no-work, imbalance, overly-serious, lack of permission to enjoy life

*Grandmother Spider* — Native American goddess of creation, life purpose, following the thread of your existence and weaving the life you want
*Shadow*: lack of purpose, being at loose ends, disconnection

## Chapter Four: Depression and Grief

*Inanna* — Ancient Sumerian goddess of the underworld journey and Queen of Heaven, release, examination, transformation, rising above, rebirth/renewal, investigation
*Shadow*: stuck in depression, wallowing in feelings, waiting to be rescued, defeat, giving up power

*Persephone* — Greek maiden/daughter goddess of innocence leading to experience, growth, transformation, rebellion, launching, excitement to take the next step, rebirth
*Shadow*: stunted growth, immaturity, enamored of darkness, gloomy, self-destructive, depressive, fear of change

*Demeter* — Greek mother goddess of caregiving, protection, fertility, abiding spirit, grief, nurturing, responsibility
*Shadow*: Codependence, self-sacrificing to a fault, over-protective, inability to let go and move on

*Hecate* — Greek crone goddess of magic and wisdom, psychopomp, guide, intuition, witch, witness, perspective
*Shadow*: inability/refusal to see your own magic or listen to inner wisdom, hardness, black and white thinking

## Chapter Five: Healthy Relationships

*Hera* — Greek goddess of marriage, wife/queen, partnership, heroism, life-giving, magnanimous, sovereignty, good communication, traditional
*Shadow*: codependence, jealousy, mistrust, insecurity, martyrdom, staying too long in bad relationship, not standing up for yourself, submission, dutiful wife

*Isis* — Egyptian goddess of sacred relationship, equal partnership, consciousness, bringer of healing to relationship, rebirth, healthy boundaries
*Shadow*: codependence, self-sacrifice, giving up, lack of agency, controlling, ineffectiveness

## Chapter Six: Body and Sexuality

*Aphrodite (Venus)* — Greek goddess of love, sex, beauty, power, self-confidence
*Shadow*: vanity, jealousy, bitterness, self-criticism, revenge, over-concern with physical appearance, judgment, entitlement, giving power to others
*Freya* — Norse goddess (pre-motherhood) of free-spirited sexuality, sensuality, desire, lust, sexual power

*Shadow*: repression, guilt, shame, indiscriminant, empty sex, disconnection from body

*Frigga* — Norse goddess (post-motherhood or post-menopause) of sexual maturity and enjoyment, aging beauty, power and wisdom earned
*Shadow*: self-conscious, unresponsiveness, passivity, giving up, lack of power, guilt, shame

## Chapter Seven: Hurt and Anger

*Kali* — Hindu goddess of destruction, fury, endings, protection, transformation, compassion
*Shadow*: self-destruction, uncontrollable rage, repression, lack of agency, loss of power

*Sekhmet* — Egyptian goddess of power, fierceness, righteous fight, anger, justice
*Shadow*: anger turned inward, people-pleasing, controlling, raging, impotent

*Black Madonna* — Ancient pre-Christian, multi-cultural mother goddess of hidden or underground power, abiding presence, witness, healing, self-compassion, non-judgment, of the earth
*Shadow*: racism, sexism, selfishness, martyrdom, uncaring or unwilling to take care of Mother Earth

## Chapter Eight: Abundance and Work/Life Purpose

*Lakshmi* — Hindu goddess of abundance, good fortune, beauty, fulfillment, love
*Shadow*: shallowness, greed, selfishness, scarcity consciousness, cognitive distortions

*Artemis (Diana)* — Greek goddess of the hunt, true aim, perseverance, independent spirit, activist, purpose, goal-oriented
*Shadow*: self-doubt, lack of commitment, lack of agency, unfocused, overly-confident

## Chapter Nine: Health and Healing

*Akhilandeshwari* — Hindu goddess of acceptance of flaws and brokenness, lack of ego, embrace of imperfection, open to repair
*Shadow*: arrogance, perfectionism, victimhood

*Tara* — Tibetan goddess of compassion, self-soothing ability, healing, limitlessness, abiding presence, liberation
*Shadow*: codependence, self-sacrifice, helpless, hopeless, invisible

## Chapter Ten: Anxiety and Fear

*Butterfly Maiden* — Native American goddess of maidenhood, transformation, calm, hope, freedom, wings to fly
*Shadow*: fear of change, rigid, frenetic, stuck, frightened by life

*Yemaya* — Yoruba mother goddess of nurturance, courage, safety and security, encouragement, protection, soothing presence
*Shadow*: uncaring, selfish, holding back in fear

## Chapter Eleven: Reparenting: Learning to Mother Yourself

*The Virgin Mary* — Christian Mother of God and goddess of nurturing, compassion, care, love of self and others
*Shadow*: martyrdom, self-sacrifice, subservience, feeling undeserving of love

*Our Lady of Guadalupe* — Christian-Mestizo goddess of grace, hope, strength, social justice, non-judgment, acceptance, and mercy
*Shadow*: acquiescence, hopelessness, helplessness, emptiness

*Kwan Yin* — Chinese Bodhisattva and goddess of compassion, abidance, protection, love
*Shadow*: selfishness, superficiality, self-loathing, long-suffering martyrdom

## Chapter Twelve: Resting and Being Present

*Hestia* — Greek goddess of home and hearth, comfort, stillness, mindfulness, introversion, domestic bliss
*Shadow*: isolation, too much busyness, workaholism, hoarding, fear of being alone

*Sophia* — Judeo-Christian goddess of wisdom and knowledge, self-sufficiency, presence, peace, self-love, acceptance
*Shadow*: disconnection from self, unsettled, frantic activity, restlessness, low self-esteem

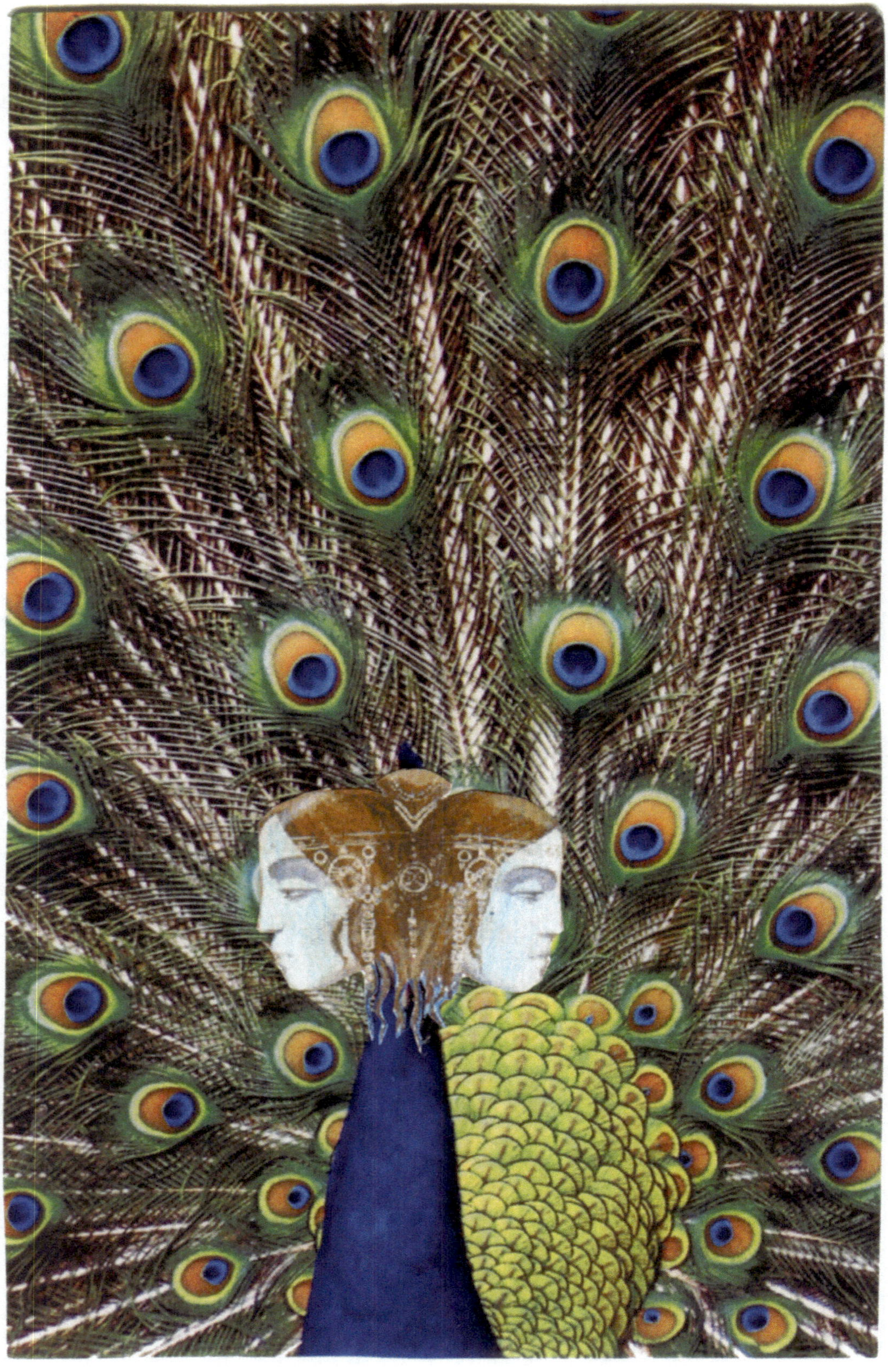

# Chapter One

# New Year, New Beginnings

LET US START AT THE BEGINNING. There are many times in life when you commence something new, leave something behind, and begin again. It could be a move to a new home, a new relationship, a new job, enrolling in school, starting a family, or embarking on a creative path. Each New Year offers a new beginning, a way to mark time and your progress, to let go of what was, and have a renewed perspective. At the cusp of a New Year, you say good-bye to the past year and welcome the future, the chance for rebirth.

There are two Goddesses of Self-Care you can turn to whenever you are beginning something. Jana is the Roman Goddess who presides over the month of January, and Usha is the Hindu goddess of the dawn. Jana is specific to the portal of the New Year and the birth of something, be it a baby or a project. Usha is an archetype to activate any time you take off in a new direction, need a fresh perspective, or want to celebrate a new day.

The New Year's guardian of the threshold, the Roman goddess, Jana, is the feminine counterpart of the two-faced god, Janus, a creator archetype, synonymous with time and space. He later came to be associated with the dramatic arts as symbolized by the two masks of comedy and tragedy, representative of the human condition. Initially, this deity was androgynous, one face feminine and the other masculine looking in opposite directions—dual energies of the divine. However, over time they became two separate entities, god and goddess.

## Dawn's Story

Dawn can't wait for the New Year to begin as it signals the beginning of a new life for her. She just moved to a town in another state and starts her dream job in January. She is nervous and apprehensive as she knows no one in her new location. She is excited about the community as it offers many more social opportunities and places to go than the hometown she left behind.

On top of that, the job is one she had been hoping to get for months, launching her on a career path she has long prepared for since finishing school. She knows she will meet people who will likely become friends, but she is unsure how to approach them and establish a connection. She has not had much experience venturing out on her own, but she is determined to go places by herself and discover all she can about her new home. Dawn doesn't want to let her fear stop her and realizes it will take courage to make the first step.

# Jana

Jana is the moon to Janus's sun, both illuminating the way into the New Year. Jana is associated with Luna and Diana, Roman moon goddesses, and over time was conflated with Juno, the goddess of marriage (aka Hera). The name Jana comes from the Latin root, *janua*, meaning doorway, gate, or path. The first month of January, the portal into the new year, is named after her, and in olden times she was honored on the first day of every month and season.

At the New Year you are like a newborn babe leaving the dark comfort of the womb you have known and emerging into the new world that stretches before you, activating a rebirth. Jana helps you gain a shiny, clean perspective after you have wiped away the dust from the moldy, old past. She invites you to leave behind what no longer serves you, drop whatever masks you have been wearing, and commit to being who you are at your core—reflecting the varied facets of your True Self.

You will discover that many of the goddesses are associated with certain animals, known as totems, which are emblems of certain qualities related to the goddess. Jana's animal ally is the peacock, whose beautiful tail feathers represent Jana's eyes, which both see you and act like mirrors, reflecting back your own divinity.

Peacock feathers bring good luck and putting one on your altar at the start of the New Year provides a way for Jana to watch over you. She is also a goddess of divination and if you align with and activate her, you, too, can imagine seeing through her eyes, using your second sight, and intuiting the right path to take in the year ahead.

# The Story of Jana

Jana, the goddess with two faces, stands at the gateway to her Roman temple, greeting the New Year's revelers. They have come to celebrate and receive her blessing in this central gathering place, a building with four equal sides and doorways, representing the four seasons.

Jana's faces, one gazing into the past and one looking to the future, remind one and all of her double-edged nature: beginnings and endings, day and night, birth and death, war and peace. Indeed, in her temple, one set of double doors stays closed during times of peace and open during times of war so that she may watch over and protect the city of Rome.

The people come regularly bearing flowers, pouring libations, making toasts to the goddess of transitions. She is the guardian at the threshold who reigns over the liminal space between two points in time. As such, she initiates all who pass through her temple doors into the great unknown that lies before them. They pray to her to guide them safely into the future.

As a goddess of lunar perception—the ability to see in the darkness—she promises heightened awareness, the gift of intuition, and keen discernment to guide her followers forward onto a new path—for every path leads within.

Jana's temple grounds abound with peacocks, whose beautiful tail feathers have eyes on the end of each iridescent plume. These are Jana's eyes watching over her beloved mortals—eyes that see all.

# Creating a Vision Board

Jana urges you to hone your vision for the New Year and imagine all of the possibilities you would like to bring forth, within and without. She is the goddess of far-reaching perception, and as such, invites you to make a *vision board* as your first creative offering in the New Year.

A vision board is a poster or bulletin board that you fill with words and images to reflect your dreams and goals for the year ahead. Setting intentions is a powerful way to manifest your personal vision on both a soul level and in the physical world.

Creating a vision board at the beginning of the year is a powerful way to imagine how you want your life to unfold in the months ahead. It sets in motion what is stirring in your subconscious, which contains your hopes, dreams, desires, destinations, and soul yearnings. It is a collage of both words and images. When selecting them, choose those that leap out at you and say, "This is me!" or "This is what I want!"

You may intentionally choose images that represent places you want to go in the year ahead, people who are important to you, and projects you want to develop; and you may intuitively select words and images that surprise you, that want to be represented even if you are not sure why. Often, the meaning reveals itself over time. All vision boards should include a recent photo of yourself because *YOU* are the center of your vision. You are the recipient of the self-care you are imagining and bringing forth in the year ahead.

Another meaningful ritual at the start of the New Year is to choose a *word of the year* that represents a feeling or quality you want to embrace and embody, and put it on your vision board. You may also want to have your word inscribed on a pendant, charm, or bracelet that you wear as a reminder throughout the year of the energy you are claiming for yourself. The list of possibilities at the end of this chapter provides some examples of words you may want to adopt as your word of the year.

As a goddess of far sight and clairvoyance, Jana invites you to select a goddess and animal guide for the year as well, and include them on your vision board. You may do this by drawing a card from goddess and animal oracle decks or randomly open this book to a page and see which goddess is there to greet you. Perhaps you already know which of these avatars you would like to have with you, and you select them intentionally because they have come to have meaning for you or you wish to bring their qualities into your life. Find images to represent them for your vision board and place pictures or figures of them on your altar as well.

**Questions to Help You Hone Your Vision**

What do I want to manifest in the year ahead?

Who do I want to spend time with?

Where do I want to go?

What project do I want to start or finish?

What do I want to feel this year?

What do I want to learn this year?

How do I see myself this year?

How do I hope my word of the year will manifest?

How can I best care for my body?

What self-care practice(s) do I want to embrace?

# Divination for the New Year

One way to envision and imagine what you can expect in the year ahead is to use your intuitive abilities to divine what is coming, what is guiding you, and what to be aware of as the year unfolds. Get out your favorite deck of tarot or oracle cards (Goddess, Animal, Fairy, etc.) and lay out a reading for the New Year.

One simple but illuminating spread for the new year is to draw 12 cards from a deck of your choice, one for each month and a 13th card for the overall energy of the year. (You may want to mix them up and draw cards from different decks.)

Ask each card for a message about what you need to be aware of that month: What do I need to know in the month of _____? What kind of self-care do I need to practice in the month of _____? How can my goddess guide help me in the month of _____?

You will learn to interpret signs and symbols by looking at the cards, understanding their meaning based on the images and figures depicted. Trust your instinct for guidance as to the card's message for you. This speaks to Jana's ability to see beyond the known world that becomes your acuity to sense what is beneath the surface using your third eye (Sixth Chakra). In this way you develop your own intuitive abilities, to know what is right for you and what is not.

You may also enjoy using runes or ogham staves, scrying with water or a mirror, or using another means of divining answers. Use whatever method of divination you enjoy or want to play with to get in touch with your inner knowing and ability to receive the guidance that is right for you as the

Dawn is excited to make a vision board for the first time to help her imagine her new life in the year ahead. She chooses the word "Courage" for her word of the year and bravely asks her affable next-door neighbor if she would like to join Dawn at home for brunch and make vision boards together. Dawn collages "Courage" onto hers along with images that represent the work she will be doing, her life with new friends, and places she wants to visit. She and her new friend each draw oracle cards and give each other readings that they both find illuminating and inspiring. They agree to meet weekly and continue the practice of drawing cards and talking about what the messages mean to them. Dawn is thrilled to have made a like-minded friend.

year unfolds. This process brings up sub-conscious, and sometimes repressed desires, truths, and internal conflicts that you are now able to explore with increased perception, seeing both challenges and desired outcomes.

## Objects and symbols to consider for your altar to Jana

**Colors:** iridescent colors, indigo

**Objects:** peacock feather, images of eyes, an image of Jana (create one!), white or blue candle

**Gemstones:** peacock quartz or sapphire, clear crystal, silver, garnet for January

**Flowers:** peacock flower, bird of paradise, carnation

**Element:** air

**Chakra:** brow or third eye (6th chakra)

# Jana Speaks

Welcome, Daughter, to this New Year. Step across the threshold and join me as we gaze ahead to what the New Year offers. Some surprises await you, as not everything in life can be seen and planned for. Good things will come to you, as will unfortunate events and losses. That is one of the truths you must learn to live with and accept. However, you have great power in intuiting what is best and in bringing positive energies, be they experiences, people, opportunities, or new paths.

It is all in how you perceive the world. If you learned from your family and society to view the world with suspicion, negativity, and doubt, you will have a harder task learning to see through the lens of hope, positivity, and good will. But that is what I offer you—the ability to see with new eyes, especially if the road leading here has been difficult. I give you the gift of rebirth.

The peacock is my companion and on the beautiful tail fan of the male peacock are many eyes through which I see. Allow yourself to see through these eyes, too. Peacocks symbolize vision and awakening, guidance and protection, as well as good fortune. Embrace us and let us carry you into the New Year on powerful wings of love that support and carry you to new heights.

Take heart that you are embarking on a journey of self-care, self-discovery, and adventure in the year ahead. Know that you are doing this for YOU and no one else. You contain the Holy Grail, the vessel of feminine knowledge, beauty, and power. You must fill your own vessel, Daughter, and keep it filled, for an empty vessel is no good to anyone, least of all yourself.

PAINTED BY T. V. KELLY

## Usha, Goddess of the Dawn

Many cultures celebrate a goddess of daybreak. These feminine deities are usually maidens, youthful spirits that represent the still young day. They illuminate what has been dark and obscured. They light the way so that you may see more clearly what you need and desire as you embark on a new path. Think of the awe you feel when the first rays of light begin to peek over the horizon at sunrise. At last! The night is done. Usha is the goddess that awakens us to the dawning of a New Day.

Usha comes from the Sanskrit word *use*, which means dawn. She is a Vedic deity, similar to other goddesses of the dawn, such as the Greek goddess *Eos*, the Roman *Aurora*, the Japanese *Uzume*, and the Anglo *Eostre*, from which we get the word Easter, a liminal time of death and rebirth. Dawn is also a liminal twilight time when we stand upon the threshold between darkness and light, anticipating what is to come.

## The Story of Usha

Usha, maiden goddess of the dawn, loves her job of ushering in the light. Her mother, Dyaus, is the heavens; her sister, Natri, is the night. Usha wakes up in the dark and dons her many-colored robes of splendor and climbs into her chariot pulled by her sacred animals. As Natri prepares to leave her post, Usha rides in on her chariot, breaking through the wall of darkness her sister has erected. Usha is beautiful to behold as she brings the first rays of sunlight with her.

Usha's robes dance across the skies, reflecting spectacular hues of pinks, yellows, oranges, and reds, transforming the black night into a golden day of possibilities. With her arrival, nightmares fade, mistakes are forgiven, troubles left behind as a new day dawns. As Usha rides, all creatures begin to stir on Earth. The birds fly up to greet her. The animals get up from their places of rest and humans stretch and rise from their beds. All can feel her breath of fresh air as her sunrise dance illuminates the sky in fiery brilliance.

Her loyal followers eagerly anticipate Usha's crepuscular arrival each morning. They look forward to replacing what has grown stale with a fresh slate. She inspires all to start something new or to begin again with hope and anticipation. Usha reminds one and all to face the reality of what is, the reality of what is in front of each person each day. This includes the understanding that life is short so that people on earth remember to embrace each day and live it to the fullest.

Usha is celebrated in the ancient *Rig Veda,* a Hindu holy text, and is the most prominent goddess in Vedic literature. Here, a hymn imagines her as multiple goddesses of dawn, resplendent in her robes of light:

*"The radiant Dawns have risen up for*
*Glory, in their white splendor like the*
*waves of waters.*

*She maketh paths all easy, fair to travel,*
*and rich, hath shown herself benign and*
*friendly.*

*We see that thou art good: far shines*
*thy lustre; thy beams, thy splendors*
*have flown up to heaven.*

*Decking thyself, thou makes bare thy*
*Bosom, shining in majesty, thou*
*Goddess Morning."*
~ Rig Veda, 6.64. 1-2 as translated by Ralph T.H. Griffith

Call upon Usha when you are ready to launch a project, a creative offering, or an untried way of living and being. Perhaps you are about to start a job, move to a different home or town, begin a relationship or project, or just greet the dawn of a new day after a dark night of the soul. With all of these experiences, Usha brings a sense of myriad possibilities and helps you see things in a new light.

It may be that you are about to begin again, to take on something you were not ready for when you first tried it, but are now. Usha helps you start over, and to know it is never too late—you can begin whenever you decide the time is right. She is the one to call when you want to reinvent yourself.

It is not uncommon to feel trepidation and nervousness when facing the unknown, when establishing a new routine or taking a new path. If it is an entirely novel experience you are facing, it requires courage and resolve to take a leap of faith. Even when you have experience with something and already know what challenges you face, it is still difficult to stand at the starting line and begin again. Usha offers a steady hand.

When it is time to walk into unfamiliar territory, Usha alights from her chariot, acting as chaperone through the tricky portal of the darkness of the unknown, gently coaxing you forward. Knowing she is with you and is familiar with the terrain ahead will help you feel more relaxed and at ease as you take baby steps into uncharted territory. She is walking right alongside you, sharing the "Breath of all breaths" and the "Life of all life," she offers, as described in the Vedas. She confidently leads, offering you a sense of safety and security as you make your way forward. She chases away the demons of fear and doubt that would hold you back. Usha has no time to linger at the gate. She is the one who reveals the treasure if you will but follow her to the end of the rainbow.

## Objects and Symbols to Consider for Your Altar to Usha:

**Colors:** red, orange, yellow, pink, white

**Objects:** candle for light, images of dawn/sunrise, chariot, red horses, image of Usha

**Gemstones:** citrine, celestite, topaz, moonstone

**Flowers:** peacock flower, bird of paradise, lotus, hibiscus, carnation

**Element:** air

**Chakra:** crown (7th chakra)

## Daily Guidance

While Jana offers a fresh perspective at the beginning of a new year, month, or season, Usha offers you a new viewpoint at the start of each day. One helpful practice is to draw an oracle card from a deck of your choice for daily guidance. Whether it is from a goddess, animal, tarot, or another of the many different types of decks available, drawing an oracle card each day is fun and offers another frame of reference, something you may not have considered until brought to your attention in this way.

You might also want to make your very own deck to draw from, providing a wonderful divination tool that is unique to you. SoulCollage® is an art practice that offers a means to create your own deck of cards using evocative found images that reflect you in your many aspects. Working with 5″ x 8″ cards, you intuitively select images and collage them to represent different aspects of your personality and soul. You can then work with the cards to discover their meaning and message for you. (See Resources at the back of the book.)

## Beginner's Mind

Jana and Usha help you develop *Beginner's Mind*, a practice taught in Zen Buddhism that offers the gift of discovery again and again. When you approach each day, experience, event, person, or lesson with Beginner's Mind, you are humble and open, ready to learn and grow. You assume you do not know everything you need to know, no matter how experienced you might be, and you allow yourself to see things with new eyes—with the openness and eagerness of a child.

It means you let go of expectations of positive or negative outcomes and just let it be, allowing wisdom to unfold. You are open to finding delight, surprise, and awe in whatever new experience or knowledge awaits you. Beginner's Mind implies trust in the outcome—no matter what it is. It is the ability to know that whatever is revealed, it is for your highest good and what you need to learn and experience.

Usha helps you practice self-care as you cultivate a new way of being. Write down your vision of how you see yourself going forward. What do you want to let go of? What do you want to nurture? What do you want to revise? Imagine yourself planting seeds of change and watering them, day by day, until one day you see the buds burst through the dark soil sending forth their green shoots into daylight. You are the gardener who makes your life bloom!

# Usha Speaks

Dear Sister, Please join me in my chariot as we cross borders and leave the darkness behind. I offer you the joy and promise of a new day dawning. My sister, Natri, the Goddess of Night, is always ready to let go when it is time for my arrival. We work hand in hand. And so you must learn to let go of whatever no longer serves you or plagues you from the past. Leave it behind and start again.

What if you just let go? Once you do, I offer you the promise of liberation—a new outlook, another chance, a fresh start.

I help you get done what you need to accomplish for the day. I help you overcome procrastination and start something. It may be that you need to give yourself more time and space to just be, to enjoy life, and not work so hard. I help you find the time for a sacred pause as much as I help you initiate something novel and different and accomplish your goals.

I am the mother who helps her child learn to walk, to feel confident in her ability to navigate the world, one step at a time. Call on me when you start something new, when you want to practice Beginner's Mind, and I will come and watch over you, reassuring you that you are not alone, that divine guidance is here. I am the promise and light of a new day.

# Journal Prompts

**Questions for the New Year:**

In reviewing the year behind you, what do you want to release and leave behind (qualities, habits, mistakes, patterns, experiences)?

What doorway(s) might you seek to open and enter in the year ahead (new experiences, relationships, opportunities)?

What inner resources do you need to call forth to accomplish the goals and dreams you have for the new year?

What new perspective(s) would you like to have going forward? What would it take for you to change your mind and see things in a different way? What would you have to give up?

How can you nurture yourself in the dark days of winter as the sun slowly returns to its full glory? What part(s) of you needs nurturing?

**Questions for a New Beginning or New Day:**

What ritual would you like to practice to start each day, to greet the dawn?

What inner qualities do you have lying dormant in the dark that it is time to bring into the light of day?

What are you hungry for or longing to begin in your life?

What is your greatest desire now?

What is it you need to feel most fulfilled in your life right now? What would it take to get it?

Where in your life can you practice Beginner's Mind? What new thing would you like to learn?

How can you balance the need for rest and stillness with the need for energetic pursuits and embarking on a new path?

# Possible Word of the Year (or choose your own)

| | | | |
|---|---|---|---|
| Abundance | Dream | Implement | Rebirth |
| Accept | Ease | Improve | Receive |
| Adventure | Emerge | Inspire | Regenerate |
| Affirmation | Endeavor | Intention | Renew |
| Alive | Energy | Intuition | Reset |
| Amaze | Enough | Joy | Resilience |
| Ample | Enrich | Justice | Respect |
| Astound | Family | Laugh | Rest |
| Attainable | Fearless | Liberation | Restore |
| Authentic | Focus | Limitless | Rise |
| Balance | Forgive | Lionhearted | Sacred |
| Be | Freedom | Listen | Seek |
| Believe | Fulfilled | Live | Self |
| Blaze | Gentle | Love | Serenity |
| Bloom | Genuine | Luminous | Shine |
| Bold | Go | Magic | Simplicity |
| Boundaries | Grace | Manifest | Steady |
| Brave | Gratitude | Mindful | Strength |
| Breathe | Grit | Natural | Strive |
| Calm | Growth | Observe | Success |
| Center | Happy | Open | Thrive |
| Change | Harmony | Organize | Transformation |
| Clarity | Healing | Passion | Trust |
| Compassion | Healthy | Peace | Truth |
| Connect | Heart | Persevere | Unstoppable |
| Courage | Hero/Heroine | Play | Values |
| Dare | Home | Possible | Verve |
| Delight | Hope | Presence | Warmth |
| Divine | Ignite | Proud | Wonder |
| Do | Imagine | Real | Yes |

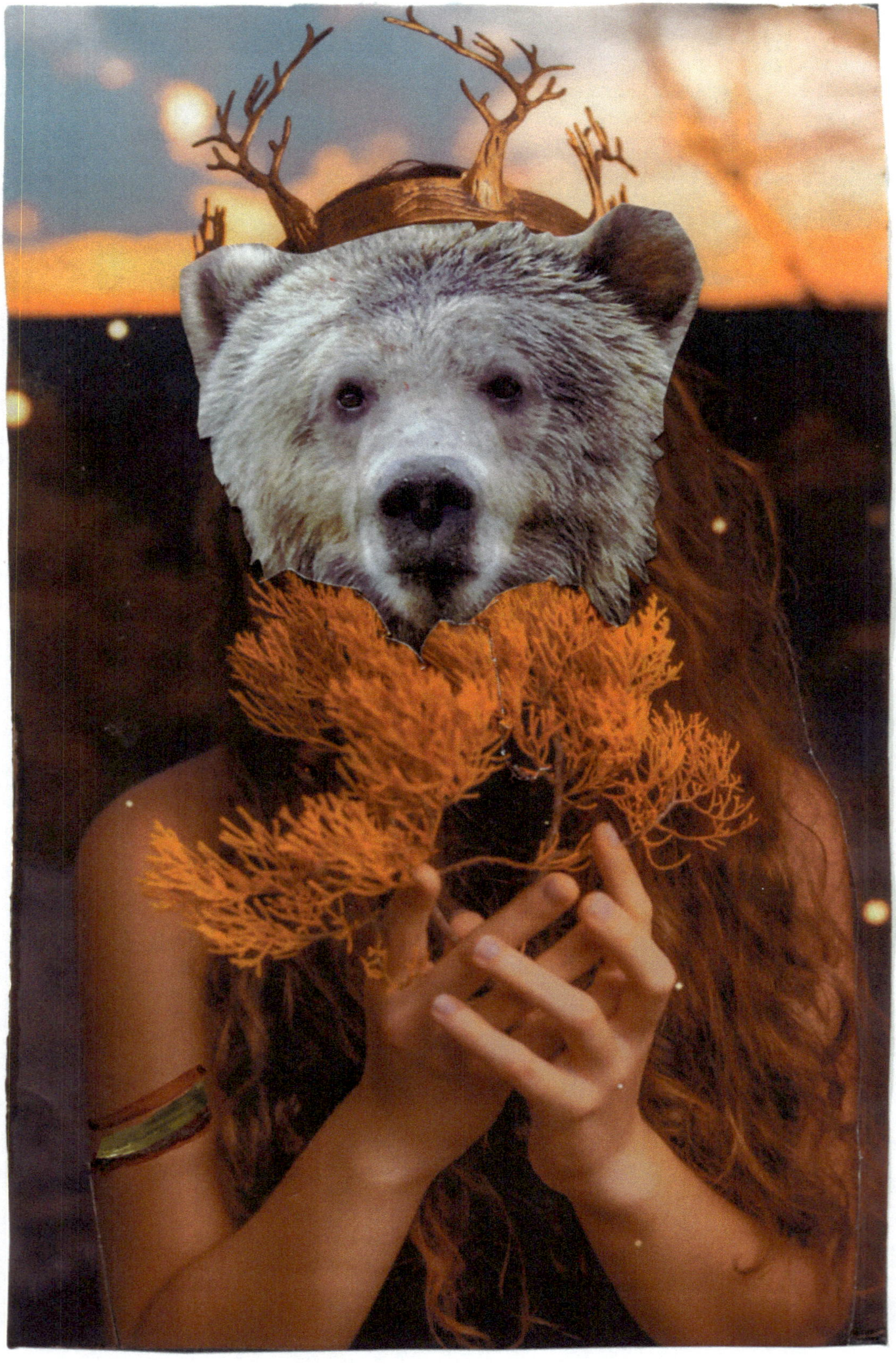

# Chapter Two

# Dreaming and Planning

IN THE FIRST CHAPTER you explored new beginnings and entering the new year. This chapter provides guidance for any time you are in a place of dreaming, visioning, and making plans. Once you imagine what you want for yourself and create a vision of the year ahead, which your vision board reflects, there comes a time to follow through. This is when your inner feminine and masculine work together: the Inner Feminine percolates with ideas, imagines, and creates, and the Inner Masculine takes action, manifesting and realizing your dreams. Remember that the Inner Feminine and Masculine are genderless constructs; self-care for any person involves a happy marriage of both.

As you sit in the place of dreaming, visioning, and planning—no matter what time of year—two goddess archetypes offer help. The goddess Bear Woman stirs inside the inner cave where you dream and conceive ideas; and Athena, Greek goddess of wisdom, industry, and strategy, motivates you to move out of the cave and turn your dreams into reality.

Bear Woman is your Inner Feminine guide who encourages you to take time to hibernate, rest, relax, and restore your strength—and dare to dream! During this hibernation and gestation period, which may very well be in the cold winter months when your energy is at a low ebb, take time to plant seeds of ideas, imagine what you want for your life, and see yourself accomplishing the goals you have set.

## Maya's Story

Something has been stirring in Maya for a while. She has been working a nine-to-five job for ten years, and while it pays well and she has moved up in the company, she is unfulfilled creatively. Her dream is to open a bakery as she loves to make breads, cakes, and desserts of all kinds. Maya cannot imagine working for another ten years at a job that doesn't fulfill her and knows it is time to make her dream come true.

She has experimented with enough recipes to know what she would like to offer customers, and she has received nothing but accolades for her baked goodies. She knows there is a lot to do, from researching how to run a successful small business, to figuring out start-up costs, to finding a storefront and possible investors. Lately, it is all she can think about. She is still dreaming, but she knows it will soon be time to make a plan.

This is a dreamy time when you feel your way into a new being, not quite ready to take action. It is a time to patiently and quietly cultivate the garden of your imagination and even allow yourself to lie fallow, trusting that your ideas will germinate when you are well-rested and ready to plan. As your vision for yourself and your life starts to take shape, Bear Woman provides assurance that it is okay to rest, dream, and just be. She is your muse during this time. She helps you trust the process and allow it to unfold in due time. When you are ready to strategize, and put plans into action, Athena steps up to guide you.

Self-care involves finding balance between doing (active, masculine energy) and being (receptive, feminine energy). You do not want to be so busy going and doing that you are not able to feel your feelings, smell the flowers, and enjoy down time. This leads to burn-out. And you don't want to be stuck in inertia, dreaming and imagining, but not following through, not daring to take the risks that lead to new experiences and accomplishments.

It is also important to recognize that not all dreams come to fruition, but attempting new things nonetheless teaches and informs; success is often built on setbacks, even failures. The point is to keep dreaming, imagining, and daring to put your dreams into action—despite any fears and doubts that pop up. Athena helps you have the courage to try something you have fantasized about. She helps activate the intrepid adventurer in you, who not only dares to dream greatly, but who dares to make it happen.

It is up to you to choose which goddess you want to work with depending on your energy at this time of Dreaming and Planning. The goddess known as Bear Woman guides you when you feel unmotivated, unready, or when you are mentally or physically exhausted from recent output and need time to recoup. She is a goddess to call on during your menstrual cycle, when your energy is low, a time when you may want to slow down, rest, and dream.

You might feel emotionally overwhelmed and need time to sort through your feelings, or perhaps your energy has not caught up with your aspirations. These aspects need to be in sync for you to move forward and take action. Bear Goddess gives you permission to take the time you need to renew your strength and visualize your next steps.

# Bear Goddesses

Bear Goddesses have been venerated by many cultures throughout the world from ancient times to the present, often associated with shamanic rituals and journeys within. In certain indigenous cultures, both men and women donned bearskins and took on the power of the bear and the ability to shapeshift, to take deep journeys into the Unconscious (or Underworld) to find answers and achieve healing.

**Some of these bear goddesses are:**

**Artio,** a Celtic bear goddess who thrived in the European region once known as Gaul that covered ancient France, Germany, Belgium, and Switzerland. It is believed that when the Gauls were defeated by the Romans, Artio became synonymous with Artemis (Diana).

**Artemis**, the Greek goddess of the moon and hunt, whose name roughly translates to *Bear Sanctuary*. She had a troop of acolytes known as "arktoi," or *bear girls*, that she mentored in the forest before they either married or continued on as priestesses in the temples to Artemis. (You will meet Artemis in CH. 8, page 182, Abundance and Work/Life Purpose.)

**Ungnyeo** was a bear who became a woman, a goddess who gave birth to a son that founded the country of Korea.

**Bear Woman** is a goddess sacred to Native American peoples such as the Ute, Cree, Pawnee, Modoc, and other indigenous tribes, whom you can call upon to guide you during dream time. Here is a story of a Modoc woman who transformed into a bear at night.

# The Story of Bear Woman

Lok Snewedjas lived alone in a mountain cave. She was a woman by day and a bear by night. Over time she grew lonely and dreamed of a more fulfilling life. She began venturing further and further from her cave until one day she happened upon a hunter. He was entranced by this strange mountain woman's beauty and intrepidness. They fell in love and lived together in her cave. She tried to keep her shapeshifting ability a secret, but one night he watched as the woman he loved turned into a bear. She was afraid he was repulsed by her and assured him he could return to his people and she would understand. But he said no, he loved her no matter what and wanted to stay with her and make a life together.

Soon they had a child and the proud father took his son to visit his family against her wishes. She feared for their son's safety, and sure enough one evening when he was playing with some children he turned into a bear and the frightened villagers killed him. Bear Woman ran to him and she, too, was shot by hunters. Fortunately, the village medicine woman knew how to restore the boy and his mother back to life with plants and herbs, and so she resurrected them. Lok Snewedjas and her husband and child returned to their cave of dreams where they were protected in the safe world they had created and were never seen by man again.

Mama bears typically go into hibernation while they are pregnant in late autumn and early winter. They find a cave or den and curl up for a long winter's nap while they gestate. Likewise, the fall and winter are fertile seasons to go within to dream and envision your life ahead during your own gestation period. This may be a time when you are literally pregnant and in a dreamy state of preparation or figuratively pregnant with possibilities, ideas, and plans that you hope to bring to fruition when you are ready to emerge from the cave. The Ute peoples have a Bear Dance ceremony and initiation rite in February to celebrate the advent of springtime and the bear emerging with her cubs.

No matter what the season, Bear Woman is a dream weaver who teaches you to journey within, to review where you have come from, and to imagine where you are going. She teaches the self-care practice of feeding your soul, eating what nourishes you (whether it is food or knowledge), and avoiding distractions or that which does not fulfill you. She shows you how to sit in stillness and hold your sacred womb vessel, your sacral chakra, and imagine a new creative form taking shape there.

Bear Woman moves in balance with nature, with the seasons, knowing when to sleep and when to forage. Bear Woman guides and protects you on the journey into the Underworld of the Unconscious, whether daydreaming or dreaming while you sleep. She abides with you as you ponder your lessons and gather inspiration and creative energy, until it is time to emerge into your cycle of power.

When you sit with Bear Woman in quiet meditation, without distraction, she helps you see what it is you need and want. If you are depleted, she helps you restore your strength and energy by allowing you to take the time needed to empty out and feel the space inside you. If you are full of dreams and plans, she allows you to sit with these stirrings until you are ready to give birth. When you do this, answers come from your inner Bear Goddess to questions such as:

- What do I need now?
- What is calling me?
- Where do I want to put my energy?
- What first step am I willing to take?

Learning to understand your dreams and work with them is Bear Woman medicine. What you dream about at night while unconscious is fodder for your conscious mind to ponder, interpret, and integrate. While you sleep, your subconscious creates symbolic stories with archetypal characters to help you better know yourself and what needs transforming and healing, as well as what path may be calling you.

The following exercise provides a way to work with dream material. Pay attention to your nighttime dreams and get in the habit of writing them down, even if they are snippets and pieces, not whole stories. They are coming to you to help you discern what is important to you, what you need to focus on, what problem is unresolved, what may be in the way that needs to be cleared out. Your dreams provide information and answers that shed light on your deepest desires and wounds.

# Dream Work

Dreams are replete with archetypes—enduring patterns and models of being—that represent different aspects of the Self. It can help to think of each person in your dream as a part of you. These dream figures appear in your subconscious mind to help you become aware of who you are in your many facets and what you need to know to achieve wholeness. Dreams give you valuable information about your inner life that you can work with and bring to your waking life to help you evolve as a conscious human being—to help you individuate and find meaning.

Start a dream journal that you keep by your bed. Write down what you remember from your dreams as soon as you awaken, even if you recall only fragments. Here are some guidelines for understanding and working with your symbolic dream life:

**Identify the Dream Elements**

- Write down everything you remember about your dream, even if scenes feel disconnected.
- List the different elements that stand out: characters, objects, locations, images.

**Make Associations**
- Next to each item on your list, write down any associations you have to it, including memories, words, ideas, feelings, or thoughts that come to you as you consider the image.
- Ask: What is the feeling I have about that image/person? What idea or word do I associate with that image/person? What recent experience, challenge, or situation does this remind me of?
- Take note of the associations that have the most resonance for you.

**Interpret Its Meaning**
- Working with each association you made, see if you can identify how the dream image is relevant to an inner dynamic or conflict that you are aware of or a feeling you have had lately.
- Ask: Who or what does this remind me of? Where have I seen that operating in my life recently? How is that like me? When have I felt that way? In what ways does a current life circumstance align with that image or association?

- Interpret the entire dream using all of your associations and correspondences, summarizing what the dream is trying to tell you or help you with. What is the most important insight you glean from it?
- Ask: How is this relevant to my life and what I am grappling with presently?
- Note if the dream calls for attitude changes or changes in perspective that might be helpful to you.
- Note any messages that seem clear to you.
- Create a collage, draw, or paint an image (or multiple images) from this dream that captures the archetypal energy, feeling, or another aspect of the dream that has meaning for you.

Call on Bear Woman to help you remember your dreams and make time to write them down and work with them. Think of her as a guardian in the darkness of the cave, who protects you from intrusions and distractions as you do your inner work. She is an ally of the dreamworld who helps you understand yourself better and envision your life unfolding in ways that best serve you.

Bear Woman is a shapeshifter who, once she leaves the cave, moves through the forest with agility and strength, trying on one form and then another, unafraid of change or challenges. She is willing to take new paths, to discover new ways of seeing herself and the world. She helps you dream yourself into being.

Maya wakes up from a dream in which she is carrying around a baby that she is very proud of. The baby is able to talk to her and brings her to a street with lots of pretty storefronts and activity. Maya goes in and out of the stores admiring the displays and items for sale. She talks with a shopkeeper who shows her around and talks to her about her business.

Maya does the Dream Work exercise and realizes that the baby in her dream is her new bakery venture that she has given birth to. It is as if she has already made it a reality and now just needs to find the space to set up shop. The street in her dream reminds her of a new area of the city that has a lot of new small businesses and boutiques and she knows that is where she would like to be. She associates the shopkeeper with a successful friend who started her own business. Maya decides to contact her to see if she would mentor her through the steps. She even comes up with a name for her future bakery inspired by her dream: Babycakes.

## Objects and symbols to consider for your altar to Bear Woman

**Colors:** brown, white, black, red

**Objects:** figurines and images of bears and Bear Woman (if you do not have one, make one!), a flower bear, or a small Teddy bear

**Gemstones:** fluorite, jasper, obsidian, carnelian

**Flowers:** sunflowers, dogwood, roses

**Element:** earth

**Chakra:** sacral (2nd chakra) and brow or third eye (6th chakra)

# Bear Woman Speaks

Daughter, it is important to be aware of your own cycle of power. Often the season you are born in is your season of power—the time when you will feel the most energy to get things done, even if it is inner work. Take note of when you were most productive last year and when you needed to rest and recover. Did these times seem in balance? To achieve balance this year, do you need more time to rest or more time to be creative and productive?

When you journey into the dreamworld for insight and visions, I will lead you into the dark cave and keep you warm. I will guide and protect you. I help you shapeshift and become Bear Woman. Wrap a soft, furry blanket around you and imagine becoming me, walking on my paws, going into your inner cave. Together we are fearless and focused. You will receive the message, the inspiration you seek, by quieting down, by asking and listening, and giving your imaginings time to gestate.

I remind you not to let your creative energies lie dormant for too long. Look for what feeds your soul and chow down when the time is right!

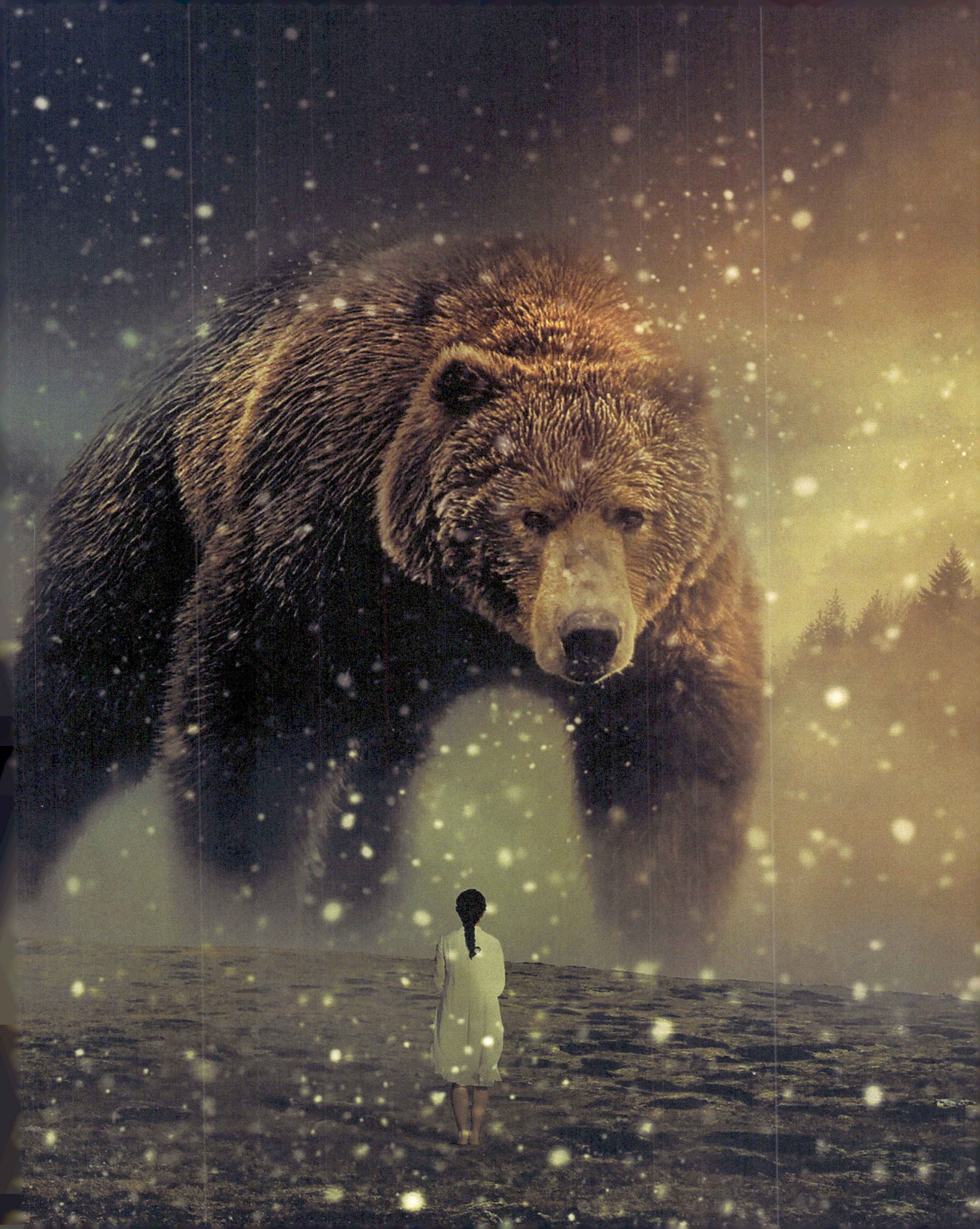

# Athena

Athena is the Greek goddess of wisdom, weaving, arts, crafts, and strategy (Minerva in Roman mythology). Her totem animal is the owl, which is often depicted sitting on her shoulder. The owl represents her wisdom and far sight, the ability to see in the dark and bring her intuitive insights into the light. You could think of it as the ability to take the creative stirrings of the imagination and bring them to fruition. Athena is a *virgin goddess*, which means whole unto herself, a goddess who thinks and does for herself and is not defined by her relationship to a man or god.

Athena's feast day, known as the Panathenea, was celebrated in ancient Greece on August 15. A statue of her was taken from Athens to the sea where it was washed, purified, and resanctified each year. In the Roman world, Minerva was celebrated on March 19th as a day to honor craftspeople.

# The Story of Athena

When Athena's mother, Metis, was pregnant with her, Zeus, her father, was told the coming child would overtake his throne. So, as gods were wont to do in those days, Zeus swallowed Metis to prevent this from happening. But soon enough he began to have a pounding headache that lasted for days. FInally, to his immense relief, his daughter, Athena, burst through his forehead in full armor, letting loose a fearsome battle cry. Zeus could not help but be proud of his warrior daughter as she came to represent wisdom in feminine form.

Over time Athena's sagacity was sought out by many a warrior, for her ability to strategize, advise, and plan. She assisted well-known heroes like Odysseus on his 10-year journey back to Ithaca, Hercules in his many labors, and Jason on his quest to obtain the golden fleece.

Athena's shadow side was exacting, punitive, and vengeful in her role as warrior goddess. The story of how Medusa, the snake-headed gorgon, ended up on Athena's aegis, or leather shield, involves a betrayal of her trust. Before she became a gorgon, Medusa was an Amazon who was seduced by the sea god, Poseidon, in Athena's temple. As punishment for the desecration of her sanctuary, Athena turned Medusa's hair into writhing snakes so that if any man looked into her eyes he was turned to stone. When the hero, Perseus, cut off Medusa's head as a trophy, Athena wore her face on her breastplate, giving Athena the same power to stop men in their tracks. The snake was a pre-patriarchal symbol of goddess wisdom, and the gorgon face on Athena's shield represented her power as a destroyer.

However, there is an earlier story set in matriarchal times before Zeus and the Olympians came on the scene. In this era, Athena was a *creatrix*—a goddess of weaving and crafts—who could turn her ideas into tangible creations. As such, she is a patroness of weavers, spinners, crafters, and artisans. All creators start with a spark of inspiration—a single thread they receive while dreaming and imagining in the formless dark and then begin to spin into reality in the light of day.

When the patriarchy usurped the goddess-loving culture (about 3,000 BCE), they gave Athena a new story—turning her from weaver to warrior, the guardian of Athens—the city-state ruled by men. She won the role of patron of Athens by introducing the olive tree and planting it at the Acropolis. It symbolized peace (extending an olive branch), as well as a source of sustenance to its people. Athena was depicted with helmet, sword, shield, and aegis as warrior and protectress, whereas in her earlier role as a weaver she wore a simple chiton, a loose dress of the times that allowed her to move about freely.

Athena carries both of these qualities—the ability to be innovative and free-thinking as well as to strategize and implement her plans. She is both a creator and a destroyer, a goddess of war and peace, a bridge between matriarchy and patriarchy. She carries these opposites within her, knowing when it is time to implement one or the other. The essence of Athena is that she knows what she wants and goes after it with vision and purpose. She is an archetype for a woman who dares to *dream it* and *do it*.

Call on Athena when you are done resting and dreaming and ready to formulate specific plans and take action. Just as she emerged from Zeus's head at birth, she helps you give birth to the creation that has been tumbling around in your head and bring it out into the world.

There are many tools available to help you plan your life and set goals. It is helpful to have a planner, calendar, or agenda so you can be specific about your commitment to realizing your dreams. When you are ready to move from imagining to manifesting, start by setting a realistic, attainable goal and then determine your course of action. It is helpful to have a one-year plan and a three-year plan. This way you can dream yourself into being and chart your progress to the end goal.

**Ask yourself these questions to hone your vision for next year and three years:**

Where would I like to live?
What job or career would I like to be doing, and what is my role?
How much money do I want to make?
What do I want my relationship status to be?
What project do I want to start (or finish)?
What do I want to learn and get better at?

Athena is a planner who thinks ahead and imagines the steps it will take and the tools she will need to get to where she wants to go. Then she follows through with deliberate actions using her innate wisdom to guide her. Follow these steps to accomplish a goal you have set for yourself.

## Eight Steps to Reach Your Goal

1. Write down your goal and why it is important to you—how it feeds your soul. Be clear about your motivation and the boon you will receive by completing it.
2. Create your action plan by listing the steps it will take to reach your goal. Consider making a roadmap, noting stopping points, turns, and milestones along the way.
3. Decide how long it will take to complete each step and a realistic end date. This can always be revised as needed. Write these "deadlines" on your calendar or planner.
4. List the actions to take at each step.
5. List the tools needed for each step.
6. Decide what reward to give yourself for accomplishing each step and reaching your final goal. This is important. It could be a night out, a vacation, or any sort of treat that feels like a pat on the back, a well-earned break, or a gift to yourself.
7. List potential obstacles you see along the way and strategies for overcoming each one. What help could you ask for? What do you need to know or learn? What do you need to let go of? What do you need to tell yourself to get past self-doubt or transform the obstacle?
8. Write down the feeling you have now at the start, what you want to feel along the way, and how you will feel at the end. Ask Athena to remind you of your hopes and dreams and to help you see yourself prevail—who, like her, crafts her life to fulfill her dreams.

### Objects and Symbols to Consider for Your Altar to Athena

**Colors:** white, gold, blue, purple

**Objects:** figurines and images of Athena, owl, sword

**Gemstones:** azurite, lapis lazuli, amethyst

**Flowers:** peony, lily, ivy

**Element:** fire

**Chakra:** solar plexus (3rd chakra)

# Athena Speaks

Sister, it is time to wake up and map out your journey on paper. This is a great tool of empowerment—a way to both remind you of how you wish to spend your time and to hold yourself accountable. My power word is: Strategize!

Whether or not you have a grand plan, use your planner or calendar to outline your week: your hours of work, times to rest and play, when to exercise, and blocks of creative time so these do not slip between the cracks. Your creative projects need to be reflected on your calendar, as the creative juices are what fill the chalice, the vessel of the feminine. It does not matter what you create. It could be making muffins, collaging or painting, writing, or a handicraft that gives you pleasure and pause. Just make time.

The vision board that my sister, the Goddess Jana, inspired helps you see the bigger picture. Your planner helps you with the day-to-day and keeps you on track to fulfill your dreams and goals, step by step.

My wisdom is helping you to know when to say yes and when to say no. Prioritize the activities and people in your life that are important to you. Be careful not to over-plan or over-budget your time. Balance your time between productivity and rest and relaxation. Give yourself days off. Enlist the help and support of friends and loved ones at times when you crave a break, and spend time with them. Ask for what you need!

At the end of each month, reassess your time management, whether or not you kept to your vision, and what you may need to modify and balance the next month. Hold me in your vision—my sword in hand, ready to cut through difficulties, my shield worn as protection from the slings and arrows of life, my trusted owl on my shoulder, providing wisdom and perspective. Your dreams are worth fighting for. Let's go!

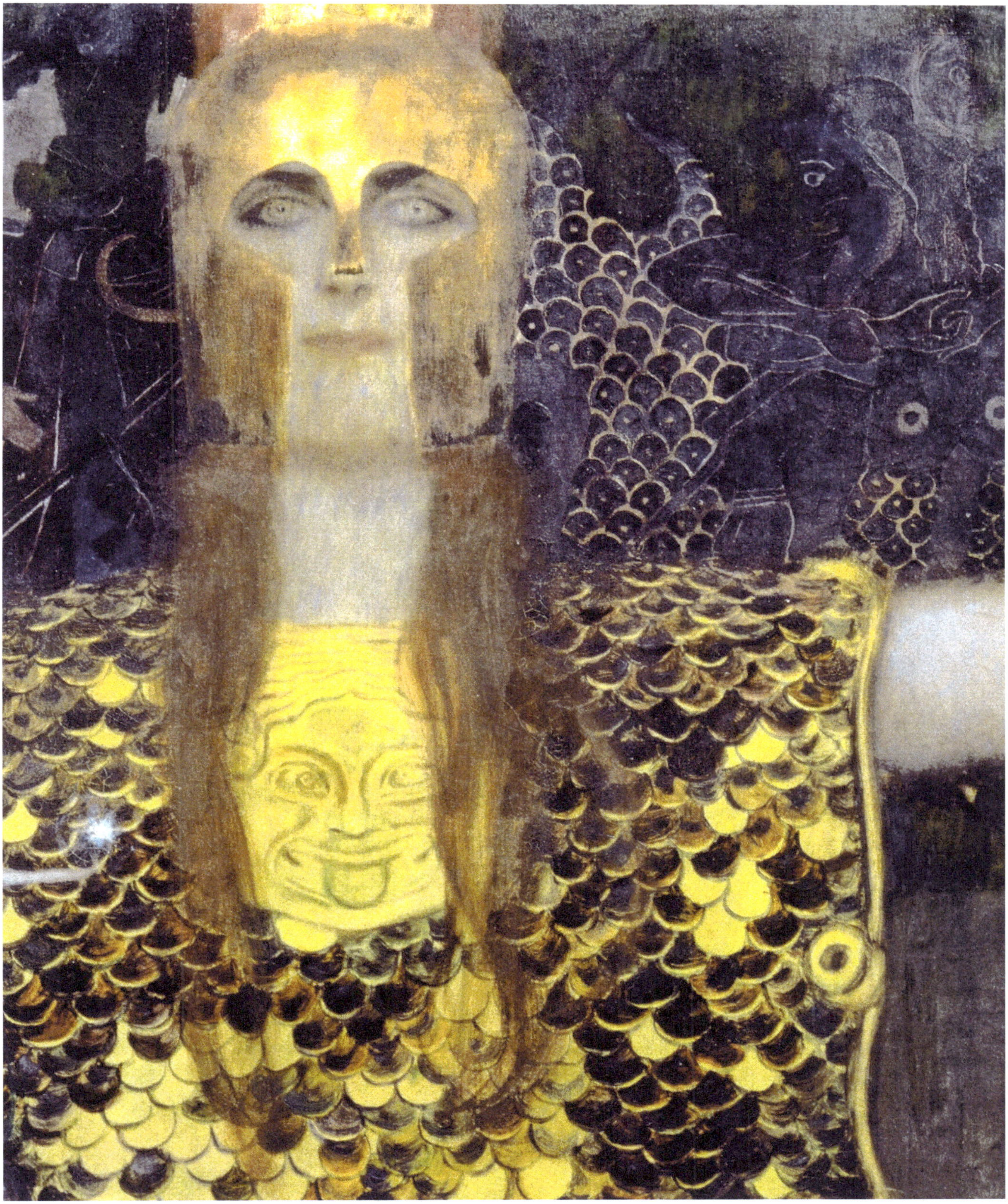

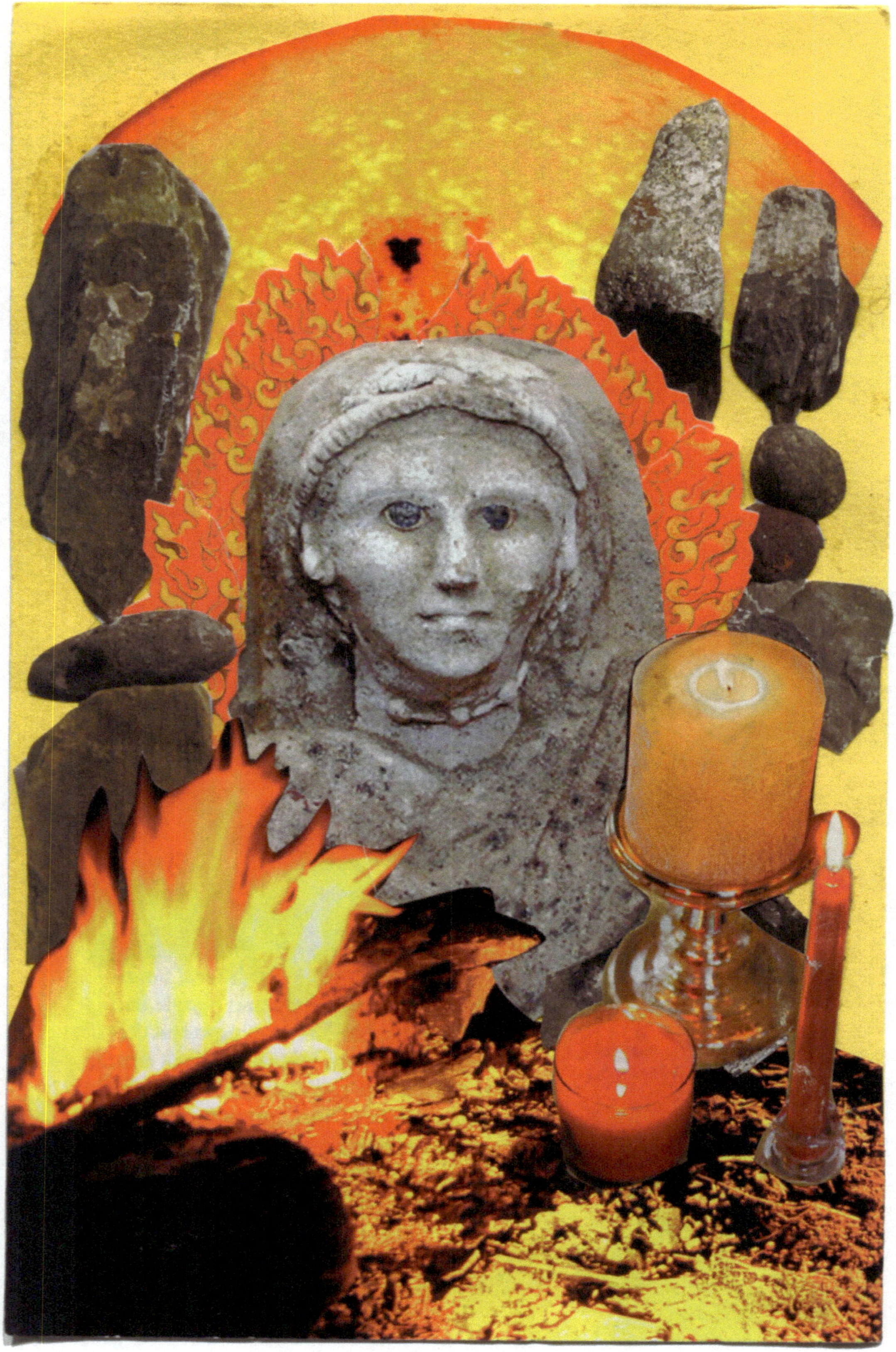

# Chapter Three

# Creativity and Play

As a therapist, I routinely ask my clients who complain of stress, overwork, overwhelm, and malaise: What is your creative outlet? Surprisingly, many don't have an answer for that. They don't factor in creative time, play time, or down time in their daily lives. Some don't think of themselves as creative at all and have no idea how to go about discovering this part of themselves.

The truth is women are creative beings with the capacity to give birth, to bring forth life from the vessel of creativity contained in their bodies—the womb. The imagination is fertile ground if watered and tended to. It really does not matter how you express your creativity, it just matters that you do—on a regular basis, like eating and sleeping. Often women don't realize that many of the things they routinely enjoy doing actually are creative expressions, such as baking, organizing, decorating a room, writing in a journal, or fixing a problem.

Some of these activities may feel like drudgery or work and are not necessarily what you associate with being creative. However, it is important to realize in what ways you are being creative, whether it is on the job or at home, cooking, or raising kids. A change in perspective or in the way you approach these daily tasks can help you feel differently about them and make them more conscious, creative explorations. At the same time, it is important to find a form of expression that you truly enjoy, that feeds

## Chloe's Story

Chloe loved to make up stories from an early age. She drew pictures to go along with the poems and fairy tales she wrote, inspired by ones she listened to at bedtime. After graduating from school, she got married and had two children. She loved being a mother—especially reading to her children and inspiring them to make art—but she began to realize she had become a bystander in her own life. She was living for her husband and children and not herself. Chloe realized she had no outlet for her creative and fertile mind. She had let her friendships fall by the wayside, too. She knew she needed to make time to play.

Chloe had a recurrent dream about an exotic flower that was dying under her care. She knew it was up to her to feed and water it so it could bloom, but she kept forgetting to. The dream reflected her dilemma.

your soul, that becomes your passion, and make time for it on a regular basis.

Being creative is a way to engage the imagination, to play—something that comes naturally for a child, but which you can easily lose touch with as an adult with responsibilities. How does this happen? Because you let your busy-ness, work life, and sense of responsibility take precedence and squeeze play and creative time out of existence.

You get stuck in the belief, "I don't have time!" or "I'm not creative!" You have forgotten how much your little girl (your Inner Child) loves to play and may indeed long to play. When you allow time and give permission for creativity and play in your life, your Inner Child not only wakes up, but lights up, and magical things begin to happen. Making space for creativity and play and allowing yourself to enjoy some "time off" from the daily grind is self-care.

Exploring the many ways to be imaginative, artistic, and playful affords you the opportunity to know yourself better and enjoy a more balanced life. Stoke the fires of your creative womb as if it were a forge where metals are bent and transformation occurs. This you will learn from the goddess Brigid, the Celtic triple goddess of smithing, creativity, and healing. She is known as Brigid of the Flame because she is a fiery, solar goddess. Fire is the element of action and transmutation. With Brigid's help, you can turn boredom, over-seriousness, and ennui into excitement, involvement, and engagement by fanning your inner fire. She is especially a goddess of creative expression through the written word—journaling, poetry, and prose.

You will also meet the Egyptian cat goddess Bast, considered the Maiden aspect of the Egyptian Triple Goddess, which also includes Sekhmet (Crone) and Hathor or Isis (Mother), goddess archetypes explored in later chapters. The playful Bast inspires you to let loose, let your little girl out, and see the world through her eyes—with childlike wonder, curiosity, and openness.

And finally, you will encounter Grandmother Spider, a Native American goddess who inspires you to weave deeper meaning and joy into your life as part of the bigger picture—how you design your life.

## How Creative and Playful Are You?

- Start by making a list of all the things you do that are *creative*, i.e., producing or transforming something, whether at work or home. It could involve making art or writing, creative problem-solving, or assembling something, which might involve cooking or building. Creativity involves transforming one thing into another or creating something out of nothing (think of a spark becoming a fire).
- Next, list things you do that are *playful*—things you enjoy doing that take you outside of yourself, that are fun, and that bring you a sense of childlike joy and a release from worries. They may involve playing with other people, animals, or playing alone.
- What on either of these lists surprises you or nudges you to see it differently?
- Number them in the order of which gives you the most joy and relaxation to the least.
- What makes them pleasurable and fun? Is there anything you can think of that would make them more enjoyable to you?
- What artistic or playful activities did you enjoy as a child but haven't made time for since?
- What would you like to add to these lists that you've never tried but want to?
- What stops you?
- What would it take to commit to learning or trying new creative and playful activities?
- Make a collage, draw, or paint a page in your journal for the creative, playful child part of you.

# Brigid

Brigid is the goddess who presides over *Imbolc*, a cross-quarter day on the Celtic Wheel of the Year, the mid-point between the Winter Solstice and the Spring Equinox. It is usually celebrated along with Brigid's Day on February 1. This is a day to honor her presence by lighting candles or by leaving a shawl or scarf outside the night before and bringing it in the next day along with her blessings and healing for the year ahead.

Imbolc means *in the belly*, and refers to the pregnant ewes at this time of year. In olden times, the birth of the lambs signaled the beginning of spring and the return of the light. It is seen as a time of "quickening," of sensing the first stirrings beneath the surface—the same feeling a woman gets during pregnancy when she feels the first movements of life within her belly. Brigid is therefore a midwife to what wants to be born, to the creative life force within you.

# The Story of Brigid

It is in Gaelic Ireland that the goddess Brigid, whose name means *Exalted One*, has deep roots. She was born of Danu, Mother Goddess of Ireland, and the Dagda, the chief god of the Tuatha Dé Danaan, a tribe of gods and supernatural beings who inhabited the ancient land of Éire. She was born at sunrise when a pillar of fire reached from her head to the heavens, earning her the name, *Brigid of the Flame*.

After many invasions and battles, the Tuatha Dé Danaan grew tired of fighting, but they did not give up Dear Éire. It is said they simply disappeared from sight, yet still inhabit the land as the invisible Faerie folk. They reside in the Otherworld, across the veil, appearing to mortals when they have good cause or on the eves of the eight turnings of the Celtic Wheel of the Year. Imbolc is the time of Brigid's felt presence and honoring.

Brigid has long been known as a triple goddess: *creatrix* of the hearth fire or smithing (transformation), arts and crafts (particularly writing and poetry), and the healing arts (especially midwifery and childbirth). She stirred the cauldron of plenty that made the healing elixirs and soups that brought people back to health. One of her miraculous powers was that her pot was always full and never empty. The poor and hungry knew they could always have a bowl of soup or cup of milk when they went to Brigid for help. It was said her cows gave milk four times a day. Whatever food was needed she made appear.

A temple was built to honor her and the eternal flame at its center was kept alive, as in the ancient Greek and Roman temples, by 19 vestal virgins, known as *kelle* in Ireland. Each took turns tending the fire on successive nights. On the 19th night, the priestess would say, "Brigid, guard your fire, this is your night," and Brigid would come to stand guard. No man was allowed to enter this hallowed ground.

In the 5th century, when Christianity was spreading like wildfire across Europe, Brigid, the sacred goddess, became Brigid, the beloved saint. Because the Celtic people were loath to let go of such a powerful force as the Goddess Brigid, the Christian church cleverly repurposed her into a saint. The goddess Brigid's story of making miracles and creating plenty became the saint's story. In the Christian version, she was sometimes referred to as Mary of the Gael, Mother of the Gaelic people, a midwife who was said to have helped deliver the baby Jesus—a way of attributing her creative power to the new religion.

The Brigid who became a saint is steeped in lore. She is said to have been born of enslaved people, her father a Druid, a pagan spiritual leader of the ancient Celts, a people made up of many tribes throughout central Europe and the British Isles. She arrived at the crack of dawn in the threshold of a doorway, two symbols of liminal states—both of this world and not of this world. Because of this, she represents the mediating force of standing between two opposites and holding the tension, e.g., pagan/Christian, freedom/enslavement, rich/poor, upperworld/underworld, fairie/mortal, fire/water.

One story goes that when Brigid was a newborn babe in the cradle, her parents left her sleeping in the house while they worked in the field. Neighbors alerted them to flames consuming the house and all came running. Upon entering, they saw that the baby lay untouched by the flames though the house burned around her.

Another story tells of how as a young adult Brigid went to the Catholic bishop to ask for land to build an abbey. The bishop scoffed at her temerity and said he would grant her as much land as her mantle could cover. Apparently he did not realize the extent of her abilities to create plenty, because when she spread her cloak, it covered many acres. The bishop had no choice but to grant her the land on which she built her abbey—on the same spot as the Goddess Brigid's fire temple where 19 priestesses guarded the sacred flame. Saint Brigid carried on the tradition and kept the flame burning. It is still burning to this day, tended by the nuns of Brigid's Abbey of Kildare.

Along with the three creative energies of smithing, creating, and healing that Brigid carries, she has another Triple Goddess aspect of the Maiden, Mother, and Crone. The Maiden is associated with spring and new life, the Mother with the abundant time of summer and fall, and the Crone (or Cailleach) with the bone woman of winter and waning energy.

Legend says that every year, Brigid goes into a cave as the Cailleach or divine hag of winter and comes out as the Maiden of spring, spreading her green mantle across the land, restoring its verdancy. Think of this as holding your creative energy inside during the winter when you dream and plant seeds in the darkness, which then burst forth with new energy and vitality in the spring. No matter the season, giving yourself time to play and let ideas germinate before you are ready to bring them into the light honors Brigid's energy.

**If you apply these three aspects to the cycle of creativity you will see how they play their parts:**

**The Maiden** as the inspiration or genesis of an idea—getting started, planting seeds, dreaming

**The Mother** as the time of giving birth to and tending a creative project—bringing your energy and fullness to it

**The Crone** as the one who knows when it is time to complete a project and release it to the world

## The Creative Fire

Brigid of the Flame ignites your fiery, solar, active nature. As a Triple Goddess she fires her arrows of creativity, healing, and smithing, right into your solar plexus. This is your chakra center of power, of getting things done in the world, fed by the sacral chakra below it of feminine creativity and infused by the heart center above it.

Brigid's shadow aspect (the unlived part), represents feeling stuck, unmotivated, uninspired and immobilized—perhaps unwilling to claim or give life to a latent creative talent. Keep in mind that being quiet and inert in the cave of winter can be by choice—a longing to rest, hibernate and gestate—or by an unconscious process that draws you down into depression. Activating Brigid in her light-bringing aspect helps you move out of this dark and quiet repose when you feel ready or inspired. Sometimes the very act of getting out of yourself and doing things in the world, particularly creative activities, helps to awaken you and move you out of a rut.

## Journaling

As a goddess of creativity, Brigid presides over poetry and the written word. Keeping a journal and writing each day or as you feel inspired helps you know yourself better. Writing down your thoughts and feelings helps you work through issues and conflicts and come to terms with them. Writing is a way to move out of a reactionary mode and into a reflective, responsive mode, especially when you feel triggered or bothered by something or someone, or overwhelmed with thoughts and emotions.

Journaling is a good method of self-care as you are allowing self-expression and listening to what your soul needs. It helps you gain perspective and work through swirling feelings or confusing thoughts. Writing is calming. It helps you process and order your thoughts and feelings and make sense of them. It assists you in being more mindful of what you need and want. A good way to start journaling is to write a line each day, noting something you saw, something you heard, something you felt.

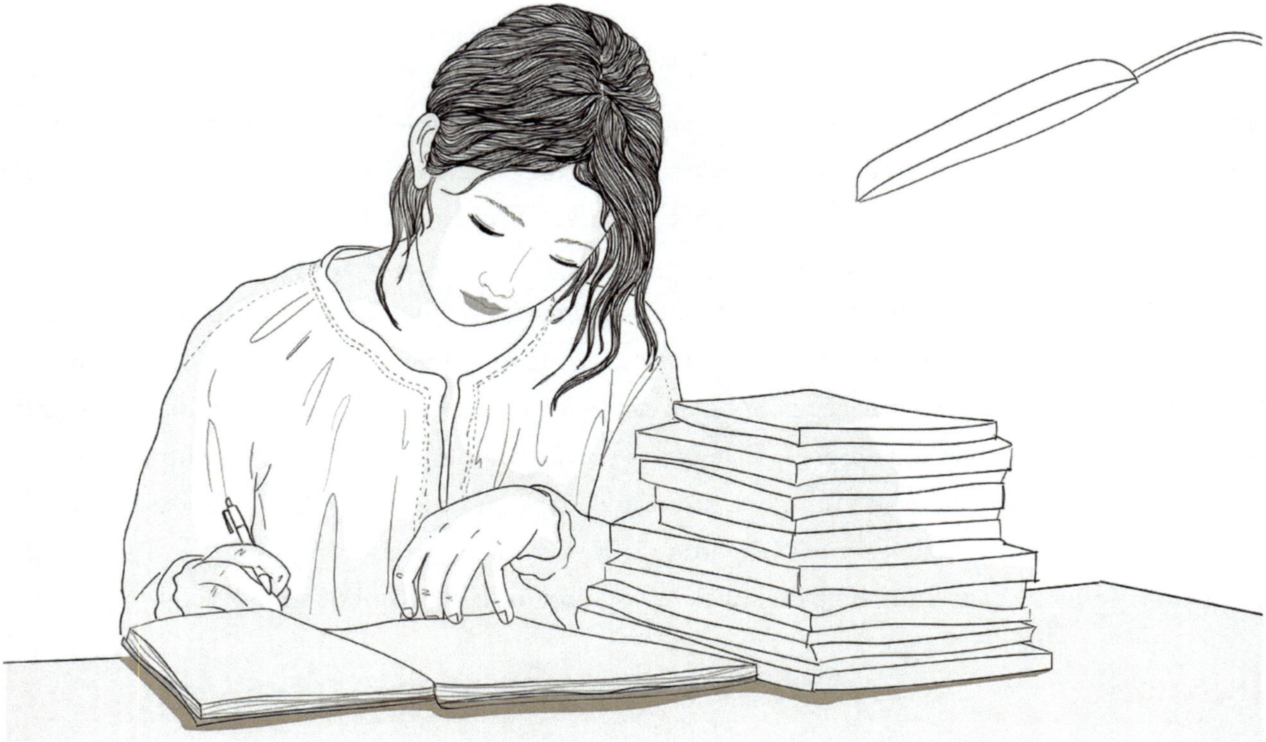

# Creative Writing

To ignite Brigid's creative flame, try these exercises:

**WRITE A LETTER TO YOURSELF**

Writing a letter to yourself from the goddess is a good way to resolve unease, fear, and doubt. Bring a problem, concern, or fear to Brigid, and ask her to give you guidance. Pose it as a question for her to answer. Light a candle to bring in her spark of inspiration and begin writing from her voice. What does this nurturing, healing, creative maiden-mother-crone goddess want you to know? Be open to receive her wisdom.

**WRITE A STORY OR FAIRY TALE**

Cast yourself as the heroine of your own story—the little girl who enters the forest to find herself—and choose one of the goddesses you enjoy working with to be your fairy godmother, wise woman, or knowing elder who helps you overcome adversity and find your way to your True Self. Imagine the heroine of your fairy tale experiencing the many trials and tribulations of your own life and how she finds her way out of the woods. What has she learned?

**WRITE POEMS**

One way to connect with Brigid and wake up your creative muse is to write poetry. Try writing a poem each day for a week or a month to flex this creative muscle. Avoid judging yourself. Just let the words flow, the fires burn bright, and see what comes.

**Try these different poetic forms:**

**ODE** — Write an ode to Brigid or another goddess using what you have learned of her sacred energy. An ode is a lyric poem that celebrates a person, place, or thing.

*Ode to Bast*
*Sleek and black her fur,*
*Oh, sweet Bastet, Come,*
*I call to Her.*
*She's there for me, night or day*
*With a soft meow*
*She purrs, "Let's play!"*

**HAIKU** — Write a haiku to capture a feeling, experience, or image that can be expressed in one breath. A haiku typically has five syllables in the first line, seven syllables in the second, and five in the third.

*Imbolc quickening*
*Stirring the cauldron inside*
*Ready to give birth*

**ACROSTIC** - Write a six-line acrostic poem that begins with the letters of Brigid's name:

*Beloved goddess*
*Roaring fire*
*Inspiration personified*
*Grace me with your presence*
*Ignite my flame*
*Daring me to become You*

Now write an acrostic poem using your own name, invoking your passion and power as a woman and goddess of fire.

**DIAMANTE** — Write a diamante, a diamond-shaped poem with seven lines and two subjects, usually opposite. The first and last lines have one noun. The second and sixth lines have two adjectives. The third and fifth lines have three nouns ending with -ing. The fourth line has four nouns; the first two nouns in line four relate to the first subject introduced on the first line, and the second two nouns on the fourth line introduce the second subject, the opposite of the first.

*Creativity*
*Imaginative, Inventive*
*Bubbling, Sparking, Bursting*
*Fire, Vision, Blindness, Ash*
*Smoldering, Waning, Deadening*
*Numb, Bored*
*Banality*

**FOUND POETRY** — Find a page of text from a book or magazine and circle words that appeal to you and form a narrative picture—a poem using found words. After circling the words, you may want to color or collage over the other words leaving just the words you have selected for your poem.

You can also cut out a variety of words from printed sources and collage a poem this way. If taken from magazines this can turn into a colorful collage of words. You can add collaged images to enhance your poems as well.

Chloe, who loved reading fairy tales as a girl, enjoyed the creative exercise of turning her life's story into a fairy tale. She could easily imagine herself as the little girl who ventures into the woods and encounters all sorts of beings—witches and helpers—as well as challenges to meet, just as she has in her own life. She realizes she is on her way to finding herself and her life's purpose. Setting down her story in such a way inspires her to begin writing a children's book.

# Brigid Speaks

Dear Daughter, I am with you in the flame of inspiration and passion that you feel in your belly. I invite you to stoke your creative fire as a way to love and express yourself. Know that your creativity is your superpower. Do not hide your unique creative viewpoint from yourself or the world. Let it be revealed.

I will help you transform fear and doubt into love and confidence. Love yourself as a good mother loves her sweet and holy child. Be the good mother who makes sure her child has time to create and provides her with the time and materials she needs to do it.

Whatever criticism, shame, or doubt may have been planted in the soil of your being, it is now time to root it out and be done with it. Name old beliefs or messages you received as a child or have come to believe over time—the lies that say you are not creative, not an artist, not good enough, not deserving, not worthy. Give them to me by letting them go into the fire, and I will help you transform them into truths you can live by. Once the old lie is burnt, write the affirmation that you wish to carry with you, the truth that will replace the lie, for you are a divine child, born of the creative fire, just like me.

## Objects and Symbols to Consider for Your Altar to Brigid

**Colors:** green, blue, white

**Objects:** candle, chalice with water, green shawl or scarf (her green mantle), Brigid's cross (often woven from reeds or grasses), Brigid doll (made from corn husks or straw)

**Gemstones:** fire agate

**Flowers:** hyacinth, heather, wisteria

**Element:** fire

**Chakra:** 2nd (sacral) & 5th (throat chakra)

Helen

## Bast

The Egyptian cat goddess Bast, short for Bastet, is a solar goddess like Brigid. All solar goddesses are creative, fiery, and dynamic. They like to inspire and shine. Like all cats, Bast is curious, adventurous, and playful, and brings these qualities into her relationship with you. She invites you to explore what it means to play as an adult with many responsibilities, an adult who may have long ago abandoned the idea that playing is important. Bast asks, "Wouldn't you like to have less seriousness and more playfulness in your life?"

## The Story of Bast

The beguiling goddess with a cat's head known as Bast was born of the Egyptian sun god, Ra, and the goddess, Isis. She was one of many children known as the "eye of Ra," meaning she carried his power, influence, and sovereignty. Her full name, Bastet, means *the soul of Isis*, so while she carries her father's masculine solar spirit, she carries her mother's feminine creative essence. She enjoyed riding with her father upon his solar barge across the sky each day, but she was also venerated for her lunar energies and referred to as *the eye of the moon*. The people looked up to her as a protector, bestower of fertility, and goddess of the arts.

In early Egypt, Bast was a fierce lioness and guardian of lower Egypt while her sister and counterpart, Sekhmet, the lion-headed goddess (you will meet her in CH. 7, page 161) was the protector of upper Egypt. During her warrior period, Bast vanquished Apophis, the serpent god of the underworld who wanted to plunge the world into darkness and chaos. Bast's feral nature became tamer over time, but she maintained her wild heart. By 1,000 BCE, Bast metamorphosed into a domestic cat who was both playful and protective. She watched over women and children, protecting them from disease, and her earthly cat counterparts were good at keeping vermin from getting into the grain.

She was the patroness of Bubastis, the ancient capital of lower Egypt and her cult center. There, a temple was built in her name with a surrounding lake. Festivities were held there in honor of her joyful spirit every year—a bawdy affair with music, dance, drink, and merriment. Her feast day is February 5.

The ancient Egyptians revered cats and considered them part of the family. When their feline pets died they mummified them and buried them alongside family members in their shared crypts. As a guardian and protector, Bast safeguards your childlike wonder and stands in the way of anyone or anything that wants to steal your nourishment or deprive you of enjoyment and playtime.

Bast is most often depicted as a black cat in a woman's body wearing a beautiful beaded dress. She exemplifies the Maiden aspect of the Triple Goddess, and as such, helps you get in touch with your innocence, playfulness, and light-heartedness—your Inner Child. She helps you be more in your body and less in your head. Cats are very sensual animals and love to be petted and held as they purr their contentment. By giving yourself more time to play, you, too, will be purring with pleasure. Besides being a protective figure, Bast is a goddess of music, dance, and physicality and can also be competitive, cunning, curious, and enjoy playing games.

**Answer these journal prompts to explore Bast's playful energy:**

*Remember how you played as a little girl . . .*
- What were your favorite activities?
- Who did you most enjoy playing with?
- What made playing with this person fun or special?
- How did you like to play by yourself?
- What did you enjoy playing as a child that you would like to do now?
- What kind of play would you most enjoy now? (See list below for ideas.)
- What steps do you need to take to make play a part of your life?

Play implies having fun, feeling pleasure and exhilaration, laughing, and letting go. Your catlike or childlike nature of inquisitiveness, exploration, and openness guides you to find what gives you joy. The wonderful thing about play is it doesn't have to have a known outcome.

Challenge yourself by choosing something from the list below to try each week. Put it on your planner or calendar, ensuring that your creative time and playtime are scheduled and balanced with work and rest.

## Ideas for play (many involve being creative, too)

- Play a musical instrument
- Dance (learn a new dance, take a class, or just do your thing)
- Sing; join a singing group
- Listen to music or go to a concert
- Sports activities (join a team?)
- Physical activities like running, swimming, hiking, biking, skiing, rock climbing
- Play games (discover new games; play favorite games; organize a regular game night with friends)
- Be spontaneous: do something fun or adventurous without planning
- Go someplace new or different and take it in with childlike wonder
- Arts and crafts: painting, drawing, sculpting, collaging, building or making
- Write: use your imagination to make up a story, poem, or other piece
- Travel to a destination near or far and discover new people, places, and ideas
- Gather with friends or relatives (who are fun, enjoyable company)
- Go to a beach and build sandcastles, swim, sunbathe, etc.
- Throw a party or attend a party or gathering
- Go to a park and explore (amusement park or nature park?)
- Collect something you enjoy having: go on treasure hunts
- Try something new (e.g., restaurant, skill, pastime, hobby, activity, game)
- Act/drama: join a theater group or class
- Comedy: learn improv, go to a comedy club, watch funny movies or stand-up
- Interact/play with animals
- Interact/play with children
- Go on dates with fun-loving, interesting people
- Go to a movie or a play
- Try a new recipe or make treats in a playful, fun way (with someone?)
- Garden or walk barefoot on the earth, dig in the dirt
- Read and escape into a good book
- Sexual play: let go and enjoy the moment with someone you love (maybe yourself?)
- Take a walk in nature: find new places of beauty to visit and explore
- Spend time with a friend or loved one doing a fun activity or just being together
- Divination: do readings for yourself or ask someone to do a reading for you
- Take a day off from work and do what gives you joy (have a Me Day!)

# Bast Speaks

I invite you, Sister, to come play with me. Lighten your load. Get in touch with your feline, instinctual nature. Make space in your life for what gives you pleasure and make time for me to be with you and show you how.

I love to laugh and be silly, to dance and sing and play games, to use my imagination. I want you to join me in this adventure of life. Is something in the way of you doing that? If so, bat it away for the day, and allow yourself to be the maiden, the carefree girl, or curious cat whose spirit is free to try new things, to do what you love, to make magic.

If it was hard for you to enjoy life as a child or if you were not allowed much playtime and spontaneity, I send you warm, cuddly cat hugs. I invite you to swat away these old obstacles. Pounce on any outdated beliefs that say you don't deserve to have fun and turn them on their ear. Notice any old messages that say, "Hard work and productivity are all that matter," and replace them with truths like, "I give myself permission to be light-hearted and to have fun. I deserve to enjoy life. I make time to play." I am with you all the way.

Let me be your companion and we will partake in the delights of life together. Come play with me!

## Objects and symbols to consider for your altar to Bast

**Colors:** pink, red, white

**Objects:** Bast or cat figurine, photo of you as a playful child, a favorite toy

**Gemstones:** alabaster, cymophane (cat's eye), onyx, turquoise

**Flowers:** pussywillow, cattails, blue lotus, catnip

**Element:** earth

**Chakra:** sacral (2nd chakra)

# Grandmother Spider

And finally, Grandmother Spider, also known as Spider Woman in some indigenous cultures, is a *creatrix* who is here to help you claim your place on the web of life. She comes from Native American tradition, where she is seen as the weaver of the world. She teaches you to trust your creative instincts and to weave them into the very fibers of your being. She encourages you to create a life worth living, a life filled with joy and purpose. No matter what circumstance you are born into, she assures that you will find your way to a well-lived life by staying true to yourself and connected to Source.

Grandmother Spider is the personification of the Creator archetype. This archetypal energy is realized through your imagination, and it is where self-expression, innovation, originality, and artistry are born. It is not only what you create but how you live your life that Grandmother Spider presides over. Her message is that you are one with her and together you co-create the world. The Creator in you gives birth to new ideas, projects, and ways of being that reflect your unique soul.

If you feel you have lost the thread to your True Self, the one you came in with and knew as a child until you were tamed, tamped down, and turned away from your original purpose and unique spark, Grandmother Spider guides you to pick up the thread again. Familial, societal, and cultural pressures to conform, to be the obedient "good girl," and hold to what others define as feminine and proper causes women to lose sight of their wild nature, to disconnect from their creative core. You can spend many years going in circles trying to live up to others' expectations, or you can circumvent this aimless wandering by finding the thread and following it to your True Self. Grandmother Spider encourages you to be creative in the way you live your life, by learning and practicing whatever it is that feeds your passion, whatever it is that gives you joy, and sticking to it. An old proverb tells us: Begin to weave and the Divine will provide the thread.

Many Native American tribes, including the Hopi, Pueblo, Kiowa, Choctaw, and Cherokee, venerate this beneficent goddess who is credited with weaving the world and the web of life, which we are all a part of.

# The Story of Grandmother Spider

Grandmother Spider loved to imagine and create beautiful things. One day she made the four races of people out of clay—red, black, white, and yellow—different colors yet equal in shared humanity. However, they were living in darkness and needed light from the sun that shone on the other side of the world.

Several animals tried to steal the sun, but Possum just got the fur on his tail burnt off, and when Buzzard tried, he singed off the feathers on his head. Grandmother Spider was nothing if not resourceful and knew what to do. She got busy and spun a great web that reached all the way to the other side of the earth. Then she fashioned a clay pot to carry fire in and away she crept along the strands of the web to the other side.

When she got there, she bided her time unseen in a dark corner, looking for her chance to pounce. Seizing the moment, she quickly grabbed a piece of the sun, stuffed it into the pot, and scurried back to the people she had created. As she made her journey home the fire grew bigger and brighter until Grandmother Spider had no choice but to fling it into the air where it stuck, shining brightly on her people. With her ingenuity, all were able to see in the light of day and thrive in the warmth of the sun she had brought to them.

A small ember was left in her bowl, and this Grandmother Spider gifted to humans to make their own fire on Earth. This, in turn, inspired them to nurture the creative flame within. It is the job of humans to use this goddess-given power to continuously generate—her gift to the two-leggeds—and become co-creators along with her.

⇉⇉⇉- ·.· -⇇⇇⇇

You are connected to her—to the Great Mother, the source of life—by an invisible thread that extends from your crown chakra at the top of your head to the center of the web that Grandmother Spider perpetually weaves and repairs. Imagine her web stretching across the universe, where she lives and watches over you and all her creations. If you visualize this connection to Source you will feel supported, seen, and ensouled.

Each of us is responsible for contributing to the great web, to its structural integrity. Spiders have the ability to pluck the strings of their web much like a guitar and to glean sensory information from it and all who come into contact with it. Grandmother Spider knows your hunger, your desire, your creative longing, and she wants to help you learn to play the strings of your own instrument.

Like Grandmother Spider, who tunes the silk by adjusting the tension and connections to build a stronger web, you, too, can adjust the way you live in the world, fine-tuning your sensibilities and capabilities so as to live up to the promise of a soul-filled life. This is what she offers you. She helps you see the obstacles that trap you and to remove them or go around them so that you can live up to your creative potential. She asks, "What is your creative gift? How will you use it?"

Grandmother Spider wants you to find what gives your life meaning. It may be something you loved doing as a child and have forgotten or set aside for more practical pursuits, perhaps settling for something that is sucking the life out of you. She reminds you of what you once aspired to. Did you want to be a musician? Did you once love to paint? Did you dream of being a writer one day? Did you like making and building things with your hands? Did you enjoy decorating and beautifying your living space? Do you love to sing? What stopped you from realizing your dreams?

Your Grandmother wants you to remember what you love and to find your way to doing what feeds your soul, even if it means starting over, beginning anew. Follow her thread and she will lead you to your True Self.

## Objects and Symbols to Consider for Your Altar to Grandmother Spider

**Colors:** black, white, violet

**Objects:** spider figurines, web images or weavings, crown

**Gemstones:** spiderweb-cut amethyst, spiderweb jasper, obsidian or agate

**Flowers:** chrysanthemum, spider mum, orchid, red spider lily

**Element:** air

**Chakra:** crown (7th chakra)

# Grandmother Spider Speaks

I am the sacred spinner, and you, too, are a weaver, Granddaughter. I am glad you have looked up to see me on my silken web. When you look at me, remember that you and I and all other beings are weavers of this world together. Each being is connected by a cord, part of the great web, tying you to me, the Great Mother, just as you were once connected to your mother by an umbilical cord. As above, so below.

When you were born, you became a part of this web and were given gifts to help you create your own unique life. It is up to you to use your gifts and manifest your dreams of a whole-hearted, well-lived life on this Earth.

Remember what your True Self came here knowing, what purpose your Soul came here to fulfill. If you are not sure of your talents and gifts, or have forgotten, now is the time to take their measure, to remember, to claim them. Now is the time to weave your destiny, to take part in the spiral dance, in keeping with your soul's desire.

I will watch over you as I continue spinning, and I ask you to join me. There is no right or wrong, good or bad, when it comes to creating art or your life. Leave behind judgment and perfection and allow yourself to find your way, to begin at the beginning, and to weave your way to the center. Follow the thread you were given at birth and you will find your way back to the Source.

# Journal Prompts

How do you imagine the unique spark that was you at birth?

What words or images come to mind when you think of who you came here to be?

What would you like your life to be like going forward?

If you could change one thing about your life, what would it be?

What gives your life meaning?

What makes your life worth living?

What, if anything, is missing from your life?

What would it take to find this missing piece and add it to your life?

What does a soulful life look and feel like to you?

What do you imagine it would take to make a more soulful, meaningful life?

~90~

# Chapter Four

# Depression and Grief

It is time to look at how to practice self-care when you are likely to need it most—when feeling down and depressed. Depression is a way to describe feelings of sadness, worthlessness, despondency, lack of motivation, difficulty concentrating, inability to feel pleasure, and low energy. It affects how you eat and sleep and view the world. Clinicians consider it a mood disorder that affects the way you think and feel. While there are varying degrees and types of depression, estimates are that at least 10% of the population will experience depression that rises to the level of a serious condition at some point in life. For some it is a short-lived episode; for others it is a long-term struggle. Learning to navigate through depression is key, and the goddesses you will meet in this chapter show you how.

Recognize that feeling depressed at times is a normal part of living. You can point to situations that cause you to feel sad and depressed that are very understandable responses. Conversely, a depressive episode may come on without any seeming provocation or cause, often experienced as a loss of meaning. However, depression can be normalized and understood as a state most people feel at various points in their lives. You are not your mood, and it is okay to feel low, sad, and depressed at times. Your mood need not define you. You can learn to both accept and feel your emotions without letting them overwhelm or control you. Learning to self-regulate helps you through these challenging periods so you come out the other side. For those whose depression

## Sadie's Story

Sadie has had bouts of depression since college, when she suffered her first disabling episode that made it difficult to get out of bed and keep up with her studies. She ended up dropping classes and felt alone and helpless as her parents went through a divorce after years of fighting, which Sadie witnessed growing up. Her preoccupied parents offered little comfort or guidance to her as a child or as a young adult.

Now in her 40s, Sadie still struggles with seasonal depression when fall arrives, reminding her of those gloomy, challenging days when depression first hit and she felt alone and abandoned. She realizes this association to a truly difficult time in her life leaves her feeling stuck in the past. She would like to find a better way to navigate these dark passages.

is related to traumatic life events, healing from the original pain and learning to self-soothe (as a good mother soothes her child) is crucial.

If you think of your life as a vast landscape of hills and valleys with some level ground in between, then it is perfectly natural and expected to encounter both low and high points. It would be pretty boring terrain if your life were flat all the time. Therefore, you must learn to navigate through the valleys and not get stuck there.

Grief can be part of depression, although grief is generally experienced as a response to loss. A loss can be a death, an illness or injury, a disappointment, an ending of a phase of life, a relationship, a home, a job. In this way, grief, like depression, is also a natural and even necessary part of living. What you do with feelings of depression and grief is up to you, and this is where the practice of self-care comes in.

First among the powerful goddesses who will help you through the darkness is Inanna, an ancient Sumerian goddess who was likely the original archetype and progenitor of Aphrodite/Venus, the goddess of love and beauty. She will help you learn to navigate through the darkness of depression and rise from it. To help you with the process of letting go and grieving, you will meet the Greek Triple Goddess of Demeter, the mother, Persephone, the daughter, and Hecate, the magical, wise crone.

# Inanna

Meet Inanna (aka Ishtar), whose story was told by the ancients some 5,000 years ago. They equated her with the planet Venus, also known as the Morning and Evening Star depending on what time of day it is visible. Her story of descending into the Underworld came about as ancient people watched this magnificent, bright planet closest to Earth seem to appear and disappear at certain times of the night and day, depending on the time of year.

A story emerged from watching this enigmatic planet's rise and fall. The myth born of this celestial cycle claimed that Inanna was in the darkness of the Underworld when Venus was behind the sun and not visible for a period of time. When the earth rotated and Venus appeared once again in the morning sky, Inanna was believed to have risen from the Underworld into the light. Inanna's story is one of the earliest resurrection myths.

Ancient people considered the Underworld a real place—not a place of suffering and damnation, but instead the seat of wisdom. It was where people went after they died and crossed over the River Styx, but it was also a place where mortals went to find themselves. It was considered a repository of ancestral knowledge. Those intrepid travelers who went there returned with the gift of acuity.

To our ancestors, the Underworld was sacred, as was darkness. You are born in the darkness of the womb and laid to rest in the darkness of the tomb. It is not a bad place, rather a space of exploration and discovery, for it contains the secrets of human existence, just like the caves humans once inhabited. Darkness holds the power of mystery, deep insight, the wisdom of the ancients, and it is a necessary counterpart to Lightness, the world above. You contain this darkness within you. You must learn to go there, find the treasure, and return. You must learn to live in both realms—the yin and yang, the light and the dark—and find balance. As an old alchemical saying goes, "As above, so below. As within, so without. As the universe, so the soul."

# The Story of Inanna

Inanna had many facets: priestess, lover, queen, and goddess. She gained her power directly from her father, Enki, the God of Wisdom, who one drunken evening bestowed upon her a set of immutable laws, wisdom, and symbols of sovereignty, known as the *holy me*. Realizing what he had done the next day, he tried to get these powers back, but Inanna considered that an act of betrayal and refused. She established her queendom in Uruk with Enki's eventual blessing.

The time came for Inanna to descend beneath the earth to pay respects to her twin sister, Ereshkigal, the Dark Goddess and Queen of the Underworld, whose husband had recently died. Decked out in her royal raiments, Inanna descended seven levels to reach her grieving sister. At each level, she was required to leave a piece of adornment: her robe, her jewels, and finally her crown, until she was naked.

When she reached Ereshkigal deep in the Underworld, Inanna humbled herself before the Dark Goddess. And what did Ereshkigal do upon seeing her sister after so long, knowing she was to be the new ruler? Enraged, jealous, and broken-hearted, she killed Inanna and hung her on a meat hook.

Now clever Inanna had planned ahead and instructed her priestess that if she was not back in three days to send for help from Enki. And that is just what her priestess did. Soon, two tiny insect emissaries arrived to bargain with Ereshkigal. The tiny creatures lamented and empathized with Ereshkigal in her grief. Finally feeling heard, Ereshkigal allowed the flies to give Inanna the food and water of life, which brought her back from the dead. Thus resurrected, Inanna began her ascent from the Underworld, reclaiming the adornments she had left behind on each of the seven levels.

The clothes and jewels that she had relinquished represented the base instincts and ego trappings she had to let go of to die to her old self. Upon her return, she reclaimed these items, now transformed into helpful attributes. Vanity converted to self-confidence, arrogance to humility, selfishness to compassion, jealousy to admiration, lies to truth. Inanna had gained wisdom through the experience of death and rebirth, of transforming darkness to light through wisdom. Now Inanna had a kind of power different from those bestowed on her by Enki. This was earned. When Inanna emerged from the Underworld, she placed her crown on her head and became the self-empowered Queen of Heaven and Earth.

---

You can learn how to descend into the Underworld and rise again, renewed and transformed. You can learn from the stories of Inanna and Persephone, both women who descended into darkness and came out the other side. You can learn to see times of depression and grief as an *Underworld experience*. You can learn to release something holding you back and make the journey consciously, letting go of what no longer serves you, and claiming what does.

When you accept what is happening when you are depressed, grieving, and descending into darkness, it is easier to find your way through. It is your task to discover the treasures hidden there, and to come out when it is time to rise again with newfound clarity and a sense of your own sovereignty.

## Objects and Symbols to Consider for Your Altar to Inanna

**Colors:** white, blue, copper

**Objects:** crown, necklace, symbols of what you wish to release

**Gemstones:** lapis lazuli, copper, tourmaline

**Flowers:** lily, orchid, rose

**Element:** air

**Chakra:** root (1st chakra) and crown (7th)

# How to Transform Thoughts and Feelings While in the Underworld

**The Descent**

Make a list of your feelings and try to identify why you feel that way. For example:

- I feel sad because I am no longer happy in this relationship/job and I don't know whether I should stay.
- I feel angry at myself for putting up with my partner's behavior/work situation for as long as I have.
- I feel scared that I will be alone and no one will love me/I won't find a better job.
- I feel hurt by my mother's/father's abandonment of me as a child and how I have not allowed myself to get close to anyone for fear of another abandonment.
- I feel sad and lonely, but I am not sure why. It reminds me of a time when…

**Hanging on the Hook: Feel the Feelings**

Give yourself time and space to feel all of your feelings. You may need to feel sad and grieve for something that once held promise but that you no longer want. You may need to rage and scream into a pillow or outdoors and move the anger through your body. You may need to feel the fear of doing something new and stepping into the unknown. Allow these feelings to be expressed and wash over you like a wave and then out to sea again in their time, knowing feelings are not forever.

Feelings come from the watery realm, and they ebb and flow naturally if you allow and accept them. You do not need to wallow in them for long periods if you name and validate your feelings and nurture yourself through them. Take time out if you need to be in your feelings and with your feelings. Talk them through with a trusted friend, family member, or mental health professional. Do not rush through this process—you may feel that you are done with these feelings because you are tired of them, but take care not to suppress them in your eagerness to be done with them. Be careful not to take them out on others; instead be patient and compassionate with yourself as you *hang out* with them.

**Hanging on the Hook: Process Thoughts**

Now make a list of your negative thoughts or beliefs about the situation or about yourself. For example:

- I am unlovable/incompetent.
- I don't deserve a happy relationship/good job.
- I am doomed to stay in an unfulfilling relationship/job.
- These feelings are all my fault.
- This feeling of depression/grief will never go away.
- There is no future for me where I will feel "normal."

Notice how you feel when you have these thoughts about yourself or your situation. Notice if any of these thoughts or messages come from childhood. Are they messages you heard a parent say? Are they messages you heard from others about you as an innocent maiden growing up, trying to find your way? Were they helpful or hurtful?

Determine which thoughts are inaccurate, unfair, and actual lies you tell yourself or have come to believe about yourself. Replace them with the truth. Even if you know you have made mistakes or have done something you regret, forgive yourself, and be determined to learn from your mistakes.

Now change the old belief to a new one—a counter-statement of truth that makes you feel better. Imagine yourself as a child, and your fear, doubt, and negative self-talk as a schoolyard bully: what defense would you offer the child? What rebuttal can you formulate against the bully's cruel words? Do all of this in writing and then read it out loud to yourself. This exercise is akin to asking your Inner Mother, Goddess, or Higher Self for help in seeing yourself more clearly and accurately, and for the wisdom and ability to transform yourself.

**The Ascent**

When you have done the work in the darkness of the Underworld and truly allowed yourself to feel sad, scared, hurt, guilty, ashamed, etc., notice when the waves of emotions have moved through you and are ebbing. When you have examined your thoughts and found clarity as well as a sense of relief and liberation, you are ready to ascend.

Claim the truth of who you really are. Speak your truth out loud or write it down. Imagine yourself rising with new power and vision as you crown yourself queen. Your sovereignty comes when you realize your feelings of shame and pain do not control you and can be transformed. You can descend into the darkness with your tender feelings whenever you need to. Be with them, understand them, allow them to be—to come and go with ease. When you have risen from the underworld, reward yourself with something that gives you pleasure, contentment, grace.

# Inanna Speaks

Hello, Daughter. What I want you to know is that you do not have to lose your Self when you descend into the Underworld. It is a time to release all things you may have thought you needed or were precious or familiar to you, but upon examination, are not. By doing so, you will discover your true power, strength, and beauty. You will claim new potency as you ascend.

I offer you a way to descend consciously. While you may not want to visit depression, hurt, fear, and sadness, there are times you know you must feel these very real feelings, not deny them. You must accept them because they are there, because you are in pain, because something triggered an unhealed wound; something caused you to hurt. You do not have to fear the underworld or avoid it. It is a part of you, of everyone. Allow yourself to sit with the feelings, acknowledge them, discover the original pain, and learn to soothe yourself through them.

When I was hung on the hook, I knew my sister, the Dark Goddess, was doing what I could not do. She was helping me die to my old self so that my new self could be born. Looking at me during those three days, you would have thought I was dead to the world. But I was noticing my thoughts and feelings, examining them, and releasing them—letting them move through me. I noticed what my ego was holding onto and let it go. When I had done that self-reflection and recalibration, I experienced a rebirth. I was ready to rise back to the surface, claiming my true power with new vision and clarity.

You can do the same. When feeling depressed, name your thoughts and feelings, write about them, talk about them, examine them. Discover where they originated and decide whether they need to live with you anymore or be transformed. When Ereshkigal let all of her sadness and grief out, what helped her return to herself was being heard, witnessed. She received empathy and felt understood. That is often what is needed to move out of stuck feelings. If there is someone you trust to give you empathy, tell them. If not, be the one to listen and provide empathy to yourself. Remember I am with you in the darkness. Follow my lead and we will rise again.

# The Triple Goddess of Persephone, Demeter, and Hecate

While it is important to learn to navigate through feelings and to change negative thoughts into more accurate ones, you can also be sad and depressed due to grief and loss. This is often the result of situations and circumstances beyond your control, such as normal life passages, endings, and seasonal changes. This is where Persephone, the Maiden or *kore*; Demeter, the Mother; and Hecate, the Crone—the Greek Triple Goddess—can help. (In Roman mythology Persephone is known as Proserpina, Demeter as Ceres, and Hecate as Trivia.)

Persephone is a goddess familiar with the Underworld and likely modeled after Inanna, who came before. The mother-daughter death and rebirth story of Persephone and Demeter is one that was enacted for hundreds of years (1600-400 BCE) and known to the ancient Greeks as the *Eleusinian Mysteries*. These annual rites involved a 13-mile pilgrimage along the Sacred Way from Athens to the hilltop of Eleusis. There, the temples to Demeter, Persephone, and Hecate stood. The pilgrims—young and old, rich and poor, men and women—who took part in this rite learned to overcome their fear of death and return to their lives renewed, reborn.

# The Story of Persephone, Demeter, and Hecate

One day, the innocent, young maiden Persephone was picking flowers in a field when the earth cracked open and the handsome God of the Underworld, Hades (in Roman mythology, Pluto), emerged. The dark god, sitting atop his horse-drawn chariot, snatched up Persephone and disappeared back into the abyss before anyone knew what had happened.

Her mother, Demeter, Goddess of the Grains and Harvest, was beside herself with fear when she realized her daughter was missing. She searched high and low for nine days without finding any sign of Persephone. During her period of searching and grieving, plants and crops died, nothing grew, and people went hungry for want of Demeter's fertility magic.

After wandering for some time, Demeter encountered a woman named Baubo, the bawdy and irreverent Goddess of Mirth. This spirited old woman joked with Demeter and lifted her skirts, flashing her vulva, which caused Demeter to break into a deep belly laugh, restoring her life essence.

However, it was not until Hecate, the magical crone goddess, heard Persephone's cries that Demeter was able to reunite with her daughter. Hecate was a psychopomp or "soul conductor," who holds the key to the Underworld. She is associated with the crossroads, meaning she could see Past, Present, and Future. She led Persephone out of the darkness with her torch and negotiated her return to the earth plane, but only for part of the year, as by then Persephone had eaten six seeds from a pomegranate. This was the juicy, feminine fruit Hades offered her before she rose to greet her mother. The pomegranate seeds bound her to the Underworld where she reigned as queen during the fallow season of late fall and winter. The other six months of the year she spent with her mother, transformed into the maiden again, heralding the coming of spring, new growth, and summer abundance.

This powerful Triple Goddess of Maiden, Mother, and Crone helps you move through the seasons of life and learn to hold conflicting emotions like sadness and joy, to reconcile opposites like dark and light, rest and activity, innocence and experience. They represent three developmental stages of life as well as three inner aspects of the feminine, no matter your age. These three goddesses help you learn how to grieve loss and change and find your way from darkness to light, and back again as needed. Their qualities and lunar aspects are:

**The New Moon Maiden**

youth, lightness, carefree innocence, beginnings, birth

Persephone offers you the gift of feeling your feelings and expressing them unselfconsciously. She assures you that when you are open to new experiences, learning and growing, you are in right relationship with yourself.

**The Full Moon Mother**

middle age, responsibility, nurturance, fruitfulness, life

Demeter offers you the gift of time off, space to grieve and acknowledge your pain in the midst of life. She also represents agency, the ability to take care of yourself and find what helps you in times of grief—from crafting, to planting, to laughing.

**The Waning Moon Crone**

old age, wisdom, perspective, enlightenment, endings, death

Hecate offers you the gift of overview, guidance, and finding meaning in experience. She helps you review the past, accept mistakes and loss, and move on from them. She comes to your aid to help you see the larger picture and not sweat the small stuff.

You can help yourself through challenging times by imagining the inner good mother, (Demeter), and grandmother, (Hecate), comforting and guiding you, the daughter, (Persephone), through life's passages and challenges. If you did not have a good mother or grandmother in your life, think of a teacher, wise friend, or role model whose kindness and wisdom you admire and seek her counsel (or remember her wisdom and love). Surround yourself with images of the nurturing mother that you have collected or created by painting, coloring, or collaging. Imagine how she would care for you, and become that Inner Mother for yourself (see CH. 11, page 231).

There will be times in your life when you are in the Underworld because you are leaving behind one period of life or age and entering another. This, too, is a form of grief, of letting go of what was to make way for what is to come. Persephone's descent into the Underworld as a maiden is analogous to the rite of passage of a young girl or adolescent to a woman.

Most mothers experience a sense of loss when a daughter enters puberty and begins pulling away to try and figure out who she is separate from her mother. This portends a loss of innocence for a daughter. As much as it is a necessary developmental stage, it is also sad for a mother to "give up" her little girl, but she must allow her daughter to begin the process of individuation. Mothers must learn to grieve through various stages of their children's lives, letting go a little more each time. Similarly, women must grieve their own life passages and concluding roles—from maiden to wife, to mother, to queen, to grandmother and crone, including divorces, job endings, physical changes, and retirement.

Because she was a goddess of the grains and harvest, Demeter, in her grief, caused the crops to stop growing and food supplies to dwindle. Similarly, when you experience an ending, whether it be a death or life passage, you may lose your appetite, neglect yourself and your surroundings, and let yourself go, both inwardly and outwardly. Demeter needed time to adjust to the shock of loss, as you do when change occurs. Take your time, feel your feelings, and find ways to nurture yourself through the sadness, no matter if it is an external situation or an internal shift that has caused you to feel depressed.

It is also important to recognize when it is time to return home, to yourself. This often takes its own time and is not a straight path of healing. Honoring the rhythm and timing of your own unique healing journey helps you know when you have reached the end.

It is helpful to consider the five stages of grief when you are trying to come to grips with change or loss: denial, anger, bargaining (hoping for another outcome), depression, and finally acceptance. These are not always experienced in order, although acceptance is the desired end. Feeling angry, sad, and hurt, denying reality for a while, and imagining another outcome are all normal thoughts and feelings to have when you experience a loss. Self-care requires you to lovingly see yourself through the process to reach the grace of accepting what is, and this takes time.

Meeting the feminine fool, Baubo, helped save Demeter while she mourned. As Demeter began to laugh again and feel other emotions besides sadness and depression, she gained perspective and energy. Fertility returned to the land, mirroring her own growth and rebounding life force. You can see laughter as an antidote to your own darkness when you are ready to let go and move on. Finding humor in things and consciously seeking experiences to make you laugh are self-care practices that help pull you out of a stuck place, especially as time spent in the Underworld gets old.

And what of Persephone, the maiden who suddenly found herself whisked away by the sexy god of the Underworld on his chariot? This is akin to times in life when you are excited and hopeful about someone or something, a time of change, when one part of your life gives way to another, sometimes unexpectedly. Perhaps someone sweeps you off your feet or a new job takes you to a new location. It can be exciting, scary, and overwhelming to face the unknown, to experience a sudden change in life circumstances, but it may be a necessary shift. It may lead you to the next chapter in the story of your life.

Persephone had to learn to navigate the Underworld without her personal mother, as does every woman. However, Persephone had her grandmother, Hecate, the magical crone goddess of the crossroads, who carries the torch to help see in the dark. If you trust her to show you the way, this goddess helps you through difficult transitions in life with her vision and knowing. When things look hazy and unclear, when the path ahead is obscured, and only darkness is visible, pulling out your metaphorical lantern to shine light on what lies hidden helps you gain insight and understanding. Like Hecate, now you can see the past behind you—to what got you here and how this may relate to childhood wounding. Standing at the crossroads, like Hecate, it is important to determine what you can do to help yourself in the *present*, so that you may step into the *future* transformed, hopeful, and healed.

When you are like Persephone, suddenly torn from what you have known and expected into a new way of seeing and being, you may feel lost, wandering in the darkness for some period of time. When this happens, call upon Demeter, imagining her as your own Inner Nurturing Mother (see CH. 11, page 230) to see you through. If you love and care for yourself during this time as a good mother would nurture a hurt and lost child, you will find your way home to your Self.

There are times in life when an illness or injury brings you to your knees. When this happens, you must find your way through pain, fear, helplessness, and at times, hopelessness. It is a challenge to accept what is happening to your body and what it means going forward, and this takes time. It is imperative to grieve what was before and what you have lost. It is also helpful to research and explore all of the ways you can help yourself on your healing journey with the assistance of your inner Wise Woman, your own Inner Hecate. The writer and psychoanalyst Clarissa Pinkola Estes calls this inner part La Que Sabe—The One Who Knows—the one who knows what is best for you, what will help you and what will not. Learning to listen to and trust your intuition, your primal knowing, is part of her magical power and yours.

While it is important to develop your own Inner Mother or Wise Woman to love and care for you unconditionally, do not hesitate to seek a helper in the outer world as well—a therapist, teacher, healer, mentor, or trusted friend who can comfort and guide you.

Sadie likes imagining herself as Persephone, who returns to the Underworld in the fall, but this time with a helper and guide, the Crone, Hecate. Picturing Hecate leading her through the darkness of seasonal depression with a lantern helps her see more clearly how her gloomy mood is rooted in the abandonment she felt as a child by her distracted parents. She thinks of her wonderful grandmother who always made her feel safe and loved, so this association with Hecate brings her comfort. She also finds a therapist to work with to better understand and let go of past hurts. At the same time, Sadie begins to journal her thoughts and feelings when she feels down, imagining she is having an Underworld experience like Persephone, searching for wisdom. She finds that by letting her feelings and thoughts go onto the page, and finding more accurate ways of perceiving herself, she is able to grieve her childhood more consciously and spend less and less time stuck in the past reliving a depressive pattern.

## Hecate Speaks

Dear Daughter, I am your inner Wise Woman. Call on me when you are shrouded in darkness, when you are grieving in the cave of the underworld. I will come with my torch, shine the light on what needs to be seen, and show you the way through.

Together, we will comb through the memories and experiences to find the jewels buried there. I will guide you through this by encouraging you to discover and accept your feelings then and now. These nuggets of truth are the treasure you seek.

I am your shoulder to cry on. There may be old wounds to heal or new wounds to lick. There is dignity in having wounds and healing them. They help you become whole.

If you need a break, time to recover, to do nothing but sit in the darkness for a while, I will abide with you however long it takes. I will remind you of the self-care needed here, the tenderness and compassion for yourself that will help you recover in due time.

I will help you discern what you need and whom to ask for help and hand you the key so you can return to the upper world feeling stronger and wiser. Our time together in the Underworld can be fertile and interesting if you choose to make it so—if you consciously explore, seek understanding, and tend to your pain. I will be with you as your grandmother and soul conductor, as wise healer and witness. You are not alone. I am with you.

## Objects and symbols to consider for your altar to Persephone

Colors: white, pink, green, black

Objects: photo of you as a girl, something from your girlhood, pomegranate

Gemstones: rose quartz, white or black onyx

Flowers: narcissus, daffodils, heather

Element: earth

Chakra: root (1st chakra)

## Objects and symbols to consider for your altar to Demeter

Colors: red, orange, brown, gold

Objects: wheat, corn dolly, bowl of earth, potted plant, seeds, cornucopia

Gemstones: garnet, turquoise, amber, petrified wood

Flowers: poppies, mint, fall leaves

Element: earth

Chakra: throat (5th chakra)

## Objects and symbols to consider for your altar to Hecate

Colors: black, gray, red

Objects: candle, wand, lantern, cauldron, key

Gemstones: hematite, black tourmaline, smoky quartz

Flowers: lily, dittany, motherwort

Element: fire

Chakra: brow (6th chakra)

# Journal Prompts While in the Underworld

What led me here?

When I shine the light into the corners of my psyche, what do I see, what do I feel, what do I know?

In what ways do these current feelings remind me of ways I felt as a child? What was happening then that resembles what is happening now? How did I learn to cope then that is not serving me now? What did I need then?

What am I needing most while in the Underworld at this time?

How can I give myself what I need?

What form of healing will best serve my mind, body, and spirit?

How can I learn to be my own best healer?

What can I learn about myself and what my soul needs with respect to this circumstance/incident/illness/injury at this time?

Who can I turn to for help? What do I need to ask for?

What change of mind or heart do I need to make to adjust to this circumstance?

What do I need to release before I can ascend?

What will it take for me to accept this situation and rise again?

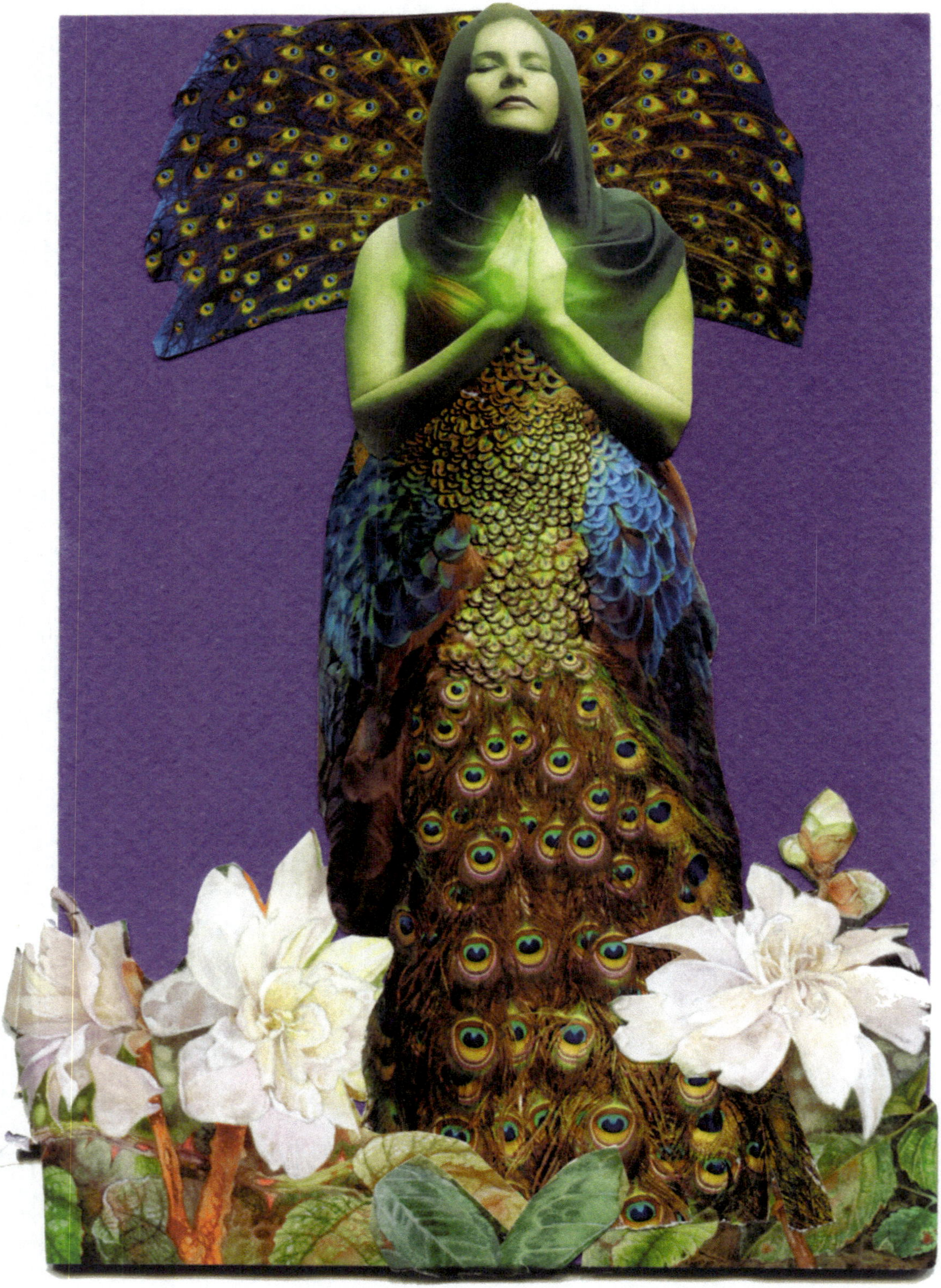

# Chapter Five

# Healthy Relationships

How do you create and maintain healthy relationships, whether with a romantic partner, child, sibling, friend, or co-worker? Do you notice that when you are in a relationship with someone you tend to focus more on caring for them and less on caring for yourself? Healthy relationships imply that two people are equally getting their needs met, share mutual respect, and communicate effectively. Self-care is extremely important to a healthy relationship because if you are not taking care of yourself, you have little to give to a relationship.

Without a practice of regular self-care you are vulnerable to caregiver burnout (and resentment) or the reverse: expecting too much caregiving from another because you have not learned to fill yourself up. While this chapter will primarily focus on intimate relationships, you can apply much of the wisdom you learn from the goddess archetypes you will meet here to other relationships as well.

In a romantic relationship, you are co-creating a sacred bond. You are looking to find balance between giving and receiving, independence and togetherness, and getting your needs and desires met as well as meeting another's needs and desires. It does not have to be a perfect balance, but mutuality is key. It also does not mean you are required to say yes to your partner's every request. Boundaries and the ability to say "No" play into the balancing act of giving and receiving.

### Jill's Story

Jill is in a new relationship, which she is determined to make work after her marriage of five years ended in divorce. She feels loved and adored by her partner, Sam, but she knows her people-pleasing tendencies are getting in the way again. She is frustrated by Sam's attempts to make decisions for her and tell her how she should be handling things on her job. That is not the kind of support she wants from Sam. However, it is hard for Jill to stand up for herself and let Sam know how she feels and what she wants, which is simply to listen, validate her feelings, and be an empathetic ally.

Jill is afraid if she speaks up Sam will get hurt or defensive, and they will end up in an argument. She left her marriage because her ex was verbally abusive and controlling. She wants to learn to communicate effectively with Sam and break her pattern of backing down and clamming up when Sam tries to help her.

A healthy relationship is held up by four pillars: Respect, Trust (which requires honesty), Kindness, and Love.

Goddess archetypes are effective models of what it means to stand in your feminine power and speak your truth. Goddesses of old embodied empowerment and made their feelings known. They had no problem asking for what they wanted.

Self-care in a healthy relationship means recognizing and owning your feelings, communicating them effectively, and then asking yourself what you need and want from your partner and requesting it. You may not always get what you ask for, but it is healthy to *request it* and not make demands or expect your partner to read your mind.

Healthy relationships are predicated on the understanding that as a strong, capable woman you can meet a lot of your own needs and certainly do not require someone else to meet *all* of your needs, emotionally, physically, or spiritually. However, being in an intimate relationship means you have some needs you want your partner to fulfill and vice versa. At the heart of a healthy relationship is the mutual agreement you make with your partner about how you understand and meet certain needs and desires each of you have. This requires communicating your needs and wants clearly and without apology.

Women have been conditioned to be accommodating and self-sacrificing. All too often I have seen that women do not ask for what they need and want from their partner, or they don't believe they have the right to ask, or even don't believe they deserve to have their needs met. They accept what they are given (sometimes scraps) and do not ask for more. All too frequently, women put everyone else's needs before their own. This leads to feelings of emptiness, resentment, and imbalanced relationships. Women must learn to fill their own cup and receive replenishment from their partner as well. Goddesses are often shown holding cups or chalices, symbolic of the holy grail, the divine feminine wellspring of giving and receiving.

There are two goddesses who will help you in this realm. The first is Hera, the Greek goddess of marriage (Roman name: Juno), who is an archetype of the *Queen* and *Wife*. She was married to Zeus (Roman name: Jupiter), the top god of Mount Olympus.

You will also meet Isis, the Egyptian goddess of sacred relationship and bringer of consciousness, healing, and magic. She had a symbiotic relationship with Osiris, her lover/husband/brother. Yes, many gods and goddesses had a brother-sister bond as well as a husband-wife bond, which symbolically speaks to their relatedness and shared values. In fact, Hera and Zeus were also siblings.

# Hera

Just as Athena's essential creative power under the patriarchy made her into a war goddess, so Hera's original role was redefined by patriarchal storytellers. In pre-Hellenic mythology, before Zeus was known, Hera was a *Great Goddess*, the Queen of Heaven (much like Inanna, who came before her), whose breast milk created the celestial Milky Way. Hera is the feminine form of the masculine word *hero*, and as such, she had her own heroic journey as a *creatrix* and mother goddess—life-giving, nurturing, and kind, but also fierce, protective, and able to stand on her own. Originally, she was a goddess of the winds, agriculture, and civilization. She stood alone as an omnipotent, seminal goddess. When she was later paired with Zeus, she became an archetype of the wife, of feminine power in relationship, but her shadow loomed large in Greek mythology. She was painted as the long-suffering and jealous consort of her notoriously philandering and all-powerful husband.

It is important to understand that Hera was originally a goddess who had authority in her own right and did not need a man to complete her. Yet she has come to symbolize marriage and the drive to *put a ring on it*. So while she represents the archetypal energy of wife—the queen to a man's king—she is also one whose sovereignty begins prior to marriage. In her evolved form she represents a woman who develops her own sense of self and self-worth before she chooses to marry or partner with someone and find fulfillment in relationship.

## The Story of Hera

Hera was one of six children of the Titan god Cronus and the earth goddess Rhea. It was foretold that one of Cronus's children would usurp him as king of the gods one day, so to prevent that from happening, the power-hungry Cronus devoured all of his children, starting with Hestia (whom you will meet in CH. 12, page 259) and including Hera.

Their last child was Zeus, but Rhea saved

him by wrapping a stone in swaddling clothes and tricking her husband into swallowing it instead of their youngest child. Rhea hid Zeus away in a cave on the island of Crete and gave him up to the care of mountain nymphs, who adored him and lovingly raised him. When he came of age, Zeus went back to free his siblings and vanquish his father. The siblings' rebirth and the overturn of the old order led to the Olympian gods and goddesses, which eventually numbered 12, with Zeus as their leader.

Zeus fell in love with the beautiful and loving Hera, but she was not as interested in him as she was in the animals she nurtured and surrounded herself with. So Zeus disguised himself as a cuckoo bird and flew to Hera's window. She easily captured him and was delighted with her new pet. Zeus eventually revealed himself to Hera and she was convinced of his love. They had a grand wedding and lived happily for a long time before Zeus started his cheating ways with both goddesses and mortal women alike. This caused Hera to fly into fits of rage and jealousy and seek revenge. She and Zeus had a stormy relationship that was both competitive and passionate. They eventually reconciled due to Zeus's persistence in winning her back and Hera's forgiveness of him.

Like Jana, Hera's sacred animal is the peacock. It symbolizes her integrity, her love of beauty, and her ability to show her true colors (or feelings). The many eyes on the ends of its tail feathers allow her to be watchful, avoid exploitation, and to notice her feelings which leads to intuitive knowing. In this way, the peacock provides protection.

Hera's strengths in the role of wife and partner are self-empowerment (being whole unto herself), loyalty, openness, generosity, a strong desire to share her life with another, and the ability to communicate her needs and wants. Her shadow side is codependency, which could be defined as caregiving to a fault, putting her partner's needs before her own, or enabling a partner who is deceptive, abusive, or addictive. Her shadow qualities of jealousy, vindictiveness, and martyrdom speak to insecurity and a loss of potency in a relationship that doesn't honor the four pillars of respect, trust, kindness, and love.

You can learn from Hera how to be a goddess who brings her own power to a relationship and holds it. This is a woman who values and practices self-care so that she does not lose her sense of self and agency in relationship. If she has been neglected or betrayed, she tries to understand her partner and work towards healing what is broken. But she can only do her part. If she is met with a partner who is unwilling to do the work of repairing and reconciling, she must put her needs first and move on.

The shadow qualities of jealousy, insecurity, and mistrust can be challenging and throw the relationship into a tailspin. Yet if you recognize and integrate these shadow parts (and not let them run the show), your relationship has a better chance of surviving, if not thriving. This requires becoming aware of the pitfalls to your sense of security and self, which are likely rooted in childhood. Through conscious effort you can change dysfunctional patterns and heal old wounds. Another shadow quality of a Hera woman is a fear of being alone and taking care of herself. Consequently, she may stay in a relationship too long, preserving the image of togetherness to the detriment of her own well-being.

A healthy Hera woman does not sublimate herself or her needs to the marriage. She is a loving partner as long as she is treated with kindness, respect, love, and honesty. She shines when she is adored and cherished as an equal partner. Without those essential ingredients, she has no need to stay in the relationship and subject herself to pain. As much as she might want a partner, she knows she will do fine on her own until she meets the right person. As a goddess and queen, Hera's wisdom is to know what you need and want from another and communicate it in a healthy and effective way.

The Hera archetype teaches you that you can say anything to your partner if you say it in such a way as to do no harm, i.e., striving to be kind and clear with your words. That does not mean you need to take responsibility for how another may feel if you speak truthfully and skillfully. In my role as a therapist, I see many people in relationships refrain from speaking their truth or communicating their feelings for fear of how the other will react or feel. This is a kind of self-sacrifice that leads to confusion, misunderstanding, and disconnection. The other extreme is to dominate and demean, which creates a painful power imbalance.

It is not your job to protect others from your feelings (or theirs). That means you must accept your feelings and allow them in your partner. There are no wrong feelings. Try not to repress them or *make nice* despite your true feelings about something. If you do, the feelings will likely pop back up, leak out in unconscious or passive-aggressive ways, or turn into seething resentment. You also want to avoid a pattern of over-reacting and using your feelings as a cudgel. Feelings are not a tool of manipulation but a means of expressing what your heart and soul tell you.

Bringing feelings out of the shadows, owning them, and conveying them in a balanced, skillful way is self-care. It does not matter what someone does with them, e.g., whether they change or not, so much as it matters that you take care of yourself by expressing what you feel and asking for what you want.

**A simple but profound three-step communication skill is to:**

1. **Say how you feel.**

"I feel (hurt, scared, angry, frustrated, sad, etc.) when you say/do _____ or when _____ happens."

2. **Ask for what you want.**

"Could you/Are you willing to/I'd like it if_____?"

3. **Reach an understanding or agreement.**

This is an agreement you can both live with. Voice it so that both you and your partner are clear about it. Write it down if you need to. This may involve negotiation and compromise. If your partner cannot give you what you ask for, you must give this to yourself or find another way to get this need met as your partner is not ultimately responsible for your care; you are.

*Nimbus omnia pene trans*

Et soror et coniux Iouis, en fratri atq; marite    Fulmina diuitijs maiestatiq; potestas:
Se sociat. Cur sic:nam bene conueniunt       Sunt Iunonis opes,fulmina dia Iouis.

Crispin. de pas Inue. fecit. et exc.

# Feeling Word List

This may help you identify what you are feeling so as to better communicate it to others:

**Angry**, *mad, enraged, furious, annoyed, resentful, disgusted, irritated, outraged, bitter*

**Sad**, *disappointed, depressed, dejected, down, pessimistic, upset, heavy-hearted*

**Hurt**, *wounded, sorrowful, grieving, aching, torn, raw, tormented, pained, suffering*

**Happy**, *joyful, thrilled, pleased, content, loving, grateful, glad, uplifted, light-hearted*

**Confused**, *perplexed, surprised, unsure, conflicted, lost, uncertain, doubtful*

If you have difficulty knowing your feelings and owning them, consider keeping a Feeling Journal. Write down each day what you notice you are feeling at various points. Name it and claim it. Ask yourself what you need to help you abide the emotion or transform it to feel better.

# The Hieros Gamos — The Sacred Marriage

The ancients performed a rite called *Hieros Gamos*. It represented the sacred union of the goddess and god enacted by humans. It is symbolic of the inner wedding that you must achieve between your own inner yin feminine—receiving, watery feelings—and yang masculine—giving, fiery thoughts. It is an important step in your individuation process that you work to achieve this balance within so as to find this complement in your outer relationships.

This requires that you take stock of where you may be out of balance. Too much ungrounded feminine energy leads to moodiness, doubt, and floundering about. Too much ungrounded masculine energy leads to confusion, judgment, and control. Regardless of your gender, you must seek to balance the feminine and masculine within you: As within, so without. Imagine your own Inner Feminine and Masculine and ask yourself: Which has more power and efficacy? What is out of balance between these two energies? What does each need from the other? How can you better achieve balance within and bring them together in wedded bliss?

Ideally, our inner feminine *inspires* our inner masculine to do; our inner masculine supports our inner feminine to imagine and create. Together, they manifest magic, an integrated marriage of mind, body, soul, and spirit.

~120~

# Hera Speaks

Daughter, I am an ancient mother who speaks to you of power—your own personal power—not the power to dominate and control, but the innate power of the Feminine. The power to receive love as much as give love. The power of holding your own and not getting knocked off your feet by surrendering your power to the one you love. The power to believe that you deserve to be loved and treated well. The power to know that you are lovable.

Do not let your story be written by the old, patriarchal code that says women are not equal to men, that a woman must do all of the emotional labor, that you must suffer in silence, take what a man gives (or does not give) without question. You are not required to look the other way and ignore your feelings when your partner hurts you with his or her words or deeds.

Neither must you go on the attack, for you give away your power in this way, too. If you think of your feelings as the ocean, you want to live in the gentle ebb and flow and not succumb to a tidal wave or drought.

It may be enough to recognize the feeling within you, allow it to be with you, soothe yourself, and let it go out with the tide. If not, determine what would help you, voice the feeling, and find resolution with your partner. This is how you maintain your sovereignty.

## Objects and Symbols to Consider for Your Altar to Hera

**Colors:** white, blue, purple, gold

**Objects:** figurines and images of Hera, swan, peacock feather or cuckoo (white feather), cup or chalice

**Gemstones:** Chalcopyrite (peacock ore), peacock quartz crystal, lace agate, pyrite

**Flowers:** white lily, lotus, hyacinth

**Element:** air

**Chakra:** throat (5th chakra)

## Isis

The Egyptian winged goddess Isis is one whose story tells of the restorative power of love. She, too, was considered a Great Goddess, the "Lady of Ten Thousand Names," including "The Mother of Life," the "Crone of Death," and "Isis the All-Goddess." The name Isis actually means queen or throne.

She was worshipped for millennia, not just in Egypt, but throughout the Mediterranean, Africa, and Europe. Temples to Isis existed as late as 550 CE, and their ruins have been discovered in Italy, France, Turkey, and Greece. As the Christian patriarchy overtook the goddess-loving tradition, these temples were repurposed or torn down. Often churches and cathedrals were built in their place.

## The Story of Isis

Isis was the daughter of Nut, the Sky goddess, and Keb, the Earth god, and so held the qualities of above and below, of spirit and matter. She and her consort Osiris were wise and just deities who ruled over Egypt in true partnership. It was their mission to provide people with the means to live in a just and civilized world by teaching them to grow food in the soil, to weave clothing from plant material, and to form communities and governments so they could live harmoniously.

Seth, Osiris's brother, was a jealous and treacherous god. Envious of Osiris's authority and popularity, he murdered his brother by dismembering him. He hid his body parts throughout the land, and then took the throne in his place. But Isis, in her intuitive and far-sighted wisdom, searched high and low and found his 14 hidden body parts except for his penis, symbol of his generative potency.

Undaunted, Isis, using her magical healing powers, fashioned a golden phallus and put Osiris back together again. Thus resurrected, he returned to his rightful place on the throne with her. Isis and Osiris conceived a divine child, the falcon-headed god Horus, the god from whom all the pharaohs descended. Together again, Isis and Osiris ruled over heaven and earth, assuring fertility and abundance to all of humanity.

Depictions of the Black Madonna throughout Europe originated from images of Isis holding her infant son Horus; these later morphed into the Christian version of the Madonna and Child. Dark-skinned Isis is the original Holy Mother.

Isis carries the *ankh*, the Egyptian symbol of life. The circle of the ankh represents the feminine, receiving lifeforce, the yoni or vulva. In the center of the loop is the ascending soul. The vertical stem of the ankh represents the masculine, penetrating lifeforce, the lingam or penis. The horizontal and vertical lines meet to form the sacred union.

Isis is an archetype that brings healing to relationship. She is not satisfied when something is broken until she is able to fix it, or at least try to put it back together in a new way. That is her magic. In that sense, she is a regenerative goddess who brings consciousness and inspiration to relationship. She imagines how it can be and works hard to create that vision. Of course, she needs a willing and committed partner to meet her halfway, but she will be the driving force to make the relationship whole; she will be the one to notice when things are slipping through the cracks and bring it back in line.

Isis carries the archetypal energy of rebirth, the willingness to grow and change and work to resurrect the relationship if it grows stale. In her shadow aspect, she resentfully does all the work and lets her partner slide.

She will fight for the relationship and not give up—until she does. While the Isis archetype is a mender and a healer and works to make the relationship whole, she has a limit, and when she reaches her limit, she is done. She seldom looks back, because she knows she gave it her all.

## Boundaries

There are times when you may need to question how much you are giving versus getting from a relationship and decide whether you want to try to revise it, discontinue it, or accept it. For example, if you are in a relationship in which you are primarily the giver and get little or nothing in return despite sharing your feelings, making your needs known, and asking for change, it is time to reconsider the value of your partnership. If you truly feel your soul is being sucked dry, you may decide it is not worth your energy to try with a partner who does not respect your wishes. It is imperative that givers learn to set limits and boundaries because takers rarely do. This is crucial to your self-care.

Setting boundaries requires you to learn to say no, to stop accepting less than the love and respect you deserve, and to love yourself enough to claim what you want and need, even if it means disappointing someone.

Being able to set boundaries is important to a sense of self and to not losing yourself in relationship. The right to privacy, the right to say no to a request, to know your limits and communicate them, the right to move freely and make your own choices without feeling controlled (which requires honesty, trust, and agreement on both sides) are all important boundary issues to establish in an intimate partnership.

On the subject of trust and honesty—as important as it is to speak your truth, you also have to be someone with whom it is safe to tell the truth. Both with spouses and children, if you over-react, defend, go on the attack, or fall apart when you hear something you do not like, it makes it difficult for others to tell you the truth. Establishing trust requires you to both speak the truth and hear the truth, even when it hurts.

Without the ability to know your feelings, express them skillfully, and set boundaries, you run the risk of losing your power and sense of Self. You could potentially succumb to a resentful victim or martyr role and founder in a dysfunctional relationship.

Both goddess archetypes teach you to hold your power and stand up for your values as well as your needs and wants. They model a willingness to do what it takes to make a relationship work and thrive without losing yourself. Hera and Isis teach you to live a fully expressed life in keeping with your True Self and not sacrifice yourself for the sake of the other.

Jill realized she needed to overcome her fear of speaking up for herself, and so she communicated her feelings about Sam's tendency to tell her what to do or how to handle situations. Jill conveyed her fears about repeating the mistakes of her marriage and told Sam she was determined not to stay silent. She asked Sam to please listen to her more and express empathy and understanding, not solutions, unless she specifically asked Sam for advice. She was able to do this in a calm, non-accusatory way, and Sam agreed to work on being a better listener and supportive partner. Working with the archetypal energies of Hera and Isis helped Jill feel empowered and emboldened to ask for what she wanted and bring healing to her new relationship.

# Isis Speaks

Dear Daughter, There are times in relationship when there is a dismemberment, a falling apart. It is often necessary to restart and reset the relationship, to do a housecleaning of sorts.

It may be that you have become fragmented, that you have lost your sense of self and sacrificed it to the relationship. If so, it is time to find your missing pieces and put them back together again. The journey to wholeness begins with your own honest reckoning, a re-membering of your True Self.

If you first look inward to see what you are feeling about this relationship and what may be missing, you have a starting point. It is also important to ask your partner what is missing, what may be rumbling beneath the surface for him/her. Bringing these deep stirrings up to consciousness is the only way to attune to each other's needs and longings, repair hurts, and forge new bonds.

Do not be afraid of what you might find by asking, exploring, being curious, and checking in with yourself and your partner. With courage, you can navigate through even the deepest, darkest waters. You can only avoid these truths for so long. At some point they will make themselves known, often through unconscious means that can hurt.

I am the goddess of life, death, and rebirth. You hold these same instinctual energies within you. With my wings you can fly to great heights of perception and discern what needs tending and mending. By connecting with your divine feminine wisdom, you can achieve a sense of wholeness for yourself and your relationship.

## Objects and symbols to consider for your altar to Isis

**Colors:** blue, white, green, gold

**Objects:** figurines and images of Isis, eye of Horus, gold or white wings, ankh, scarab, cobra

**Gemstones:** lapis lazuli, amethyst, bloodstones

**Flowers:** lotus, rose

**Element:** water

**Chakra:** sacral (2nd chakra) and solar plexus (3rd chakra)

## The Threefold Path: Ten Agreements for a Healthy, Happy Relationship

The keys to a successful relationship are based on concepts poetically described by the poet Kahlil Gibran:

*Give your hearts, but not into each other's keeping.*
*For only the hand of Life can contain your hearts.*
*And stand together yet not too near together:*
*For the pillars of the temple stand apart,*
*And the oak tree and the cypress grow not in each other's shadow.*

When you enter into partnership or marriage with the assumption that you are a fully capable adult who can take care of yourself, you acknowledge responsibility for your own path and your own happiness.

It is useful to see the *relationship path* as separate from your *individual path*. You do not need to give up your individual path when you enter into relationship. It is important to continue walking your own path and to also walk the path of relationship out of choice, not obligation or duty. The path of relationship is created with your partner, together, as equals.

That does not mean that you do not sometimes step off your individual path to help your partner or sacrifice things you like to do to be with your partner, as long as you do so out of love, by choice, and without resentment. It certainly does not mean you give up your path completely for the sake of the other. You essentially agree that you each need to have your own path regarding work, career, hobby, pastimes, interests, childcare, friends, etc., as long as you and your partner are respectful of the agreements you make about your marriage or partnership.

When you walk the path of relationship together, it is important to keep in mind that you do so out of choice, knowing you are not abandoning your individual path and will travel it as need be. Your individual path is of your own making, and it is important to your sense of autonomy, well-being, and wholeness. Determining your individual path is up to you. Neither partner has the right to define the other's path or take the other off their path to meet his or her needs. You endeavor to support and respect each other's path at all times. The following agreements, if accepted by both parties, make for a balanced relationship of equals. They can be seen as vows you make to each other in love and mutuality.

1. I have chosen to be in a relationship with my partner for which there is mutual respect and equality. I agree that no one is "the boss," and that we will agree on how to live together as well as communicate and negotiate our differences. I will at all times endeavor to accept, honor, and respect those differences, even when I do not see eye to eye with my partner. We can respectfully agree to disagree.

2. I am responsible for my own thoughts, feelings, and actions. I cannot make my partner feel or behave a certain way, and my partner is not responsible for my feelings or actions. I will not blame my partner for my feelings or my choices. I can only take responsibility for myself, and I can only change my behavior.

3. I am responsible for communicating openly and honestly with my partner. I have the right to express my feelings in a way that does not *demean*, *diminish*, or *destroy*. I will use good communication skills, including using "I statements" to express my feelings without the expectation that my partner do anything other than listen, acknowledge, and accept them.

4. I accept and validate my partner's feelings. There are no "bad" or "wrong" feelings. I have the right to my feelings and my partner has the right to his or hers (as our children have the right to their feelings). I will not tell my partner what he/she *should* or *should not* feel; nor will I negate, belittle, or disrespect his/her feelings. I do not need to correct, take care of, or fix my partner's feelings. I will take my partner's feelings into consideration and attempt to do what I can to improve my own behavior as necessary.

5. I have the right to ask my partner to do something for me or to help me, but I do not have the right to expect or demand it. I ask for what I want, using words like, "Would you?

Could you? and Please…" My partner has the right to say no. If my partner cannot help me or meet my needs when I ask, it is my responsibility as an able, independent adult to take care of myself and meet my own needs or to seek help elsewhere. If my partner asks me for something and I cannot give it at that time, I may offer a time when I can and be good to my word. I do not expect my partner to meet all of my needs or desires.

6. I am with my partner out of choice, want, and desire, not exclusively out of need. I do not need nor do I expect my partner to prop me up, make me feel good about myself, take care of me like a parent would a child, make me whole, or otherwise be responsible for me and my well-being. I am responsible for loving and taking care of myself as part of my own path. As part of our relationship path, we may agree to a division of labor that includes one person working and providing income while the other is the primary childcare provider; this does not change the equality or power dynamics of the relationship.

7. I refrain from telling my partner what he/she "should" do. I attempt to eliminate the word "should" from my vocabulary, as it conveys an expectation and a judgment that I, as an equal partner, do not have the right to project onto another. I recognize that "should" is a word that conveys shame and it is not motivating. I can express my feelings, tell my partner what I would do if asked, or say what I would like, without expectation that they will do what I want or think is best.

8. I agree to make my partner and my children a priority over the needs of parents, friends, family members, or others who might want or demand my time and energy. I will help others and give my time and energy to others out of choice, not out of obligation or by demand, and as my partner and I agree is in the best interest of our relationship and our children. I will share my feelings with my partner about family members, endeavor not to judge them, and do my best to get along with them (even if I do not agree with or like them).

9. I have the right to disagree with my partner, to say no to my partner, and to choose my own path. However, I will at all times endeavor to work with my partner to resolve conflict, come to a resolution, or reach a compromise. In doing so, I will not hold onto the past and hold grudges. Once a conflict is resolved or we agree to disagree, we will let it go and move on unless the conflict becomes a destructive pattern, in which case we will seek help.

10. I agree to honor and respect my partner's path as long as it does not step outside the bounds of what we agree we want for our partnership or marriage. For example, I have the right to leave or end the partnership if there is deception, addiction, or abuse and my partner is unwilling to seek help, change the destructive pattern, and make amends.

# Relationship Exercise and Journal Prompts

Choose a relationship with someone that you would like to improve. Ask yourself:

What do I value most about this relationship?

What is working?

What is not working (or what is missing from this relationship)?

What do I truly need from this relationship (if anything)?

What do I want from this person?

How am I letting my needs and wants in this relationship be subverted?

How can I better communicate my needs and wants?

What am I afraid of if I say how I feel and ask for what I want?

What would it take to work through my fear and communicate honestly?

What self-care is needed in this relationship?

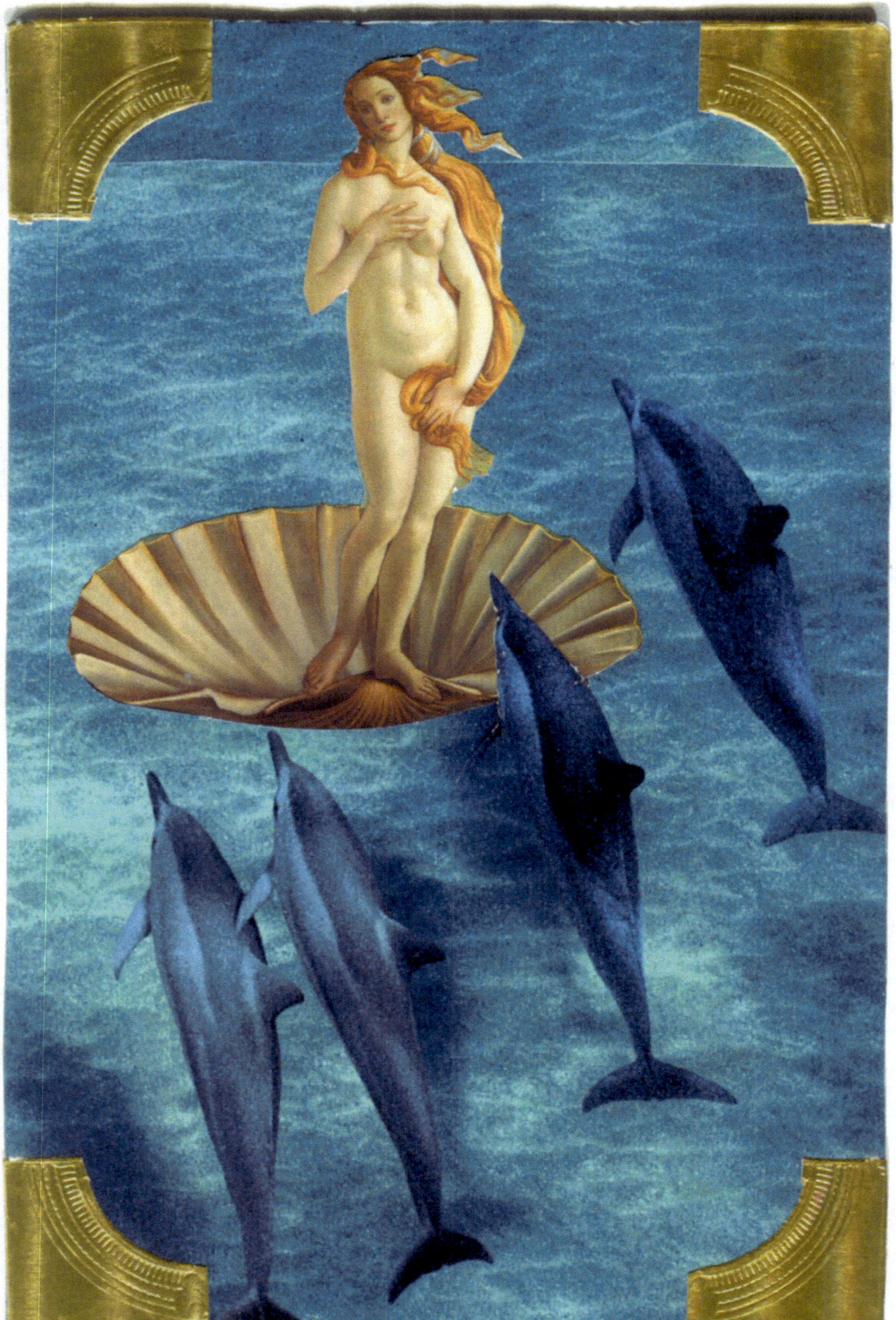

# Chapter Six

# Body and Sexuality

THERE IS PROBABLY no other area of a woman's life in which she needs to practice self-care more than in the way she perceives and takes care of her body. How you think and feel about your body, and consequently, your sexuality, is probably the one issue for women that is universally fraught with insecurity, self-criticism, and shame.

Women tend to be accepting of other female shapes and sizes and sympathetic towards those who struggle with body image, yet have little acceptance of their own body or compassion for their own struggles.

It is easy to get stuck in the comparison game, always finding someone else who is doing a better job at caring for her body or whom you perceive to have better hair, skin, breasts, butt, belly, legs—you name it!—than you do. Most women would admit they would like to be more loving towards their body. It is time to embrace body positivity! That is, loving your body no matter its size, shape, color, or any other aspect of your body and identity.

Unfortunately, in our society and most cultures worldwide, women have long been scrutinized and judged for their looks, physicality, and sexiness, starting from a very early age. Women have been cast as objects (and seen themselves as objects) of men's desires. You have most likely tried to live up to a certain standard of beauty set up by an outdated, outworn, and impossible model of feminine perfection, depicted in art and advertising, and

> **Julie's Story**
>
> As a recent college graduate, Julie looks forward to starting her life on her own, but she has long-held hang-ups about her body that started in middle school when she went through puberty and classmates fat-shamed her. Her mother also made comments whenever she put on a few pounds and implied she would not find a partner if she was overweight.
>
> Consequently, Julie shut down and doesn't allow herself any sensual pleasures. She has not wanted to explore intimate relationships with anyone for fear they would scrutinize her body. Julie wants to learn to love her body as it is and explore sex with someone who is not judgmental and will love her for who she is.

largely dictated by men. Women have internalized male standards of beauty and projected them onto themselves.

It is plain to see from images of women from thousands of years ago that women's bodies were celebrated as curvaceous vessels of life and nurturance—their roundness a mirror of the large-wombed Mother Earth.

There was a time when a woman's body was honored for its creative, life-giving capacity, not for its seductiveness. There was a time when pleasures of the body were respected and practiced without concern for how one woman's body compared to another's. There was a time when a woman's body and her enjoyment of her sexuality was a holy sacrament. Is it too far-fetched to imagine returning to such a mindset and way of being?

The truth is women's bodies come in all shapes, colors, and sizes, and none of those myriad possible forms deter from her singular beauty. If only women fully embraced the idea that they are beautiful because of their many varied facets and figures, then perhaps we could dispense with comparing, contrasting, and competing. It helps to consider body types as existing on a spectrum of feminine and masculine, youthful and elderly, small and large—realistic images that stray from the typical renderings of goddesses that are perfectly proportioned according to male artistic interpretation.

Take a look at the *Venus of Willendorf*, for example. She is a model of woman as full-figured, fulsome, and fat-accepting—a body to approve of and celebrate. Though there are no known myths attached to her, this small, 26,000-year-old statue was called a Venus figure, as were other such ancient figures when discovered, because they were believed to be icons of creative fertility and feminine beauty. She was considered an early representation of Aphrodite or Venus, the Greek/Roman goddess of love and beauty, one of the goddess archetypes you will meet in this chapter. The Venus of Willendorf portrays a womanly shape that has only recently begun to be embraced again as luscious, acceptable, and beautiful.

A little-known intersex goddess to consider in this discussion is Aphroditus, with the breasts of a woman and the phallus of a man, who dressed and identified as a woman. In this form, she was seen as the daughter of Aphrodite and Hermes, the Greek messenger god. This archetype took another form known as Hermaphroditus, who identified as male and dressed in clothes typical of men at the time. These archetypes help us recognize and accept the sacredness of intersex, transgender, and non-binary people and bodies.

In general, the goddesses of old provide a model of what it means to be a woman who is powerful and in charge, a woman who loves and accepts her body and takes pleasure in her sexuality. These strong goddess archetypes existed before the patriarchal religions changed the story by stripping away feminine potency.

In Christianity, the story of Adam and Eve set the stage: woman as temptress, woman as belonging to man, woman as disobedient, woman as sinful because she is sexual. The story that has been told for the past two millennia or more is that women are subordinate to men, and any open expression of sexuality is shameful and forbidden. If any of these archaic beliefs persist within you, it is time to change the story and tell yourself a new, more liberating one.

In this chapter, you are going to meet and work with three goddesses who fully embrace their bodies and sexuality and whose myths reflect their feminine power and influence. Aphrodite is the Greek Goddess of Love and Beauty, known to the Romans as Venus. Freya is the Nordic Goddess of sensual love, sex, lust, and power. Freya has an older woman counterpart named Frigga, considered the aging goddess, both mother and crone, who still sees herself as a beautiful, sexual being as she matures and changes.

# Aphrodite

The archetypal Aphrodite woman likes to look good and feel good about herself. She defines her own beauty and style without concern for others' approval. She is just fine with who she is and how her body looks, and she likes to accentuate all that she is as a feminine being. She appreciates the many ways beauty is reflected in women of all ages, colors, ethnicities, shapes, and sizes. She is happy in her own body and encourages women to be proud of theirs, no matter the shape or size. She is creative in the way she sees and experiences the world and appreciates things of beauty.

The shadow side of this archetype is prone to self-criticism, comparison, and envy, so any time these inner voices show up, it is time to take a look at your negative self-talk and work to transform and integrate these parts so the Aphrodite goddess within you can shine.

Inanna, the ancient Sumerian goddess and queen of Heaven and Earth that you met in CH. 4, page 93 is an early incarnation of Aphrodite/Venus. They share many of the same qualities as goddesses of love, fertility, and feminine power and beauty in their many forms.

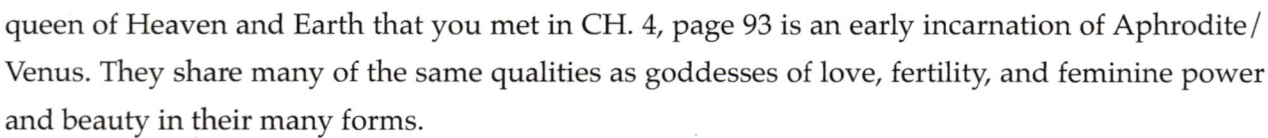

Aphrodite's feast day is February 6, when in ancient Greece a festival called Aphrodisia celebrated her power and wisdom. You may want to prepare a sensuous feast on this day for your lover or loved ones to honor the spirit of the goddess of love and beauty.

# The Story of Aphrodite

Once upon an ancient time in Greece, the Titan god Cronus was in a battle for supremacy with his father, Uranus, the sky god. Cronus severed the genitals of Uranus and cast them into the sea. This caused the feminine waters of Mother Ocean to become impregnated, and out of this union emerged the goddess Aphrodite, whose name means "foam-born." She surfaced as a fully-formed woman from the watery womb of the sea.

She had singular standing as a wild and beautiful instinctual goddess and became Mighty Aphrodite, in command of her life and loves, of which there were many. Aphrodite married Hephaestus, the god of smithing, but she took many lovers—gods and mortals. After all, she was the goddess of love and beauty.

Aphrodite's affair with Ares, the god of war, led to the birth of Eros (Cupid to the Romans), the god of love, whose arrows caused people to fall in love. One of Aphrodite's greatest loves was the handsome mortal, Adonis, whom Persephone, goddess of the Underworld, also loved. A pact was made whereby Adonis spent four springtime months of the year with Aphrodite and four winter months in the Underworld with Persephone. He had the choice of how he wanted to spend the other four summer months of the year, and he chose to spend them with the seductively powerful Aphrodite. They became inseparable until one day Adonis was gored to death by a wild boar. As Aphrodite ran through the woods overcome with grief, she stepped on a white rose and her blood turned it red, creating the red rose of passion.

---

While Aphrodite is an icon of feminine beauty as depicted by countless artists throughout time, what she shows is how to love yourself and your body unequivocally and unapologetically. She helps you embrace your own unique beauty whole-heartedly. Women are but a reflection of the divine feminine in all her many and varied permutations—expressions of the goddess in human form.

You could say that Aphrodite is born within you when you love yourself unconditionally and see yourself as a sacred, sexual being, complete and whole—even holy. She is ultimately a goddess of love; with her guidance you can learn to love yourself and find love that may have been alluding you out there. Love amplifies beauty, and so through her eyes you begin to see the world differently, including yourself and others.

# Ten Ways to Love Your Body

1. Every day write down three things you love about your body or are grateful for, remembering your body is a sacred vessel. Are you grateful for a body that brought you through trauma? Strong legs that help you run? Breasts that fed your child? Do you love your hair? Say thank you for a bootylicious butt, a belly that has birthed babies, good eyesight. (And don't add a "but," "if only," "when…") Learn to love your imperfections, as there is no perfect body. Be willing to turn even things you have historically disliked or come to believe are not good enough into a positive affirmation of your unique body.
2. Let go of comparing yourself to anyone else. Affirm your uniqueness and sense of self. Show up as You by owning your power and embodying it. When you think you are beautiful, you are.
3. Honor your body's sense of emptiness and fullness. Make a practice of eating when hungry and choosing nourishing, whole foods (not junk food). That does not mean deprive yourself of tasty treats now and then. Give yourself the time and space to enjoy eating. Eat in a balanced way while enjoying the sensual pleasures of yummy food.
4. Move away from "weight" consciousness and into "health" consciousness. Avoid dieting, depriving, or starving yourself. If helpful, find a nutritionist or alternative healer to learn what your body needs and does not need and explore what foods best serve you.
5. Do one thing every day to move your body for at least 20 minutes, whether it is walking, dancing, running, yoga, or any number of physical practices. Did you know that having sex is the equivalent of a 20-minute run?
6. Take care of your sexual needs, whether alone or with a partner. Give yourself the gift of bodily pleasure. Be willing to experiment and play. If sex is not pleasurable to you, but you would like it to be, seek help with sexual healing.
7. Choose to be with people who are supportive, kind, and non-judgmental, and who appreciate the uniqueness of your being, both inside and out. The more you do this with yourself, the more you will expect it and get it from others.
8. Notice when you are tired and give your body the rest it needs, including naps or just vegging. Practice good sleep hygiene (See CH. 12, page 256). Give yourself time to unwind and relax each day and don't overwork.
9. Ask your body each day what gift you might give it. Could it use a massage? Facial? Stretch? Swim? Hydration? Bubble bath? Nap? Essential oils? Love? Sex? Honor your body

by checking in with it and caring for your sacred temple. Don't ignore what your body needs and wants!

10. Notice what you say to yourself about yourself. Would you talk to a friend or loved one the same way? Replace criticism and negative self-talk about your body with affirmations of love and respect for your body. Research shows us that self-compassion helps us lose weight if that is our goal, while self-criticism leads to weight gain. Similarly, studies have shown that body dissatisfaction leads to lowered sexual desire and fulfillment, whereas positive feelings about your body leads to greater arousal and sexual satisfaction. Change the story! Practice radical self-love.

Be kind to yourself as you seek to change your perceptions or something about your body. Self-care involves recognizing and accepting your imperfections (because nobody is perfect!), while also loving yourself and finding ways to feel better—compassionately.

## Aphrodite Speaks

Dear Daughter, You are an immaculate manifestation of the divine feminine. I implore you to love yourself as an earthly goddess, as I do, and be all that you are!

If you believe you are whole, lovable, wonderful, delicious, and all that, then you will be. That is all it takes—Believing the Truth of who you are and not the lies that you have been fed by society and others out there. Your truth is in here: Inside. Your body is your truth, your temple. It is yours to own, claim, and carry with pride and joy.

I invite you to embrace life in all its beauty and sensuousness. Notice what gives you pleasure and give yourself that gift. Pay attention to your six senses. It is through your senses that your body and soul communicate. Notice and name your response to your felt experience by doing something each day to honor each of your sacred senses:

*Smell*—Practice aromatherapy, light a scented candle, burn incense, cook something and savor the aroma; go outside and notice the scents that abound in nature as well as the unique smell of your lover.

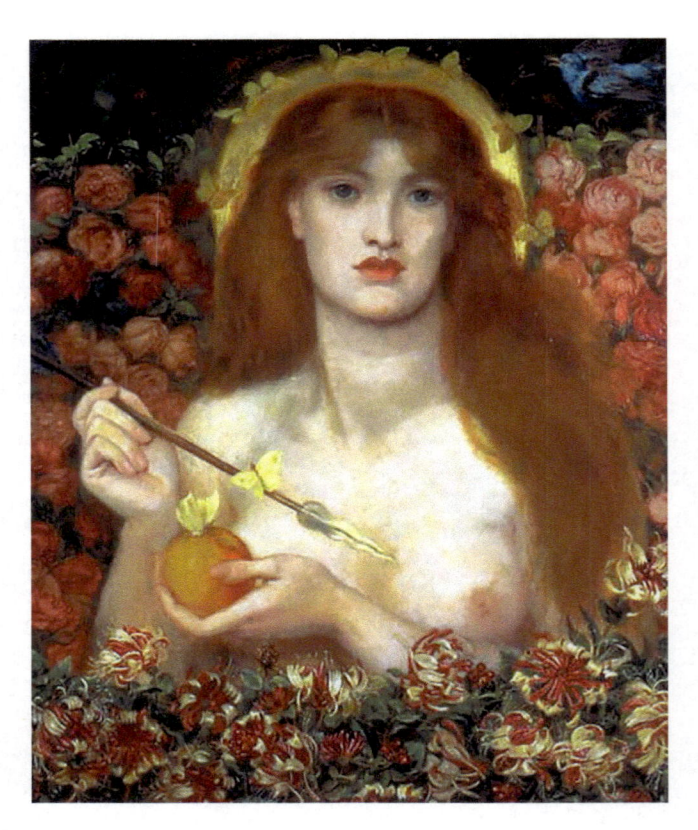

*Taste*—Enjoy something sweet or juicy, spicy or savory, a soothing cup of flavorful tea, a treat you baked; savor the juice of your favorite fruit; eat slowly and notice how it feels and tastes in your mouth; taste your lover's salty skin.

*Touch*—Luxuriate in the feeling of something soft and silky, furry, or filmy against your skin; caress your skin, apply lotions and oils; pet your favorite animal or your lover.

*Sound*—Listen to music, a podcast, audio book; tune into the sounds of nature as you sit outside attentively; hear the patter of rain against your window, enjoy the sounds of silence or the sound of your lover's breath as you lie near.

*Sight*—Look at the sunrise or sunset, the stars in the night sky; go out in nature and observe the flora and fauna, peruse a book of art or enjoy your own art; take in beauty, including your lover's face, hair, eyes, nose, mouth, body.

*Intuition (your sixth sense)*—What do you notice when you tune in to your body's wisdom? What message do you get? What image do you see? What do you know on a deep level? Your body knows if you will but listen. Sense what your lover desires and provide it.

Honor me through an art form that celebrates self-love and my archetypal energy as a lover and fierce feminine icon.

## Objects and symbols to consider for your altar to Aphrodite

**Colors:** white, red, aqua

**Objects:** heart, red or aqua candle, Venus figurine, shell, swan or dolphin figurine

**Gemstones:** rose quartz, pearl, ruby

**Flowers:** red roses, anemones, violets

**Element:** fire

**Chakra:** heart (4th chakra)

**VENVS**

    Julie decides to start by working with Aphrodite and learning to love her body and feel powerful in it just the way it is. She explores self-pleasuring, something she has not allowed herself to enjoy before. She begins looking at her body in the mirror and expressing gratitude, love, and approval for each part. Whenever she hears the critical voice in her head, she reminds herself of the truth that she is a beautiful, wise woman with much to offer someone.
    She awakens her senses by listening to music, trying different essential oils, lighting scented candles, and treating herself like a goddess of love and beauty who savors sensual delights. She creates an altar and fashions her own Venus of Willendorf figurine out of clay, letting her fingers lovingly recreate the curves of her own body in the doll, which has a prominent place on her altar. Over time her inner Aphrodite awakens, and Julie feels ready to start dating.

# Freya and Frigga

These Norse goddesses are sometimes viewed as separate beings and at other times as two aspects of the same Great Goddess of Northern Europe: Freya, the free-spirited, spring maiden, and Frigga, the wise mother and crone.

Consider this goddess as two aspects of your life in terms of developmental and life changes. Freya is the young, lustful lover, the woman who dates and explores her sexuality through partnership (which really could occur at any age), while Frigga represents the archetypal goddess of maturity, after menopause, whose body—and possibly her sexual needs and desires—has changed.

When this Norse goddess is activated, you are willing to embrace your sexuality at any age or stage. She shows you that it is natural to remain a sensual, sexual being throughout your life, even as your body, needs, and desires change.

For some women as they age, sex becomes less of a concern. Desire may wane, and they are content to live without it. And for other women, regardless of age, sex is never a strong urge, and they may find peace with their asexuality (feeling no sexual desire) or gray-sexuality (intermittent or inconsistent sexual desire). What is important is that you are honest about what you want and need and do your best to find your own fulfillment through loving self-care.

Sometimes what you need is permission from your Higher Self or Inner Goddess to be sexual and feel pleasure. You may have challenges to overcome if you have been steeped in a patriarchal religious paradigm that equates sexuality with sinfulness and relegates women to a subordinate or passive role. But you can find your way to sexual freedom and enjoyment through loving self-care and healing old cultural or familial wounds.

Freya/Frigga can be seen as a two-in-one archetype—the maiden and the mother/crone within one body. The names both mean "beloved lady or wife." "Frigg's Day," better known as Friday, comes from her name. It was considered a lucky day to get married. Her feast day is May 30.

## The Story of Freya and Frigga

Freya is a free-spirited goddess with a healthy love and lust for life and men (or women). She lives in Asgard with her husband, the Norse god Odin, who is often away on travels. Not one to sit and wait for him (as he is a free-spirit, too), Freya takes many lovers. She wears beautiful objects, like a circlet of amber tears around her throat known as the Brísingamen. How she came to own it says everything you need to know about Freya's sexual power.

Awakened early one morning by dreams of gold, Freya sets out in her chariot drawn by two cats. As if being pulled by a magnetic force, she drives her chariot to a cave on the edge of the woods and enters, hearing sounds of clanging metal within. As she enters the dark passageway, she sees the fire of a forge burning brightly ahead. Out of the flames a dwarf pulls a magnificent necklace of golden amber stones, and Freya realizes this is what she dreamt of the night before.

She knows she must have the Brísingamen—the magical, glowing necklace of power. With it she will be able to shapeshift and resurrect men slain in battle. She asks the four dwarfs who have fashioned the necklace if she can buy it from them, but they say no, they have enough gold. They tell her she can have it if she sleeps with them. After four nights of bedding the dwarfs, she fastens the necklace around her neck and cries tears of gold.

The four dwarfs Freya frolics with represent the four directions and the elements of earth and water (feminine), air and fire (masculine). So through sexual union with these four elements she absorbs these creative, elemental, life-affirming aspects within herself. They become part of her magic.

Freya/Frigga also wears a cloak of falcon feathers that gives her oracular powers. Wearing it, she can foresee the fate of all beings. Freya is such a vibrant life force that she is able to bring Viking warriors killed on battlefields back to life and provide them sanctuary in her heavenly *Fólkvangr*, meaning *field of the people.* As a goddess of fertility, life, and love, she invites the soldier's wives to join them in celebration of their rebirth. Women look up to her life-giving abilities and pay homage to her when they wish to conceive a child.

As Freya aged, Frigga came to be the more subdued wife and queen of her own domain, less promiscuous than Freya, yet still fully in her sovereignty.

---

Freya/Frigga is a goddess who is comfortable in her own skin. Freya's cat-drawn chariot indicates she is wild and free and in tune with her instinctual nature. So desirable was she that men, gods, giants, and faerie folk fought over her. Her sexuality was a kind of healing magic in itself. Through her sexual adventures she exercised her power as a woman without shame. Her sexuality was simply a way to live fully and pleasurably in her body.

You can bestow such life-giving power to yourself by allowing the older, wise woman—the Frigga within—to counsel the younger Freya part of you who may still be afraid to be all that she is. Frigga is a mother who gives permission to be free, to come out of your shell, and to engage with life in all ways. Through her, you can discover your own passions and allow them to stir and ignite.

Sexuality is a normal and healthy part of being human, of being a woman, but guilt and shame around sexuality as well as the feminine body have long been imposed by patriarchal attitudes—old programming from family, religion, society—messages as old as Eve.

You may have been told not to touch your body or not to dress a certain way; you may have been called slut or whore or other derogatory names because you were in a woman's body or had sexual desires and acted on them. (Notice there are no such terms for men who express their sexual nature.) You may have been told sex is bad, evil, wrong; only for procreation or marriage; that it is a woman's duty to submit to a man, and that you should not want it; that sex is a sin; nice girls don't do that—the list goes on. But the truth is that sex is as normal and natural to being human as breathing and eating.

**Good Sex = Good Communication**

Having a safe, committed partner to play with, explore with, and talk to about your needs and desires helps you overcome shame and any wounding around sexuality. If you were sexually abused, work with a trusted therapist to help you heal from this trauma and reclaim your body.

You can teach your partner how to give you pleasure and how to love you. It is important that you do so as a matter of self-care. Otherwise you are living in your head (not tuned into your body), wishing and hoping your partner will read your mind and know what you like and want them to do. It seldom works that way.

Sometimes it is a dance—you find a rhythm that works for both of you, and few words are necessary—but not always. As with learning any dance steps, it is important to find a willing partner, communicate what you like and do not like, what steps work and do not, and practice!

For example, you may want to ask your partner to make eye contact with you when you are having sex, to talk to you, or reassure you. You may want to let them know you are trying to get more comfortable with sexual expression, to feel safe in your body during sex, and would like to go slow and both be present. Creating a safe container for intimacy can be both healing and liberating. You may also want to play in ways that feel wild and free, and experiment with different ways of expressing your sexuality and feeling good in your body. This also requires a trusting partner with whom you can communicate your desires and share mutual consent.

It goes without saying that it is important to choose a sexual partner wisely, practice safe and protected sex, and only consent to what you want and are willing to do for your own or your partner's pleasure and well-being. It is imperative to say no to anything that makes you uncomfortable or causes you pain.

**Sex Is Good for You**

Having a healthy sex life reduces stress, depression, and anxiety, thanks to the endorphins that are released. Sex involves physical exercise and benefits the heart and overall health. It also makes for better sleep and helps you look and feel both vital and relaxed.

Some people harbor the belief that it is wrong to pleasure themselves when alone. But if you truly want to practice exquisite self-care, do for yourself what you would do for someone else or give to yourself what you wish to receive. Why? Because you matter. You deserve love, kindness, joy, release, and all the attention and care a goddess is due. If there is no one to do it for you, do it for yourself.

> Note: If you have been sexually abused it is important to heal the trauma with the help of a qualified professional. This way you learn self-compassion and self-love so that you may enjoy a healthy sex life. Taking charge of your own healing is fundamental to self-care.

# Freya and Frigga Speak

Dear Sister, When you embrace us, you give yourself permission to be a sensual, sexual being in whatever way suits you.

We ask that you experiment with getting to know your body and your desires.

Make time for yourself. Touch your body. Pamper it. Oil it. Delight yourself.

Read erotic literature (or write your own story!). Watch romantic or sexy movies that turn you on.

Fantasize about a lover who meets your every need; in fantasy there is nothing off limits.

Caress or massage your body, slowly moving from one body part to another noticing what feels good; try this with a partner, taking turns to touch and communicate what feels good without it necessarily leading to sex or climax—just for the pure pleasure of it.

Take a warm bubble bath with your favorite essential oils; add flower petals; dim the lights and play music.

Sleep on soft cotton or satin sheets with a few drops of essential oils on the fabric. Wear sexy lingerie or nothing at all to bed. Tickle your skin with feathers.

Dance alone or with a partner to sexy music with the lights down low.

Buy a new sex toy and have fun playing with it.

Practice flirting, feeling your power as a woman. It does not have to lead to sex unless you want it to.

Wear something sexy and go out on the town and flaunt it, or just wear something you enjoy feeling next to your skin.

Prepare a sensuous, delicious meal for yourself, or make one with your partner, and eat by candlelight. Feed each other dessert.

Buy yourself flowers (or pick them from your garden) every week, and put them on your table or altar in honor of your beauty and love for yourself. Make it a practice.

Remember you are a sensual, sexual goddess who deserves to feel good about your body, your experiences, and your choices. You have permission to be a sexual woman. The world is your oyster. Be the pearl that grows within it.

## Objects and symbols to consider for your altar to Freya and Frigga

**Colors:** green, yellow/amber, gold

**Objects:** phallic and yonic symbols or images, necklace, cat figurines, falcon or other feathers

**Gemstones:** amber, topaz, emerald, pearl, gold

**Flowers:** orchid, primrose, daisy

**Element:** earth and water (feminine)

**Chakra:** sacral (2nd chakra)

# Journal Prompts

**Exercise: Turning Old Lies Into New Truths**

Write down as many messages as you remember hearing as a girl or young woman about your body or sex on one side of the page. On the other side, counter each of these old lies with the truth that you now know or want to accept. The truth is that every woman deserves to love and be loved, to be proud of her body, to have sex and enjoy it if she desires it, whether giving pleasure to her own body or giving and receiving pleasure with a partner. Claiming the truth is liberating!

| Old Messages | New Truths |
|---|---|
| | |

**Dialogue With the Inner Critic**

Everyone has an Inner Critic, a sub-personality or inner part that can have greater or lesser sway over your sense of self and well-being depending on how much power you give it.

Envision this shadow part and give it a name, e.g., Shamu the Shamer, Chrissy the Critic. Make a SoulCollage® card or create an art journal page imagining what your Inner Critic looks like. Does it still harangue you with old messages about your body and sexuality and what it means to be a woman? Does it like to shame you with particular directives learned from patriarchal institutions or misguided people in your life? Take note of outdated beliefs and hurtful words and determine to change them.

Create a dialogue with this part by asking it questions and writing down the answers that come spontaneously. Listen to what it needs and wants and tell your Inner Critic what you need and want and reach an agreement. A shadow part can be helpful at times if you listen to its intention. Learn how and why it is trying to get your attention. It may just be going about it the wrong way. It is possible for the shadow aspects of your personality to grow, evolve, and transform into more helpful parts. You may want to ask:

- When did you come into my life?
- What was your purpose then? What is your purpose now?
- What do you want me to know?
- What is your fear?
- What do you need?
- How can I (the Core Self) help you (a part of me)?
- How can you help me (and not hurt me)?
- What agreement can we make (my Inner Critic and I) so that I can be happier and healthier in my body and with my sexuality?

# Dialogue With the Goddess

Now make a collage, art journal page, painting, or sculpture that represents Aphrodite/Venus or Freya/Frigga—the part of you that embraces your sexuality and opens itself to love. This is the Inner Goddess or Higher Self that gives you permission to be sexual and whole-heartedly enjoy sexual pleasure, no matter your age, shape, size, gender identity, or other factors. Create a dialogue with this goddess guide and ask:

- How can I better accept my body and my sexuality?
- What wisdom do you have for me?
- What do I need to let go of?
- What do I need to embrace?
- What message or affirmation can I take with me to remember myself as a wholly (holy) sexual being who is worthy of love?

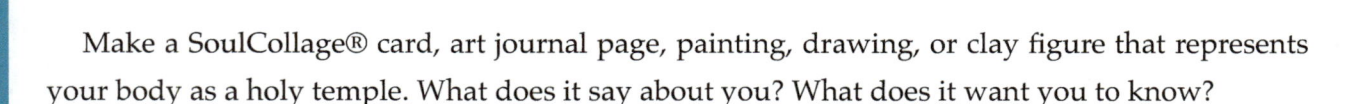

Make a SoulCollage® card, art journal page, painting, drawing, or clay figure that represents your body as a holy temple. What does it say about you? What does it want you to know?

Write a prayer to your body and say it to yourself often.

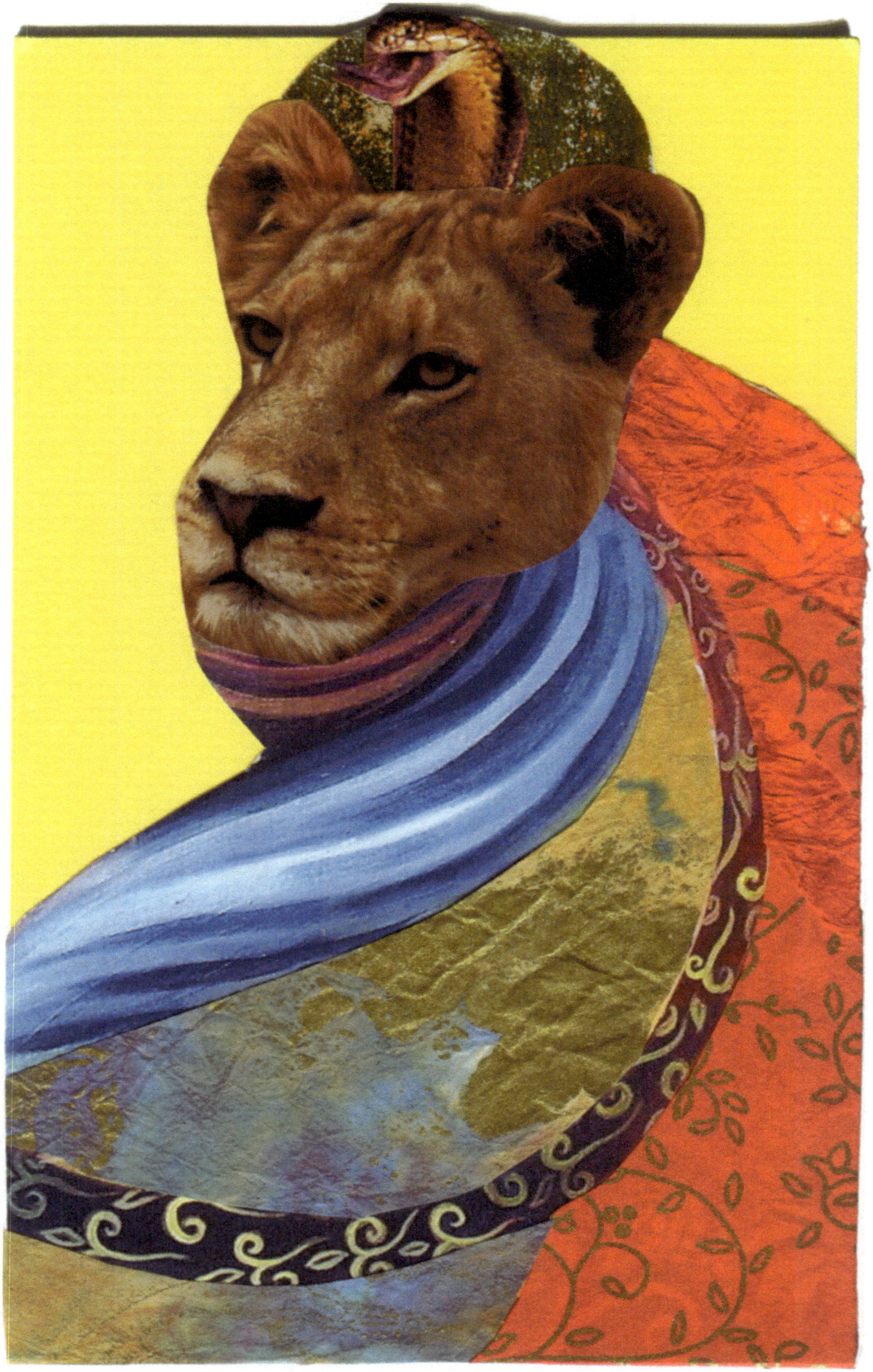

# Chapter Seven

# Hurt and Anger

The two emotions of hurt and anger go hand in hand. Beneath most anger is hurt. Anger is a way to express hurt, of lashing out, of saying, "I can't believe you did that!" or "How dare you treat me that way!" or "I won't allow you to hurt me!" Your vulnerable Inner Child feels hurt, and if she does not feel safe expressing that hurt it can come pouring (or roaring) out as anger. And that is not always a bad thing.

Anger is potent; it gets people's attention. Hurt is a more vulnerable feeling, often one that women are loath to acknowledge for fear of being ignored, humiliated, ostracized, or shamed, as may have happened when they cried as children. The underlying message is: "You are a woman. You are supposed to *mend* the hurt and take care of others' pain, not admit to your own woundedness, let alone fury."

For too long, society has made women feel that their anger is wrong, but it is not. It is a perfectly normal, natural emotion, a primal one that helps you survive potentially dangerous situations. It helps motivate and galvanize you to speak up, take action, right a wrong, change the status quo, stop abusive behavior, or end a relationship or circumstance that has reached a breaking point—when you are ready to scream, "I'm mad as hell and I'm not going to take it anymore!" Instead, women feel they are "damned if they do and damned if they don't" express their anger—deemed either rageful shrews or repressed bitches.

## Melanie's Story

Melanie grew up in a family in which "good girls" never showed their anger. She got the message that she should be happy and pleasant all the time, and if she was not, her parents would disapprove of her and even ignore her. As a teenager her anger spilled out at times. She was furious that no one talked about feelings, no one recognized them, and if they did show up, they were to be pushed back down.

Melanie came to believe there must be something wrong with her. Yet deep down, she knew her angry feelings—about being bullied by her brother, about not being able to talk about her pain in her own family—were justified. As an adult, Melanie held her feelings in until she exploded. She realized she never learned how to be angry in a healthy way, let alone accept her feelings as legitimate. She wanted to be able to feel all her feelings and not be ashamed of them, to understand where her hurt came from and how to talk about it.

Meaningful self-care involves accepting your feelings of hurt and anger and expressing these feelings, not bottling them up. When you are able to communicate these emotions in effective ways, you are able to stand in your power, to be heard and understood. It is time to stop shying away from the righteous anger women in the world feel now more than ever with the rise of the "Me, Too" and "Time's Up" movements as well as resistance to patriarchal oppression more generally. Women need to stop being afraid and ashamed of their well-deserved wrath and allow it to both inform and transform them (and others).

Anger takes many forms—from irritation, frustration, and resentment to fury, outrage, and explosiveness. Navigating through these forms of anger can feel like walking through a minefield. There are three goddesses who will help you find your way, give you permission to be hurt and angry, teach you how to communicate these emotions in a healthy way to feel authentic and empowered, and see your hurt and anger as a part of your authentic being.

They are Kali, the Hindu goddess of destruction, and Sekhmet, the lion-headed goddess of ancient Egypt—both personify the fierce feminine. And thirdly, the Black Madonna, who serves as a witness to women's pain and suffering. All three can help you feel and accept hurt and anger, as well as transform them as necessary.

# Kali

Kali is the wild, dark, protector goddess, usually portrayed in warrior mode, blue- or black-skinned, symbolically bare-breasted (naked truth), with long, tangled hair (inner wild woman), her tongue lolling (devourer of illusion). She wears a necklace of skulls (infinite knowledge), and has four to eight arms—one holding the severed head of a demon (that which plagues you), another a sword or scythe (to cut through illusion).

Her other arms offer blessings: one signals, "Fear not!"—a good reminder when you must stand up for yourself and fight the good fight. Around Kali's waist dangles a girdle of human hands (to work out karma), and she is often portrayed with one foot resting on the god, Shiva, her consort and masculine counterpart. He has laid down before her to absorb her rage.

## The Story of Kali

The Hindu warrior goddess Durga was in the midst of a great battle against an army of demons. For every drop of blood a demon spilled, another would be born, exponentially increasing the size of the enemy hordes. Durga desperately needed help and called upon the gods and goddesses to lend a hand. Heeding her call, out of Durga's head sprang Kali, the goddess of destruction, to help her sister win the battle. With her great, long tongue, Kali slurped up the demons' blood before they could multiply.

With the advantage of Kali's power and rage, Durga won the war. However, Kali was on such a destructive rampage she could not stop. It was Shiva who finally allowed Kali's out-of-control frenzy to dissipate. This god of destruction, like Kali, could also be an empathetic ally. He flung himself in her path and transformed into a baby. She, who is also known as Kali Ma—the compassionate mother—seeing the helpless infant, returned to her conscious self, bent down to pick him up, and the conflict ended.

---

Kali helps you recognize the hurt and pain you carry and have not acknowledged or have kept hidden. Imagine past and current hurts and outrages as inner demons you do battle with. They will win the inner war as long as you allow them that power and do not confront them.

The more you ignore your own hurts, the more powerful they become. They may even come to define you if you do not face them, transform them, and integrate them.

Like Kali seeing the baby Shiva, see your own hurt Inner Child. The little girl who screams in frustration, pain, and anger, afraid to let anyone see her agony, is the one lying before you, vulnerable and innocent, asking to be seen and acknowledged. When you behold your Inner Child and all that she has been through and stop to comfort her, you stop the inner destructive rampage and begin to heal.

Kali helps you know the truth, know what is needed to be your own best healer. She is a liberator who stands with you as you confront these inner demons, perhaps for the first time, as relics from the past, as unhealed wounds. Were you criticized as a child? Were you neglected? Abandoned? Abused? Did you have to take care of a parent or sibling rather than being taken care of? These hurts can haunt you, becoming "demons" that interfere with your health and happiness. They can cause you to lash out, displacing your original pain onto others in your life. When you recognize and acknowledge these injuries and grieve the loss and the pain you carry, you stop the internal bleeding. Kali is the fearless destroyer goddess who helps you vanquish the inner demons and transform your old wounds into healing strength and wisdom.

Write a letter to your Inner Child letting her know you see her vitality, her unique spark, as well as her woundedness. Promise to listen to her needs and wants and do everything you can to help her, to see her, and to take care of her. Place this on your altar.

# Kali Speaks

Dear Daughter, I am here. I hear your pain, I feel your hurt, I know your anger. I will help you see your pain so that it does not destroy you, but so that you, instead, destroy that which no longer serves you.

I am here to tell you to feel the hurt; to acknowledge the pain, the rage; to wail; to weep tears of sadness, loss, and grief. I am here to tell you to accept these feelings and allow them to be with you for a while, for as long as it takes to feel them, for as long as it takes for them to run their course, for as long as it takes for you to finally see and release them.

You are not meant to carry hurt forever. Hurt can be transformed through love and forgiveness, but first you must get through the anger. That is my gift to you—to allow yourself to be angry at whoever hurt you, whatever circumstances led to your pain, however you were let down, abandoned, neglected, or abused. You must let the fire of your anger burn out. You can do this without destroying others or yourself.

Your anger is the fire of transformation. Through it you will find the release from the heaviness of hurt. Let it go into the fire. Write it all down, burn it, or scream it into the flames, and watch it go up in smoke.

Only when you have expressed and released your anger can you get to forgiveness. When there is nothing left, when it is burned up, you will feel transformed, uplifted, detached from the past pain. Yes, you know it was there, you know it happened, you will not forget, but you will no longer carry it. It will no longer weigh you down. It will not define you. You will be free.

## Inventory of Hurts

Kali will protect you as you name and claim the things you have been holding onto, the past pain, the ongoing hurt and anger—the "demons" that live inside you.

List them. What are you still carrying? Now, next to these, list the antidotes to these hurts. What do you *need* to heal these wounds? What is it *you* can give to yourself or ask for from another to help you heal?

| Inner Demons (Source of Hurt, Pain) | Antidote For Healing (What do you *need*?) |
|---|---|
|  |  |

## Objects and Symbols to Consider for Your Altar to Kali

**Colors:** black, red

**Objects:** figure of Kali, knife/dagger/scythe, skull, black or red candle

**Gemstones:** black obsidian, tourmaline, smoky quartz

**Flowers:** hibiscus, orchid

**Element:** air

**Chakra:** throat (5th chakra)

## The Story of Sekhmet

Similar to Kali's genesis, the Egyptian lion-headed goddess, Sekhmet, sprang from the head of the sun god Ra to dispense justice and provide healing. Ra was angry at the people on earth who had lost their humanity and were at war with one another. Sekhmet attacked the inhumane, blood-thirsty rebels with such fury that Ra feared she would annihilate the entire human race if he did not intervene. He tried to convince her to retreat, as her work was done, but being the instinctual force of nature that she was, Sekhmet could not be swayed by reason.

So Ra ordered 7,000 jugs of beer mixed with pomegranate juice be poured upon the earth to tempt her. Sekhmet lapped up the red liquid in great gulps, thinking it was human blood. Intoxicated, she eventually passed out, and her rampage ended before she could decimate all of humanity.

Sekhmet is one part of the Egyptian Triple Goddess along with Bast, the playful cat maiden (see CH. 3, page 78), and Hathor, the mother goddess of pleasure (and sometimes Isis). Sekhmet represents the crone aspect of this holy triumvirate, the dark goddess who means business, who uses her anger wisely to put an end to injustice and inhumanity.

Sekhmet represents the power of the crone: she has no time to dilly-dally and make nice. She gets to the point and does not suffer fools gladly. At this point in a woman's life (after menopause), she may speak her mind more often or take a stronger position than she ever has before. She cares less what other people think. She feels the fear but does it anyway. She will stand up to an overbearing, domineering, or abusive boss or partner. She may leave an intolerable situation and start over, doing something she has always wanted to do but never allowed herself. She has learned through experience to temper her rage and anger with wisdom to bring about desired change.

Anger is a powerful emotion that few women learn to deal with in a healthy way growing up. Society historically makes women feel ashamed of their anger, even afraid of it. Women sense they are not allowed to be angry, while men are. This can lead to feeling overwhelmed by anger with no safe place to direct it. Or you may feel your anger gets the better of you or is out of control because you have not been encouraged to feel it, nor taught how to communicate it effectively. You can change the way you express it and deal with it through the alchemical fire of change—the metaphorical fire that transmutes the base metal, lead, into gold. Sekhmet's power allows anger to transform you, not destroy you. Sekhmet is a teacher who shows you how to be angry without hurting yourself or others.

Remember, anger is a normal emotion. It is not shameful or wrong to feel angry. It can be quite appropriate and motivating. It can be a healthy or destructive emotion, depending on how you use it. If pushed down or turned inward, anger hurts you and turns into depression. If accepted and released appropriately, your anger helps you heal and feel lighter. Sekhmet is your goddess ally to steer you through the inferno. Ask for her help, strength, and guidance as you try the following…

## 12 Ways to Express and Transform Anger

1. Name it and claim it. Meditate on it. It may dissipate the more you detach from it, or you may need to address your feelings with someone in a constructive way.
2. Write about it. Create an *anger journal* and let out your feelings there, or write a letter to the person you are mad at (without the intention to give it to them, understanding this is for you to get your feelings out). Do not censor or edit yourself. You may want to use a red or black crayon to scribble out your rage, and then bury or burn your writings later. Once you have written them out, you may decide to address your feelings with the person you are angry with in a more tempered way than what you wrote (see #7).
3. Release your fury by yelling and screaming into a pillow, in a closed room, or outdoors where no one can hear you. Let it all out. Say every vile thing that is swirling inside, using

swear words, name-calling, and all. (Remember, you are not saying it *to* someone; you are saying it *for* yourself, to give it a voice and get it out.)

4. Let go of the anger and tenseness in your body through physical action without harming yourself or anyone else. Hit pillows or kick boxes as you scream or speak your anger and pain out loud (good for releasing old or new wounds).
5. Throw a tantrum. Let your angry Inner Child cry, rage, yell, say what she wants or needs (you and the goddess need be the only witnesses to this). Soothe yourself afterwards in a loving, mothering way.
6. Do some physical exercise or sport that allows you to feel a release: dancing, kickboxing, martial arts, hitting a ball or punching bag, running, jumping. Consciously release your anger with each physical exertion. Let it move through you and out of you. Rant and rave while you do this, if you can.
7. Tell the person you are angry with in a way that does not demean, diminish, or destroy. Say, "I feel angry when you/about…" without blaming or shaming. Just express your feelings and ask for what you need and want without expectation. See what happens.
8. Make a piece of art and pour all of your grievances into it. Express your feelings through colors, symbols, images, brush strokes. You can later destroy it, paint over it, or keep it as a portrait of your impassioned self.
9. Tear up paper and then write down all your enraged feelings on the torn pieces, then one by one, throw them into a fire, naming and releasing them. Declare your new intentions or affirmations. Who are you without your rage?
10. Ask someone you trust—who is strong and cares about you—to witness your anger and allow you to vent (just be careful not to use them up for this purpose).
11. Practice tolerating and witnessing anger in others (as long as they are not demeaning, diminishing, or destroying you) without taking it personally or assuming it has anything to do with you. Let them own it. See it as separate from you.
12. Stand up to any abusive treatment by stating firmly that you do not like it and will not tolerate it; reach an understanding with the person hurting or abusing you or walk away. Keep your boundaries firm around this. Seek help if you need it. Take care of yourself.

Consider enlisting a therapist or other healer to guide you through the process of acknowledging and healing hurt and anger, and to learn and practice effective ways to express it.

Melanie creates an Anger Journal for the express purpose of releasing her rage. She finds that by journaling and using paints and crayons to express her feelings, especially through the use of color, she is getting to them, allowing them out, able to see and feel again what was lost.

She senses that she has unlocked a cellarful of repressed emotions. Through words and images, ripped pages, and splashes of color, she starts to feel a reawakening of her True Self. She works with an art therapist who helps guide her through the process.

She learns for the first time to speak her truth and not feel ashamed of her anger and her hurt. At the same time, she learns to transform her explosiveness into healthy communication skills that get her point across.

# Sekhmet Speaks

Dear Daughter, I am the goddess who can help you activate your solar plexus chakra, your place of personal power and ego strength—necessary for channeling and transforming your anger.

This is where your willpower, your self-esteem, your sense of individuation and identity are centered. Are you reflecting your true self to the world? Or are you hiding behind a mask to hide your shame and fear about how others might perceive you? What do you imagine will happen if you reveal your true feelings, if you show how mad you are? Remember, it is not your responsibility to take care of another person's feelings when you express your anger in a constructive way.

Take a look at how you deal with anger, how you express it. Do you tend to explode or hold it in? Finding the middle way is key: learning to respond, not react. That does not mean you cannot ever raise your voice or show passion or indignation through your words, but it is important not to leave a path of destruction, as I learned.

Acknowledging your irate feelings is the first step. Accept them as real and valid. Then consider what would help you. Do you need to be seen and heard? Decide how to go about getting these needs met by communicating what you are upset about and requesting what you need and want. You do not need to demean, diminish, or destroy another with your anger. You need to own it and work through it by staying true to yourself.

There are times when you must act to end a situation that is toxic to you, to destroy what was, so something new can be born. This ability to end a bad relationship or circumstance comes from the solar plexus, above the navel, your center of personal power. You'll know it's active when you have the will and the impetus to heed your gut instinct, to know when it is time to act, and to follow through.

Too little fire in the belly can indicate weakness, victimhood, and people-pleasing to the point of self-sacrifice and martyrdom. Too much fire can lead to control, dominance, and uncontrollable rage. I can help you find the right amount of energy for your solar plexus cauldron:

Lie down and hold your hands to your belly above your navel as you breathe deeply. Feel the circular energy moving here. Is it too fast, too hot? Or sluggish and cool? Gently rub your hands in a circle over your belly and breathe slowly and deeply as you imagine setting the right speed and temperature for this energy center. What image or symbol do you see when you feel the fire is just right?

Make a collage or draw this symbol in your journal along with an image of me to help you remember what it means to stand in your power and transform your anger with wisdom and knowing.

## Objects and Symbols to Consider for Your Altar to Sekhmet

Colors: black, orange, yellow

Objects: figures of Sekhmet or lion, ankh, yellow and orange candles

Gemstones: fire agate, yellow jasper, chrysoberyl (cat's eye)

Flowers: dandelion, red lion amaryllis, orange lion flowers

Element: fire

Chakra: solar plexus (3rd chakra)

# The Black Madonna

She is the first goddess, the deep, chthonic one who comes from the earth, who holds you in her arms like great, soft tree branches, who watches over you and protects you through all eternity. She is the dark moon teacher of mysteries and mysticism. She is the witness to your pain, anger, and woundedness. She beckons you to walk through the darkness with her before you reach for the light of understanding and forgiveness.

# The Story of the Black Madonna

She is as old as time—she carries the power and beauty of all the dark goddesses that exist in all cultures and corners of the world. She comes in many forms: Isis, Artemis of Ephesus, Inanna's twin Ereshkigal, Kali, Sekhmet, Oshun, Oya, Yemaya. Early depictions of Mary, the mother of Jesus, the Virgin of Guadalupe, and Isis with Horus reveal the Black Madonna.

Mary Magdalene, and indeed, Jesus, had dark skin. Religious scholars suggest that the erotic, biblical Song of Solomon is about the love between them or perhaps an even earlier divine couple—Inanna and Dumizi. In the New Revised Standard Bible the bride says, "I am black and beautiful, O daughters of Jerusalem."

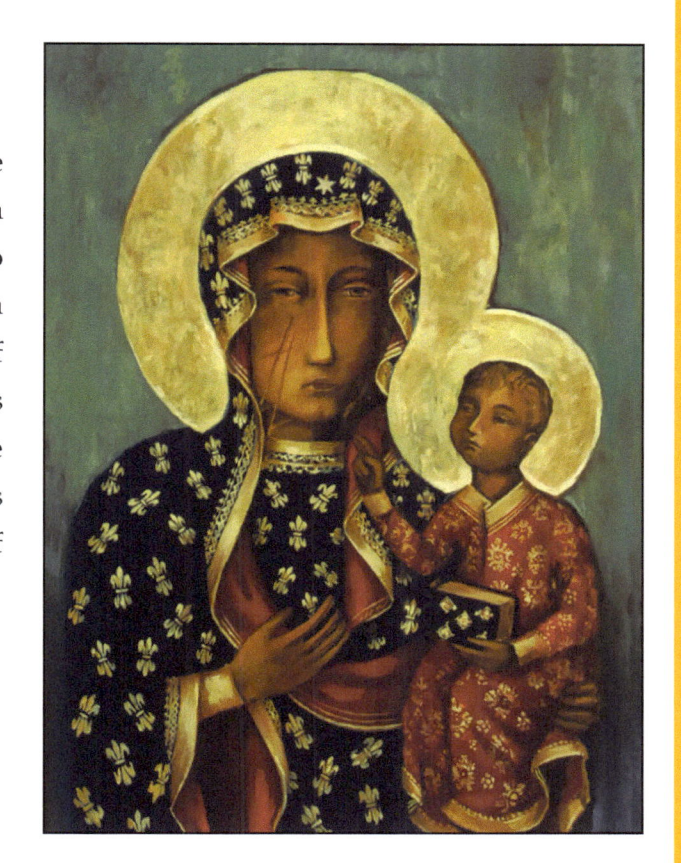

There are a number of Black Madonnas to be found in churches throughout Europe, Africa, and the Middle East, remnants of the ancient goddess, the archetype of the Great Mother. These depictions come from a time before the early Christian church appropriated her and made her into the mother of Jesus. Over time, she became whiter and whiter to reflect the Europeans who embraced Christianity and the artists who depicted her over centuries. Eventually, her blackness was all but forgotten. Some Christian officials tried to say these remaining icons in churches and cathedrals were black because of the candles and flames that burnt near them for so long, becoming *discolored* with soot over time. But this is not true. They were made to be dark, carved and painted in all shades of brown and black, the original mother who rose from the depths of the earth.

Shrines to the Black Madonna at Chartres and Mont-Saint-Michel, two cathedrals in France, are called "Our Lady Under the Earth" and "Our Lady of the Underworld," a nod to her continued underground worship as well as her origins as a Mother of the Earth. The idea of going underground can be seen in more ways than one: early Christian worshippers such as the Cathars, who believed in the sacred marriage between Mary Magdalene and Jesus and the dual principles of the divine feminine and masculine, were decried as heretics. In the 13th century, the Catholic Church wiped out most of the Cathars in France and Spain because of their unorthodox views, making them victims of genocide by the church. Those Cathars who survived continued their underground worship and understanding of a divine feminine and masculine.

At about this time the Black Madonna all but disappeared. She went underground, as most goddesses do in their journey of transformation before they are reborn. Her time underground relates to her hidden aspects, which speak to a compelling love story of equality and partnership, of her power to move between the worlds, as well as the power of the feminine in this world, so long repressed. Today some 400-500 black Madonna figures can be seen throughout Europe, Africa, and Asia, a testament to her resilience. As women of color reclaim their voice, power, value, and authority, women of all colors rise together and take their place on the throne again—as equals to men—testament to the divine feminine living alongside the divine masculine.

The Black Madonna helps you witness your own hurt and anger and not beat yourself up for having these feelings or for inadvertently taking them out on someone. She is the compassionate mother who sheds tears with you, holds you, and lets you know it is okay to make mistakes; it is okay to hurt, to feel anger. Through her abiding love, grace, and understanding, she helps you find acceptance for your feelings, learn from your errors, and to grow. You become more like her by feeling compassion for yourself and others, not to mention Earth and all her creatures.

She and the other dark mother goddesses, like Isis, Kali, and Sekhmet, work in concert with masculine gods or counterparts. They remind you that your Inner Feminine and Inner Masculine work in partnership. The masculine represents logos, your rational thinking function, reason, and the ability to understand as well as to activate and achieve. The feminine represents eros, your feeling function, emotional intelligence, and the ability to create, to empathize, to receive and contain.

Both the head and the heart are needed when you feel hurt and anger. One can inform the other and function best when they are in balance, when one does not control the other. If your head dominates your heart, you may intellectualize your hurt and anger or you might tend to criticize and condemn. You might try and talk yourself out of your feelings without allowing yourself to experience them fully and accept them as natural and normal. If your heart dominates your head, your feelings can overwhelm you and others, leaving you without the ability to reason and talk yourself through understanding them and getting your needs met in productive ways. The Black Madonna is a reminder of the need for a peaceful inner marriage of equals between your Inner Masculine and Inner Feminine, head and heart. Out of this union, the divine child of grace and redemption is born.

## Objects and symbols to consider for your altar to the Black Madonna

**Colors:** black, brown, blue, purple

**Objects:** images and figures of the many Black Madonnas, black or dark candle, heart

**Gemstones:** obsidian, jet, black pearl

**Flowers:** Madonna lily, dark roses

**Element:** earth

**Chakra:** heart (4th chakra)

# The Black Madonna Speaks

I am the first Mother. I am Kali. I am Yemaya. I am Isis. I am the Virgin of Guadalupe. I am the Hopi mother, the Navajo mother, the Yoruba mother. I am the two Marys—mother and consort. I am Mother Nature. I am all of the goddesses throughout time.

I am of Dark Skin, Dark Moon, Dark Earth, and Dark Sea. I am the womb and the tomb, the beginning and the end. I am the whore and the holy one, the sacred and the profane. I am cosmic and I am earthly, the vast black sky and the fertile black soil.

I live in the depths of your soul, the divine darkness, where wisdom is born through experience, by grappling with life, through pain and suffering, through joy and exaltation. I will birth you through the darkness and secure roots in the marl of your being so that you may grow strong and free—free from others' judgment, free to be true to your Self.

I am a witness to your being, and I am a part of you. I am your creative mother, your sexual and sensual being, your anger and your rage, your sorrow and your grief, your empathy and your compassion, your love and your forgiveness, your body and your mind, your knowing and your healing, your blood and your bones, your humanity and your divinity. These are gifts we share.

I am the throne of your being. Let us see the world together, laugh and cry together, and be in it together, Daughter, for all of eternity.

## Journal Prompts

Which of the three goddesses—Kali, Sekhmet, Black Madonna—do you most resonate with and why?

Do these goddesses scare you? What is it about them that you find frightening? What does this say about your own fears in the world? How could you better face your fears?

What was the spoken or unspoken message to you about your anger as a girl growing up in your family?

How has your family of origin's way of expressing pain and anger affected you?

What would you have liked to hear or have happened when you were sad or hurting as a child?

What would you have liked to hear or have happened when you were angry as a child?

Which is harder for you to admit to: hurt or anger? What makes it hard?

What are you afraid of when expressing feelings of hurt and/or anger to someone? What would help you alleviate that fear and speak your truth?

What would it take to forgive yourself for past mistakes, for hurting someone?

What would it take to forgive someone else for hurting you?

How does the Black Madonna challenge your preconceived notions and images of the white, Christian icon of Madonna and child? What can you learn from her?

~172~

# Chapter Eight

# Abundance and Work/Life Purpose

HOW DO YOU ALIGN YOURSELF WITH ABUNDANCE? How do you find purpose in life—both in the work you do and in the way you live your life? These are questions to explore as you learn that creating a meaningful life is a form of self-care that leads to fulfillment.

Abundance can mean anything from money and the material things you need and desire coming your way, to filling your heart and mind with that which gives you joy, to having enough time and energy to do and be all that you imagine for yourself. It is a way to see your life as full and complete as opposed to empty, wanting, and depleted. You might think that abundance is a matter of luck or just hard work, but really it is a matter of how you see the world and live your life, especially *how you create your life*.

Being open-minded and willing to see possibilities, not just limitations, helps pave the way for abundance to come to you. Fear-based, negative thoughts shrink you down. Hopeful, positive thoughts in keeping with your dreams lift you up. Abundance comes when you believe you are worthy of all good things, when you open yourself up to new ideas, new ways of being and seeing—and when you are willing to make a paradigm shift. What does this mean? It means checking in to see how much you view the world through the lens of scarcity, negativity, and lack versus abundance, positivity, and plenty and being willing to change the lens.

The goddess who will help you see opportunity and possibility and open yourself to a more bountiful life is

## Aimee's Story

Aimee has always loved animals and wanted to be a veterinarian when she was a little girl. However, her parents convinced her to join the family business. But as she approached 30, Aimee knew her heart was not in it. The job involved long hours that left little time for her to follow her own passion and purpose.

She dreaded telling her parents she did not wish to continue down this path any longer. She wanted to make her own path. She researched various jobs that would allow her to work with animals and struck on the one that seemed best suited to who she was now and that she truly felt excited about. She enrolled in a program to get the necessary training, and the relief she felt was palpable. Even though she knew her parents would be disappointed, she also knew she had to follow her own North Star to create a life of abundance, which for her meant doing what she loved and having time to enjoy life.

Lakshmi, the Hindu goddess of prosperity, good fortune, fertility, and abundance. She helps you find the richness in life—both materially and spiritually. She is also considered a goddess of beauty, for in embracing your own beauty—inside and out—you walk in abundance. She symbolizes living in sync with your desires to achieve success. Lakshmi invites feelings of worth, wealth, and well-being. She has a generosity of spirit and brings a sense of *joie de vivre* to living a rich, exuberant life.

The goddess to help you get clarity about your dreams and goals and aim for what you really desire is the Greek goddess of the moon and hunt, Artemis, also known as Diana in the Roman pantheon.

You are born with a life purpose, and it is up to you to discover it. Ask yourself: Am I subsisting and existing but not truly living my best life? Am I doing the kind of work in the world that aligns with my dreams, my highest good? If you are not doing what you really want to be doing in the world, ask: What is stopping me?

Artemis knows how to aim for what she wants in life and hit the mark. She may not hit it right away, but she will keep trying, getting better and better at reaching her target with experience. The Artemis archetype is not afraid of failure and considers it a stepping stone to success. Through each setback, she learns what she wants and does not want, and gains strength through adversity. Artemis is not afraid to dream big and take risks. Use her to determine your life purpose and find a path that aligns with it.

# Lakshmi

Lakshmi comes from the Sanskrit word *laksme*, which means goal or destination. She helps you achieve your goals of living harmoniously and abundantly, attracting what you need and want into your life with grace and beauty. She helps you believe you are deserving of all good things that come your way, as well as to be open to receive.

# The Story of Lakshmi

Like Aphrodite, Lakshmi was born from the stirrings of the milky ocean, the womb of the Earth Mother, during a great battle between gods and demons. She arose from the vast sea on a lotus flower bearing her fully formed, graceful presence upon it. With her rise the demons descended, vanquished by the power of her light. Lakshmi's presence allowed the earth to become a bountiful and blossoming home for humans and gods alike.

Lakshmi had many lovers—mostly gods of the waters—which made her fluid in the ways of love and passion. She was fickle in her dalliances, and suffered disappointments and break-ups. But eventually she came to love the god, Vishnu, preserver of the world, to whom she remained faithful.

In the Lakshmi Tantra texts, she says, "I am inherent in existence. I am the inciter, the potential that takes shape. I manifest myself. I occupy myself with activity and finally dissolve myself. I pervade all creations with vitality, will, and consciousness. Like oil that keeps a lamp burning, I lubricate the senses of living beings with the sap of my consciousness."

Symbolically, Lakshmi's attributes of fickleness and eventual faithfulness speak to the unpredictability of fortune and the faith needed to overcome adversity. Sometimes you are granted good fortune and blessings, and at other times you must suffer losses and ills. But Lakshmi learns from experience and is always able to rise above challenges and let-downs and find her way to an enriched life again.

Lakshmi bestows abundance and good fortune to those who see themselves as deserving, who embrace her confidence and love of inner and outer beauty. She is the power, the divine creative impulse, that helps you turn dreams into reality through her eight emanations.

## The Eight Emanations of Lakshmi

1. **Maha Lakshmi — The Great Goddess**
   Like many Great Goddesses throughout the world, she is seen as a powerful mother and protector of all who want what is best for you; she helps you nurture yourself.
2. **Dhana Lakshmi — Goddess of Wealth and Prosperity**
   Dhana refers to money or gold as well as inner "golden" qualities like talent and creativity, resolve, determination, and perseverance.
3. **Dhanya Lakshmi — Goddess of Grains**
   She provides an abundance of food and nourishment, helping you feel healthy in body, mind, and spirit.
4. **Gaja Lakshmi — Elephant Goddess**
   The protector of all that has been gained through hard work, she helps you remove obstacles and retrieve that which has been lost.
5. **Santana Lakshmi — Goddess of Progeny**
   She bestows fertility and healthy, happy children, or she helps you birth creative projects.
6. **Veera Lakshmi — Goddess of Courage**
   *Veera* means courage in Sanskrit; she helps you overcome difficulties by being brave and fearlessly facing all that life throws at you.
7. **Vidya Lakshmi — Goddess of Knowledge**
   She brings knowledge of the arts and sciences and helps you create bounty through what you know and have learned through study and life experience.
8. **Vijaya Lakshmi — Goddess of Victory**
   She represents the sense of accomplishment you achieve when you have done your best and reached your goals.

Consider these eight emanations as examples of how you can approach life as well as what you need to do as a self-care practice to experience abundance. For example, you may need to:

- seek new knowledge to find a line of work you enjoy
- take care of your body and eat nourishing food to have an abundance of good health
- have the strength and courage to overcome obstacles in your path
- develop your talents and creativity to bring forth an abundance of ideas and compensation for your efforts
- be a good mother and love yourself so that you may pass this along to your children

Lakshmi demonstrates that continual self-care is a goddess's responsibility to herself and leads to a sense of well-being and a life of plentitude, which is her due.

In many ways, abundance is a state of mind. The way you think creates a road to abundance or obstacles to abundance. One way to practice self-care is to change your negative, often fear-based, perceptions which leave you in a state of perpetual anxiety. Here are some common thinking mistakes or cognitive distortions that get in the way of an abundant worldview. Notice which of these you employ in your daily life, and replace them with more reasonable and helpful thoughts as a self-care practice.

# Common Thinking Mistakes

**Black and White / All or Nothing** — when you see things as either one extreme or the other, e.g., either perfection or total failure, with no ability to see the in-between, the infinite possibilities that exist between them. The antidote is to look for the shades of gray, the other options, nuance—the myriad ways of seeing something.

**Emotional Reasoning** — when you let your emotions color your reasoning or even reality; you might think that because you feel scared to try something new, it is not worth it or not right for you. This can be turned on yourself, e.g., deciding that because you feel insecure you must be incompetent or worthless. To counter emotional reasoning, do reality checks and ask yourself if just because you feel a certain way makes your conclusion true. (This is different than trusting your gut.) You can also learn to feel the fear and do it anyway so that when you look in the rear-view mirror, fear is but a tiny speck.

**Yes, but** — discounting the positive: when you negate the good by coming up with a negative to counter it or diminish what you have accomplished. Learn to drop the "but," and accept compliments and accolades and even pat yourself on the back for a job well done or completed. Remember that perfectionism is a soul-killing exercise.

**Over-generalizing** — commonly accompanied by the words "always" and "never" and seldom accurate. It is a way of taking one negative occurrence and applying it to an entire category, which creates a sense of self-defeat. The way back to normalcy is to check your tendency to use extreme words and instead accurately report what happened without predicting what that means or overstating your case.

**Exaggerating and Catastrophizing** — when you magnify an event or the importance of your problems and make it seem as if it is *the end of the world* and *the outcome is doomed*. This is rarely the case, so learning to see things in realistic proportion to life helps you maintain an even keel. Again, this requires giving yourself reality checks, asking yourself if it is really as bad as you are making it, questioning whether you really know it will turn out badly, and reaching more reasonable conclusions. Using less extreme language helps.

**Making Assumptions** — when you employ mind-reading and fortune-telling by deciding you know what someone is thinking or feeling without checking in with them. This often leads to taking the crystal ball and running with it instead of stopping and recognizing that you do not actually know the truth and the only way to know is to ask. Clarify before you leap to conclusions.

**Blaming** — this could take the form of self-blame or externalizing blame—when you look for a scapegoat for things going wrong or bad things happening and are unwilling to take responsibility, see your part, or accept that it is no one's fault. You can get a better perspective by noticing when you want to cast blame and looking at how you or another may have simply made a mistake. Blaming and shaming does not help anyone self-correct. Self-care involves being kind to yourself and others. Learn to replace blame with self-reflection, understanding, and problem-solving.

**Taking Things Personally** — when you assume that someone's comments, attitudes, or feelings are about you when they may not be. The only way to know is to check it out with them and to look at your tendency to make others' feelings and behaviors about you. Knowing that you are not responsible for others' feelings and that you need not take others' words or behaviors as commentary on you helps you move through life easier.

Similarly, **personalization** is when you hold yourself responsible for things that are outside of your control, e.g., thinking "it is my fault he hurt me." You can turn this around by checking your perceptions, getting an accurate read, and not finding fault with yourself when there are other causes.

**Shoulding** — when you tell yourself what you "*should* do" and "*shouldn't* do." Shoulding is a form of shaming and leads to guilt and frustration with yourself. It may lead to you giving up on something important because you *should* have done it this way or that, better, or different. It is a self-defeating mantra that needs to be abolished from your inner dialogue. By the same token, telling someone else what they *should* or *shouldn't* do is equally shaming, demeaning, and unnecessary. It is not a motivating form of communication. Instead, ask yourself: What *could* I have done differently? What am I *willing* to do? What do I *want* to do?

**Labeling** — when you name-call or demean yourself or another with negative words like "loser" or "stupid," or when you call yourself a "failure" instead of realizing you (or they) made a mistake or did not know something. Calling yourself names or otherwise beating yourself up is dehumanizing and brings about feelings of inferiority and low self-esteem. Make an agreement with yourself to be kind, to stop labeling and name-calling. Be willing to see other ways of understanding a situation and forgiving yourself or another.

By turning around these cognitive distortions and replacing them with more positive ways of seeing and being, you will create a more abundant and beneficent worldview. While fairly common, these thinking mistakes are self-limiting and cut you off from the good that could come to you—once you transform your negative thinking habits into accurate perceptions that promote self-care.

# Lakshmi Speaks

Dear Daughter, I am here to help you create abundance.

As a goddess you are worthy of a profusion of blessings in every aspect of your life. You are worthy of a loving partner, a peaceful life, material comfort, robust health, adventure, nice things, a home to call your own, a fulfilling career, people who care about you, good fortune—of having any and all of the riches you desire. Perhaps you already have such blessings and you do not know it. Look about you and consider if you have enough. If you want something, go after it. If you already have it, savor it, and spread the wealth.

Do not limit yourself; expand your mind and your heart.

Do not tell yourself the reasons you cannot have something; tell yourself the reasons you can.

Do not fear the unknown; bravely open yourself to the infinite universe of possibilities.

Do not worry about having enough; know that your needs will be met through your effort.

Do not despair about the past; nurture hope for the future.

Do not see the worst in people and situations; seek the best in them.

Do not close yourself off to new people, places, and ideas; open yourself to all that life offers.

Do not tell yourself that you are not deserving; trust that you are.

Do not believe you are lacking; believe in abundance and it will be yours.

# Objects and symbols to consider for your altar to Lakshmi

**Colors:** red, white, pink, blue

**Objects:** figures of Lakshmi and Ganesh (elephant), lotus candle holder and white or pink candle

**Gemstones:** citrine, star sapphire

**Flowers:** lotus, tuberose, white chrysanthemum

**Element:** water

**Chakra:** sacral (2nd chakra)

# Artemis

Artemis, the Greek goddess of the hunt, also known as Diana in the Roman world, is a *virgin goddess*, like Athena and Hestia. This means she is whole unto herself and does not define herself in relationship to any man.

She is the archetypal woman with an indomitable spirit and a will to match, a woman who knows what she wants and goes after it, and will even do battle for it. She is a woman who does not just accept the status quo but instead tries to change it. She is the one who will dare greatly, who will veer from the direction mapped out for her and blaze her own trail.

You need Artemis when you are contemplating what to do with your one wild and precious life. Let Artemis guide you to do what is true for yourself, to be true to *yourself*.

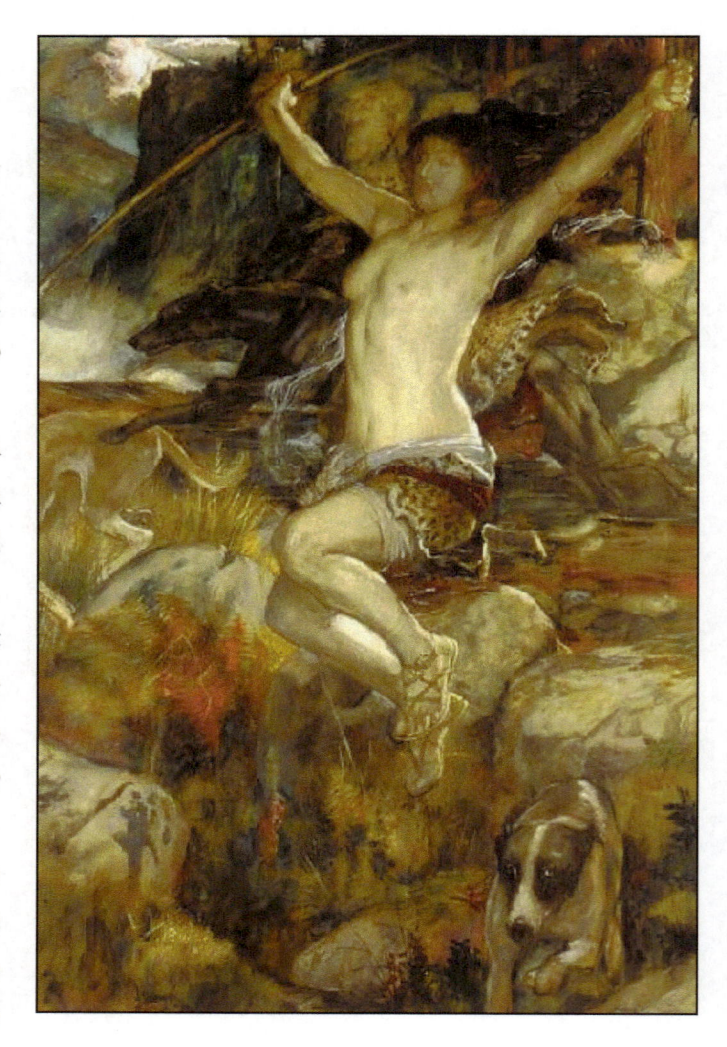

Artemis asks you to know what your purpose is in life and to follow through on the dreams you have imagined. It is not uncommon to set out on one path and then reach a dead end or crossroads and chart a new course. If you stick to your mission, you will not go wrong. If you follow someone else's path or idea for you, or give up on your path for the sake of another or because you have lost your compass, you can end up feeling lost or stuck.

# The Story of Artemis

Artemis and her twin brother Apollo were born from the affair Zeus had with Leto, a Titan goddess of great beauty. When the goddess Hera, Zeus's wife, learned Leto was pregnant, she cursed Leto and sent her away to a deserted island to give birth. Leto's labors with Artemis, who was born first, were quick and easy. However, she labored long and hard with Apollo, and after nine days of this, the newborn Artemis went to work as midwife to assist her mother, presaging one of her abilities—helping pregnant women and those wishing to conceive.

On Artemis's third birthday, Zeus sat her on his lap, delighted by his little girl's precociousness, and asked what presents she would like from him. Artemis, knowing her own mind at an early age, had a list prepared. She knew who she was and what she wanted: a silver bow and arrow for hunting, the freedom to live in the wilderness where she was happiest, hunting dogs, a sisterhood of forest nymphs to run with and teach, and clothing of her own choosing—a short hunting tunic, not a gown!

Zeus readily agreed to her requests and treated her as a favored daughter. Indeed, she became one of the twelve Olympians and wielded her power as huntress and goddess of the moon with passion and determination. She led a group of young female apprentices called the Arktoi, or *little bear-girls*, who learned from her the art of being a priestess—self-reliant, resourceful, and competent, and under Artemis's tutelage, able to survive in the wilderness. Some girls stayed on as priestesses and tended the many temples of Artemis; others returned to civilization, married, and bore children, all the wiser and more confident for their early education with the Goddess of the Wild Heart.

Artemis is usually depicted with a silver bow, its curved shape representing the moon and feminine receptive container, while her silver-tipped arrows symbolize the masculine energy of going forth in the world, aiming for something, and hitting the target. Her ability to act as midwife and protector of expectant mothers and newborn babes—both human and animal—became one of her primary attributes. This Artemis energy translates to a woman's ability to give birth to her True Self. In these ways, she is a goddess with a well-developed and balanced inner feminine and masculine.

Artemis helps you define your true nature and align it with your soul's purpose. She assists you in claiming a life that allows you to live out who you really are at your core. If you are not sure what this is, it helps to take a look at who you were as a little girl before all the taming and buffing, polishing and programming, and donning of masks began—before adults and institutions attempted to shape you to conform to cultural norms of what it means to be a girl or woman. Or perhaps you conformed to what a parent wanted for you rather than listening to what your soul thirsted for. Artemis helps you reclaim your own wild heart and desires.

Answer these questions, and see if you might be overlooking a part of yourself that has lain dormant for too long and needs to be rebirthed.

**When you were a girl...**

What did you truly love about yourself?

What did you dream of becoming?

What activity gave you the most joy?

What were you good at?

What came naturally?

What made you feel truly alive?

The kind of self-care needed as an adult involves getting brutally honest with yourself and assessing what your passions are and what you want your life to look like. Then, like Artemis, take aim and shoot your arrow of determination at the target goal—no matter how old you are, no matter how far you have come from your initial starting point. It is never too late to take a different route, to pursue a new goal, to start down an unfamiliar path. Artemis tells you that *you get to choose* what your life looks like and follow your dreams to fruition. She helps you midwife your own birth (or rebirth) as a woman who knows what she wants and makes it happen.

# Work-Life Balance

Many women struggle with maintaining a healthy work-life balance, one where they are able to enjoy both work and play or downtime in roughly equal measure. It is particularly challenging for women raising children. While men have made strides in the past 30 years or so in sharing household and childrearing duties, women still bear the brunt of it—recent studies show that this work takes up an average of two-thirds of a mother's time compared to one-third of a father's.

For a working mother, this inequity creates a severe imbalance in her life and may lead to depression and burn-out. Self-care involves negotiating childcare duties and household tasks with your partner on a coequal basis so that you can have more time to rest, relax, play, and enjoy life. Even working women who aren't mothers need to be aware of the need for rest and relaxation and not let their productivity supersede their enjoyment of life. As a goddess of the moon, Artemis needs to have her evenings free! She reminds you to gift yourself downtime.

Women have to start by *believing* they are deserving, even entitled, to time off and a healthy, balanced life. Changing this mindset is the starting point; following through is the next step. That is where Artemis can be most helpful. As an archetype, **she knows what she needs, she asks for what she wants, and she goes after it**. She is not a victim and does not allow herself to be taken advantage of at home or at work. Self-care in this realm means speaking up for yourself and getting your needs met. This might mean rocking the boat when the expectation is that you as a woman are supposed to know your place and not ask for anything more. An Artemis woman will make waves when necessary.

Self-care requires a commitment to yourself to meet your needs first and foremost and not wait for someone else to meet them or rescue you. There is nothing wrong with asking for certain needs to be met or for help, but if someone can't or won't give you what you ask, it is up to you to meet your needs. Ultimately, it is up to you to take care of yourself. Having a partner or other person in your life to share the workload generally makes life easier when you are able to negotiate an equitable division of labor and mutual caregiving.

It is important to take a look at the kind of work you are doing in the world and assess whether it is truly what you want to be doing:

Are you following your passion?
Are you enjoying the work that you do?
Do you like who you work with and the conditions of your job?

If not, you owe it to yourself to do something about it. This is how you take care of yourself on your life path. You may not find the "perfect" job, but you may be able to find a job that is better suited to your values and long-held dreams. You may also be able to create space in your life to follow your desires and interests, even if it is not what you get paid to do. This involves creating time and space for you and your creative outlets. It has been said, "If you do what you love, the money will follow." Even if you are not always sure how that will happen, find a way to do what you love.

## What Is Your Soul's Purpose?

Write a mission statement that describes your soul's purpose. Put it in a prominent place where you can see it and remind yourself of who you are and what you want out of life. As you craft your mission statement, you may want to ask yourself:

- What do I love?
- What am I here to accomplish?
- Why am I here on this planet at this particular time?
- What are my gifts and contributions?
- What do I long for and desire to create?
- What are my core personal values? (Name five.)

For example, Aimee's mission statement is: *I am here to be an advocate and aide to all creatures great and small. As an animal-lover and fierce defender of the environment, animals, and habitats, I bring my gifts of caring, compassion, conviction, and courage to my work and my life. My core values are to be of service, kindness, freedom, to find meaning and purpose beyond making money, and to stay true to myself by doing what I love: working with animals. I give myself time and space to relish the life I create and the pets I adore.*

Writing her mission statement helped Aimee focus on specific goals related to her passion and not get off-track. It helped to enumerate her core values and to see that she is responsible for creating the life she wants.

# Objects and symbols to consider for your altar to Artemis

**Colors:** white, blue, green, silver

**Objects:** figure of Artemis/Diana, deer, dog, bear, moon symbols, arrow

**Gemstones:** moonstone, blue kyanite

**Flowers:** amaranth, artemisia, anemones

**Element:** earth

**Chakra:** solar plexus (3rd chakra)

# Artemis Speaks

Dear Sister, My father Zeus asked me what I wanted when I was a child, and I already knew myself well enough to ask for what I wanted and needed to live out my soul's purpose. The things I asked for were what I needed to grow into the woman I knew I wanted to be—wild and free, close to my instinctual nature, with the ability to draw my bow and hit my target once I set my mind and heart on something.

    I know the value of having dreams, of having a clear vision of what you want your life to be, determining what tools and skills you will need, and deciding how to go about acquiring them. Make sure your goals align with your values and your soul's purpose. In this way you will live an authentic life, true to yourself and no one else.

    Find balance and practice self-care as you make your way in the wilderness. Call on me for strength, determination, and direction. I am happiest when I am walking under the verdant canopy of the forest with my dogs and stags by my side, my sisters available when I need them, knowing that my path is the one I set for myself. How about you?

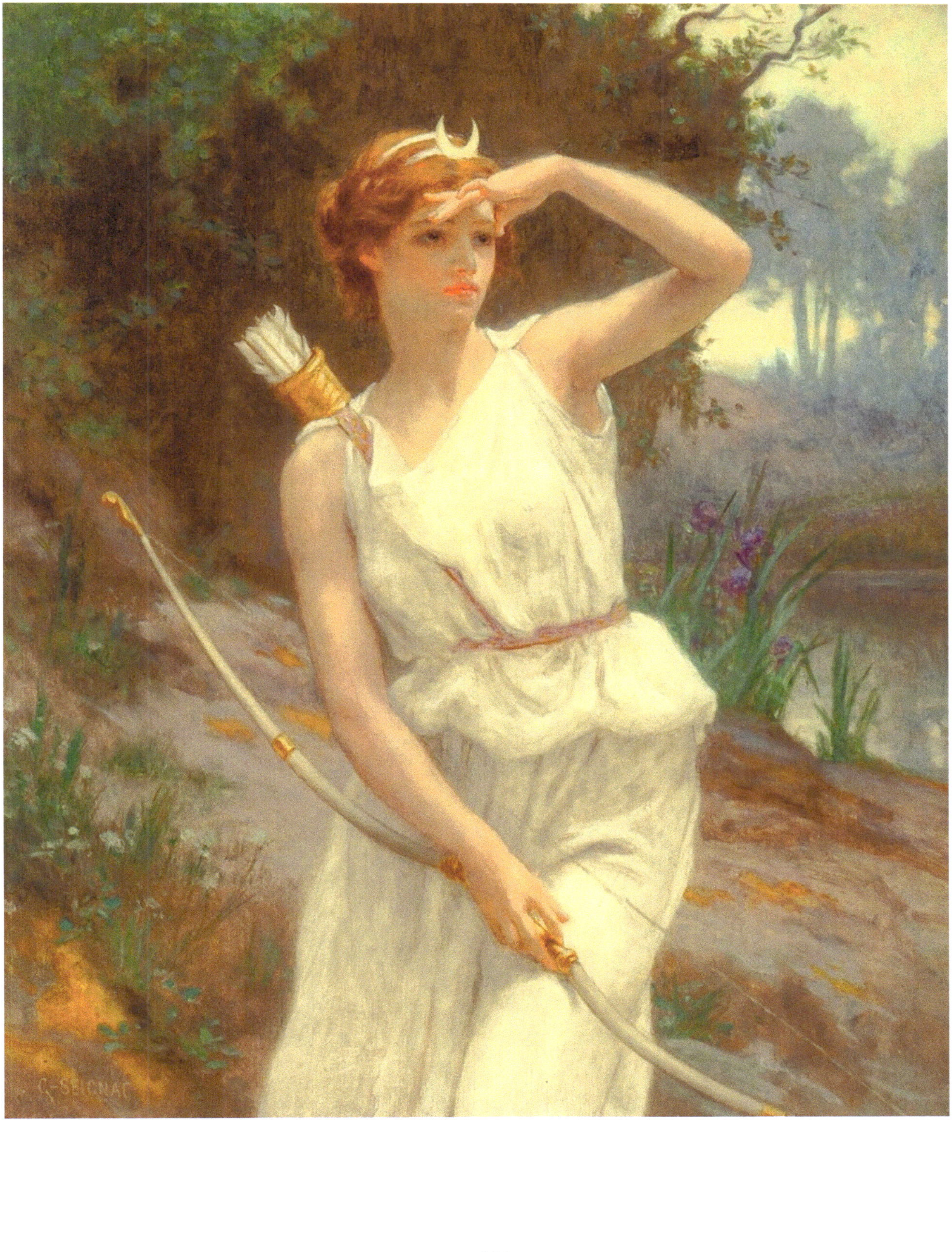
G. SEIGNAC

# Journal Prompts

As a little girl, what did you want to be when you grew up?

What was it about that dream that drew you to it? What was it about you that made that dream attractive?

Did that dream change or did you follow it? How do you feel about where you are now?

How is the work you are doing fulfilling your soul's purpose? If it is not, what would you like to do to change that?

What qualities of life do you enjoy as a result of your work, creativity, and effort?

Which thinking mistakes are you most familiar with? How can you amend them?

Assess your work-life balance by making a list of what you do with your time while working versus playing or relaxing. What can you do to bring it more in balance?

How is your life abundant?

In what areas of your life would you like to have more abundance? How can you create abundance?

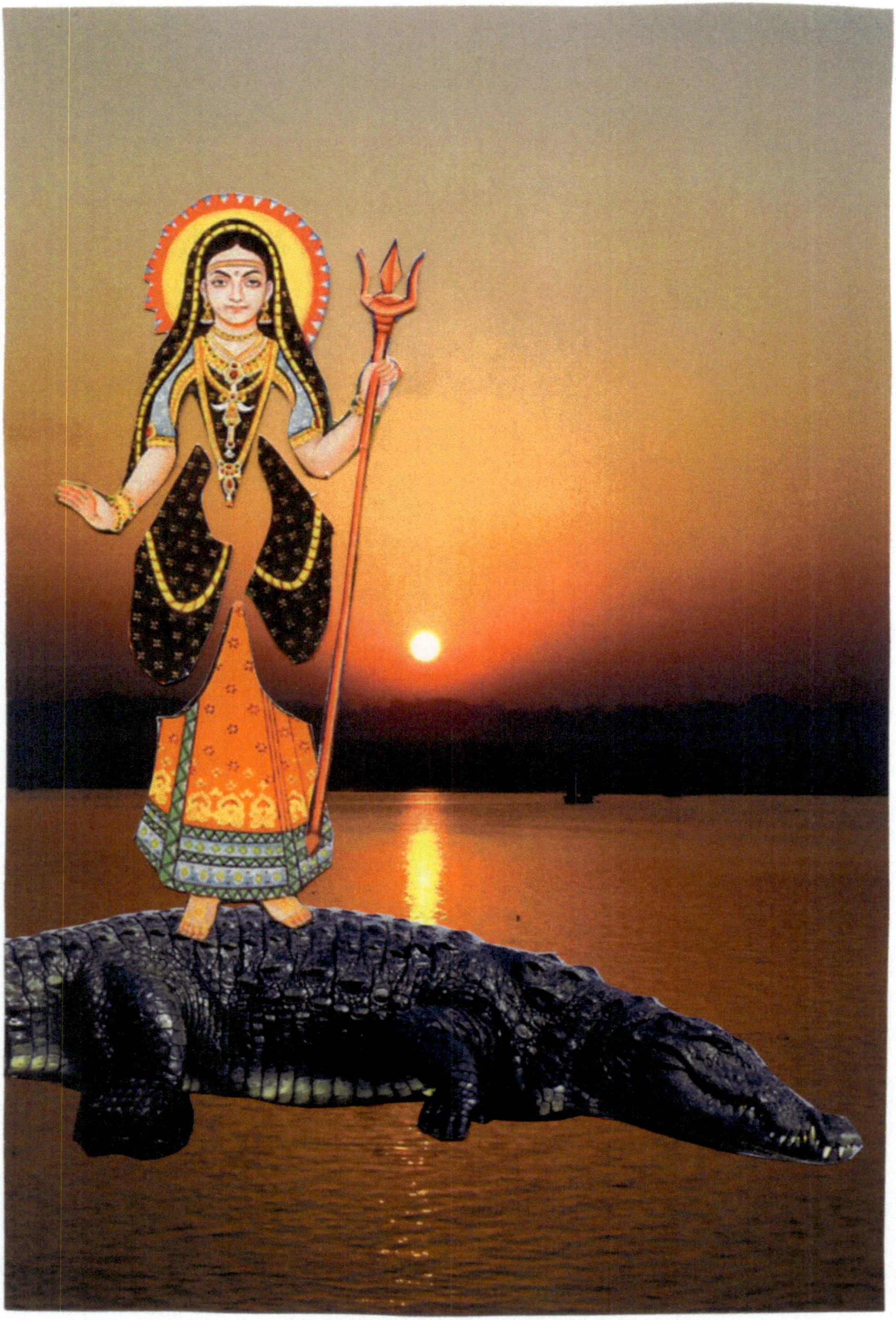

# Chapter Nine

# Health and Healing

HUMAN BEINGS ARE always in various states of good or ill health. Think of health and well-being as a continuum on which you move from minute to minute, day to day, year to year, decade to decade. When you aim for healthiness, it is important to consider the various realms in which you feel healthy or not: mental, emotional, physical, and spiritual.

You are always healing in one or another of these realms. This presupposes that human beings are never perfect, never fully healed and whole in all realms at once. When you experience that state of healthy and healed grace for a time, it will likely not last forever. This is part of what it means to be human—to suffer, to not be perfect, to be continually evolving and accepting change.

It is natural to strive for good health, to want to feel in balance, if not robust. Not too much and not too little; like Goldilocks, the goal is to feel "just right." And that is relative, since humans are born with the potential to be blessed with general good health or to be prone to certain conditions and inherited afflictions, which may or may not manifest. Sometimes it feels like luck and other times like fate when you recognize the variability of your state of health and the states of those around you. But you do have choices in how you live your life and how you choose to take care of yourself, with or without such blessings (or curses, if you will).

Self-care is crucial when it comes to your health. It is worthwhile to take inventory and see where you could feel

## Emma's Story

Emma reeled from the news that she had thyroid cancer. Her doctor explained the course of treatment, which would involve surgical removal of her thyroid. She had broken up with her partner six months before and felt very alone, shattered, and afraid. She was not sure where to turn.

She knew she needed divine guidance, and one night she sat very quietly by the window of her apartment gazing out at a large, bright star that seemed to be shining just for her. As she breathed slowly in and out with the rhythm of the twinkling star, she suddenly felt inspired to seek more information about her condition and what she could do to help facilitate her own healing. She thought of friends and family members she could call on for support. She felt help coming in the form of a sacred feminine goddess who could see her through what she knew would be a profound journey of healing.

You will also meet Tara, the Tibetan goddess and bodhisattva of compassion. A bodhisattva is one who is on the path to Buddhahood, but remains here on earth to help all who suffer. Tara has 21 manifestations and colors. You will meet two: White Tara, the goddess of healing and long life, and Green Tara, the goddess of regeneration and growth. They both offer understanding, comfort, and protection from the sufferings of the world, including your own. Tara as a feminine Buddha helps you liberate yourself from *maya*—illusions or false beliefs of the mental realm, negative feelings of the emotional realm, pain and illness of the physical realm, and soul sickness, meaning a life devoid of meaning and purpose in the spiritual realm.

better, where you are out of balance. Is it your emotional life where you suffer most, or is it physical? Are you spiritually wounded or in a mental fog? Wherever it may be that you feel dis-ease, you are your own best healer. You may need the help of others—whether earthly healers or divine guidance and intervention—but your body knows when you pay attention. You can help yourself by turning to the Goddesses of Self-Care to help you through the hard times and to achieve balance.

The first goddess to guide you on the path of Health and Healing is the Hindu goddess Akhilandeshwari. She is known as *The Goddess Who Is Never Not Broken* and is often depicted riding a crocodile through the river of life. She reminds you that, like all human beings, you are always broken in some way and always striving for wholeness.

# Akhilandeshwari

She is the antidote to the illusion of perfection. Perfectionism is, in and of itself, a kind of sickness—the hubris of believing you could ever reach a godlike state and never be wanting. It sets you up for an impossible-to-reach goal. If you tend to think you need to be perfect, Akhilandeshwari is the one to remind you that you do not. Indeed, you cannot. For even she, a goddess, is not perfect and does not strive to be. She is whole in her imperfections, and she helps you find wholeness, too.

Akhilandeshwari helps you know you are not alone and are part of the human race that exists in various forms of brokenness. She gives you permission to not have it all together all the time, to not feel good all the time, to not know where you are going all the time, to not have all the answers. The wisdom of this goddess is knowing you will be dismembered at times so you can *remember* yourself into *Being*, discovering what matters most, what needs to be healed.

In Sanskrit, her name means *the sovereign ruler of universal brokenness*. She is a manifestation of Parvati, a feminine aspect of Shiva, both a protector and destroyer god, who, like Kali, brings about endings so that rebirth can occur. Akhilandeshwari, like Parvati, is a Virgin Mother goddess—both whole unto herself and protector and regenerator of life in the Hindu tradition.

# The Story of Akhilandeshwari

Akhilandeshwari was fierce, angry, and perfectionistic, which caused her to lash out at others and be hard on herself. So Shiva provided a temple for her as a place to find sanctuary and release her strong emotions. She lived there alone, wanting to heal but unsure what would help her. One day Shiva arrived and presented her with a beautiful pair of earrings that reflected the seven chakra centers of the body. The overwhelming energies the goddess had not been able to contain entered the earrings. The colorful jewels transmuted her inner turmoil into a more balanced state, her chakras no longer deficient or excessive. Embracing her brokenness, accepting what is, allowed Akhilandeshwari to achieve healing. She was able to return to the world and live in acceptance of the cyclical nature of brokenness and wholeness.

---

The crocodile Akhilandeshwari rides through the river of life represents the primordial power of the mother—her innate strength, patience, abiding presence, and ability to be in the flow. The crocodile has a tough skin and can weather many challenges. It is a root chakra ally that protects and preserves life, even as it has the ability to devour that which is no longer needed.

Akhilandeshwari reminds you that you are not alone in your brokenness—when you are sick or hurting in mind, body, emotions, or spirit, she is one with you. When you are suffering from emotional overwhelm or dis-ease, it is easy to fall under the illusion that no one else knows how you feel, no one else has ever experienced what you are going through, no one else can possibly understand your pain. But she is here to tell you that all humans exist in various states of brokenness, pain, and suffering, and that she is a goddess who is broken too. You are not alone.

She helps you see the gold in your pain and suffering. Through these obstacles in life you grow and learn and become more fully human, awake, and alive. Without challenges, humankind would be made up of undifferentiated, one-dimensional, superficial beings. Through your brokenness, you find meaning. You find the essence of your being. Through your brokenness, you give up the illusion of control and perfection. You give up the idea of being only one way and not the other. You are free to discover yourself on your life's journey of healing and transformation.

And in beautiful paradoxical wonderment, Akhilandeshwari is the remover of your sense of brokenness, for in accepting and allowing yourself to be broken, she permits you to find wholeness. It is found through the healing power of knowing yourself, accepting yourself, and loving yourself.

जै गंगा जै जै जग जननी जै संतन सुख दैनी ।
तारन तरण पाप बल खंडन महिमा बरनी न जाई ॥

श्री गंगाजी.

# Dialogue With the Inner Perfectionist

If you have an Inner Perfectionist—a sub-personality, an inner part, a voice in your head that harangues you for not being perfect—get to know this part of yourself and find out what makes her tick. As you get to know her needs and fears, you can transform this inner part to help you, not harm you.

Envision this inner part and make a SoulCollage® card or an art journal page for your Inner Perfectionist. Give her a name, e.g., "Little Miss Perfect," "Pamela Perfect," etc.

Create a dialogue with this part as you did with your Inner Critic (see CH. 6, page 151) by asking it questions and writing down the answers that come spontaneously. Listen to what it needs and wants and tell your Inner Perfectionist what you need and want and reach an agreement. Remember, your shadow aspects need not run the show. You can integrate this shadow so that you are listening to your Higher Self and not following the dictates of a primitive, under-developed sub-personality. You may want to ask:

- When did you come into my life (at what age or stage)?
- What is your purpose?
- Where did you get the idea that I have to be perfect?
- What does it mean to you to be human and make mistakes?
- What is your fear?
- What do you need from me to stop pushing for perfection?
- What keeps you with me?
- How can I (the Self) help you (a small part of me)?
- How can you help me and work with me (not hurt me)?
- What agreement can we (my Inner Perfectionist and I) make so that I can be free to grow and make mistakes and learn from them?

# Health Challenges

Most likely you will encounter a health challenge in your life, whether you are born with a genetic predisposition or whether you experience a medical condition, mental health struggle, or injury along the way. For some people it is chronic pain; for others it is an autoimmune condition, cancer, or any number of emotional or mental states, minor and major. There are many permutations of ill health, and if you are fortunate you will only suffer the normal slings and arrows of a long life—short-term bouts of the flu, colds, headaches, stomach aches, anxiety, depression, etc. No one achieves perfect health at all times.

When you meet these challenges with self-care, facing your fears, putting your needs first and foremost, asking for help, and taking care of yourself like a caring mother would her precious child, you will find your way to a sense of balance and well-being—to feeling that you are always enough.

If, instead, you continue to put others' needs ahead of your own, make sacrifices at the expense of your own health, beat yourself up, or turn your power over to others, looking for healing only from "out there," you will likely continue to suffer—often with the hope that someone will come along and rescue you.

When that does not happen you are left feeling helpless and hopeless, a victim of circumstance. It is at these times that you are tested, that you must hold your power, claim sovereignty over your own mind, body, emotions, and spirit, and find your own healing path. In essence, you must rescue yourself with the goddess's help.

This is where Akhilandeshwari can aid you. She says that no matter how broken, injured, or helpless you may feel at any point in time or in any sphere of your life, she will help you find the power and strength to find your way through it. Her message is to be mindful, loving, and accepting of yourself and whatever feels broken. She helps you seek wholeness through self-care, knowing that you are always learning, growing, and discovering more about yourself and how to live in healthful balance.

# The Four Realms of Health and Well-Being

## Emotional

Feelings of general happiness, contentment, and satisfaction with life; a sense of balance and developed emotional intelligence, i.e., knowing what you are feeling and being able to empathize with others' feelings; the ability to identify your feelings and communicate them effectively; not being stuck in any one particular emotion; non-reactionary approach to life

Self-care approach: say how you feel and ask for what you want; share your feelings with a friend or loved one who validates them; write them down, work them through, and let them go; channel feelings into art or physical exercise; do something kind and caring for yourself; witness strong emotions and give them time to wash back out to sea or seek help in understanding and transforming them

## Physical

Relative stability of bodily health; eating a balanced diet and exercising in keeping with your body's needs; manageable levels of aches, pains, and health conditions, if not relief from them; awareness of your body's needs and willingness to care for it, seeking help and healing as needed; treating your body like a sacred temple

Self-care approach: take a walk in nature, dance, exercise, stretch to move through aches and pains and transform them; give yourself the gift of rest; learn which foods your body needs and responds well to and which it doesn't; research medical conditions you have been diagnosed with and seek answers and potential alternatives that feel right for you; get massage or energy work; take baths in water, forests, or under the sun

## Mental

Having a balanced state of mind with respect to your thoughts, attitudes, beliefs, judgments; the ability to use logic and reason, to problem-solve, and to communicate effectively based on clear thinking, flexibility, and imaginative approaches to life; being non-obsessive and open-minded

Self-care approach: journal to empty out your mind each day; notice what thoughts and false beliefs cause you suffering and replace them with soothing, realistic thoughts; affirm the truth of your being; think about what you want to say and how you want to say it so your message can be effectively heard; practice meditating; notice and let go of troubling or obsessive thoughts (replace them with accurate and helpful thoughts)

## Spiritual

The ability to experience meaning and purpose in life; loving relationship with Self and others; connection to a higher power, god/goddess, or Higher Self, as well as to nature, art, literature, music; living a life that reflects your beliefs and values

Self-care approach: give yourself regular personal time or "me" days to do what fulfills you and connects you to your *Self*; create an altar, spiritual ritual, or devotion that helps you feel connected to Source; get clear about your values and make sure you are living in alignment with them (let go of what does not serve you); find a creative outlet that gives your life meaning and make it part of your practice; learn to accept and love yourself

It is important to be aware of the mind-body connection, knowing that your thoughts, feelings, attitudes, and beliefs can affect your physical health and biological functioning. Well-documented studies show that stress has a negative effect on health, so it is important to manage stress in your daily life, to seek balance and peace. If you are having bodily symptoms and you know you are under pressure in some part of your life, do your best to find ways to lower your stress levels and change something about the way you are living.

# Akhilandeshwari Speaks

I am the one who sees the beauty in brokenness, in the cracks and flaws. When you give up on the cherished idea that you must be perfect, loved in all ways, unblemished and unwounded, you will finally be able to love yourself fully and wholly (holy)—warts and all.

I am here to remind you to send love into the parts of you that feel broken now. Where are you feeling the most fragile? Are you struggling with self-limiting thoughts or beliefs about yourself? Are you harboring feelings of inadequacy? Are you judging something about your body, your appearance? Are you thinking you are not deserving? Are you feeling unlovable, not enough? Are you hurting in your mind, body, emotions, spirit? Is some part of your body in pain? Name this discomfort or dis-ease. What does this pain want you to know? Hold or caress the part of your body that is in distress and tune into what it needs.

Know that it is not unusual to have disparaging thoughts and feelings about yourself at times, and that they speak to the human condition. Replace the unhelpful, hurtful thoughts with the Truth of who you really are—one who is always learning, growing, and healing. See yourself as one who makes mistakes and is able to fix them, to learn from them. Know you are one who will suffer at times and who is also able to heal. Embrace your imperfections as I do.

In my honor, I ask that you create an image of yourself or me in a broken state—dismembered. Borrowing from the Japanese art of kintsugi, which means "golden joinery" and is used in repairing pottery, cut or tear up an image of yourself or me and reassemble it, filling in the broken lines with gold pen or paint. This is a way of recognizing that you need not hide the broken parts, but may fill the cracks with gold—the highest state of alchemy—and not be ashamed to show them to the world.

It is the art of mending that I want you to learn and practice. This art is a way to preserve that which is broken yet still beautiful, valuable, and precious.

## Objects and symbols to consider for your altar to Akhilandeshwari:

Colors: red, blue, green

Objects: image of Akhilandeshwari or broken goddess figure, kintsugi (object repaired with gold), crocodile, Ganesh (her son, the elephant god, known as remover of obstacles), earrings, chakra stones (7 colors of the chakras)

Gemstones: emerald, aquamarine, cinnabar

Flowers: lotus, begonia, water lily

Element: water

Chakra: root (1st chakra)

## Tara

In the Buddhist tradition, she is called "The Savioress," "She Who Saves Us," or "She Who Ferries Us Across." Tara represents your potential to save yourself, to be your own best healer, to practice self-compassion. Her name means "star," and she steers us to True North. The North Star, used for millennia for navigating on the vast, dark seas, is known in Tibet and Nepal as "Dhruva-Tara"—the immoveable star. She is always there, the pole star leading you home to yourself.

Tara has twenty-one manifestations or separate goddesses that make up the one Great Goddess. These myriad incarnations come from Green Tara, the originator, who helps you renew and rebound through your own Inner Healer. You will also get to know another of her emanations, White Soothing Tara, here to help soothe your weary soul and alleviate your suffering.

# The Story of Tara

There once was a Hindu god named Avalokiteshvara, who watched over all of humanity and promised to liberate all human beings from suffering. So great was his compassion that his tears fell from the heavens, forming a great lake upon the earth. One day, out of these lachrymose waters arose a lotus flower with a beautifully serene goddess sitting upon it. It was Tara, come to help.

When Tara was offered the opportunity to become a Buddha herself, an enlightened one who is able to rise above human suffering and reach nirvana, she instead made the choice to stay with humanity as a bodhisattva. She is forever *becoming Buddha*, the enlightened one who alleviates suffering here on earth. She remains always in her feminine form as she refused to incarnate into masculine form like the Buddha, making her a true feminist goddess. Tara nurtures *Buddha-nature* in everyone.

---

Tara is depicted either sitting upon a lotus or standing, holding the lotus flower in one hand. Remember that the lotus is a spectacular flower that grows out of the most neglected of places—mud, refuse, and contamination. Yet the lotus remains pure and unsullied as it blooms on the surface, above the muck. The lotus flower represents your ability to rise above the darkest and most challenging of situations and find your way in the beauty of your own truth and regenerative ability.

*"As upon a heap of rubbish*
*Thrown out by the highway,*
*May grow a lotus*
*Delightful and of pure scent.*
*So, among defiled beings,*
*Among blind, unawakened beings,*
*The disciple of the Fully and Perfectly Awakened One*
*Shine with wisdom."*

~ The Dhammapada

**Green Tara**

Green Tara represents the green that abounds in nature—of growth and renewal. She is the green of the heart chakra. She helps you heal whatever ails you by urging you to grow beyond your perceived limitations. She releases you from ignorance, which could be understood as the inability to see the truth of your own liberation. She protects you from succumbing to fear. Both ignorance and fear are like quicksand, pulling you under and knocking you off balance.

She teaches you to let go of restricting beliefs about yourself and the state of your health. She helps you see potential for healing and growth in all aspects of your life and to act by seeking answers and remedies that feel right to you. She gently guides you out of any sense of stagnancy or victimhood and into a sense of agency. She is an active force who spurs you to take action on your own behalf, to find answers to end your suffering.

Green Tara sits on a lotus blossom with her right leg extended, ready to stand up for you, representing the action of compassion and healing. Her left hand is in the *mudra* or symbolic gesture of protection or refuge, and her right hand is open, ready to give you the gift of whatever your heart desires.

**White Soothing Tara**

White Tara is pictured seated on a lotus blossom with both legs folded beneath her, feet up, in a meditative position known in yoga as lotus pose. She is sometimes called the "seven-eyed" goddess, because she has two eyes on her hands, two on her feet, and three on her face, including the third eye, between the brows—the all-seeing, all-knowing eye and sixth chakra. With seven eyes she can always see when you need soothing and come to your aid. You have only to call upon her and she will come and offer you her blessing and healing.

White Tara helps you tap into your self-compassion and to find compassion for others—even those who vex you or cause suffering. She helps you overcome fear of illness or dis-ease. As a Mother Goddess she protects you from pain. She brings serenity and abides with you through your suffering until the energy is ready to shift. She acts as a great mirror, allowing you to see yourself healed and whole through her eyes.

Aligning with her gives you the promise of longevity. White Tara's left hand is raised in the mudra of "Fear Not," and her right hand is open in the mudra of compassion. She is white because she is associated with the crown chakra of enlightenment, transcendence, and connection to all that is.

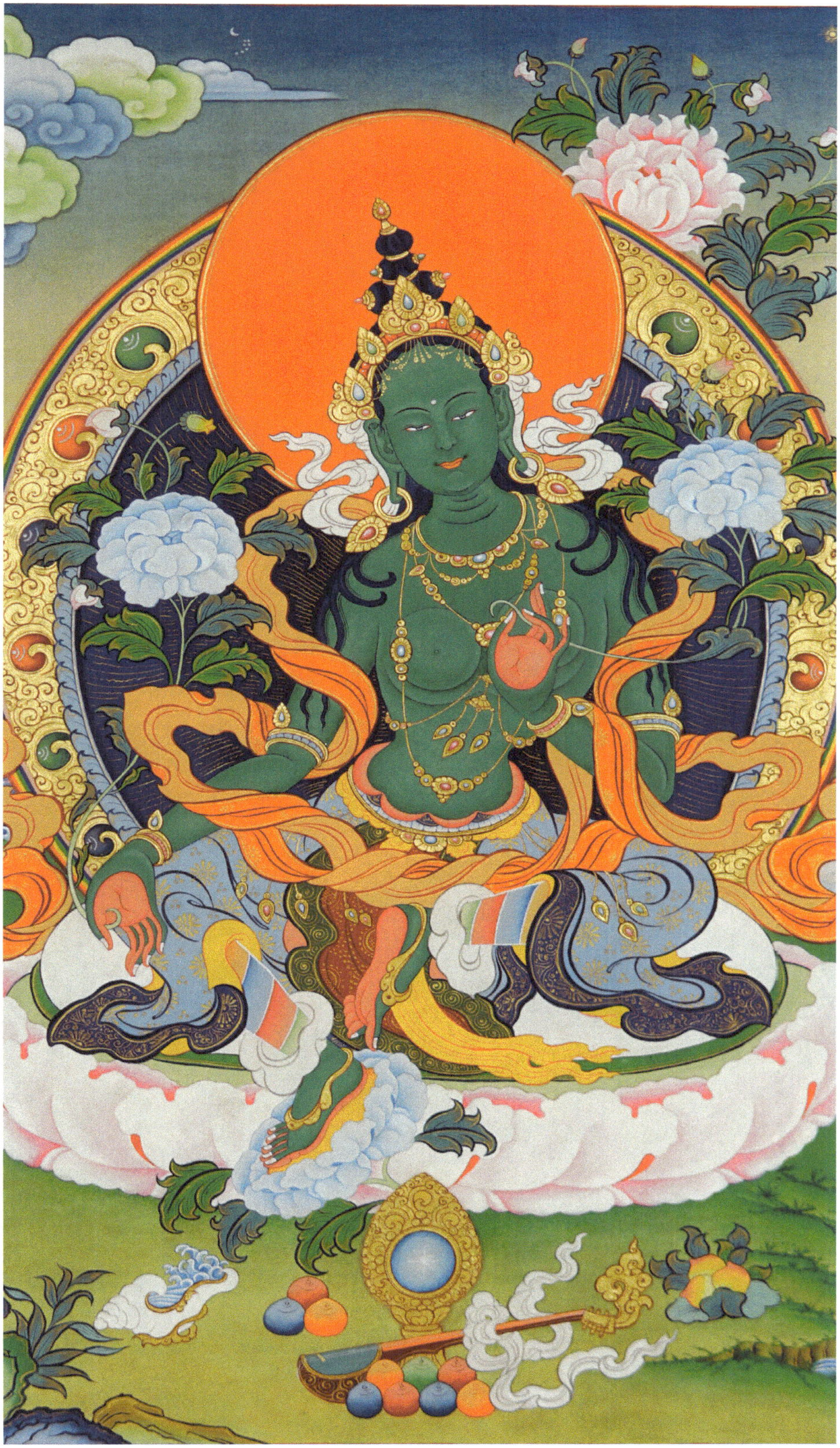

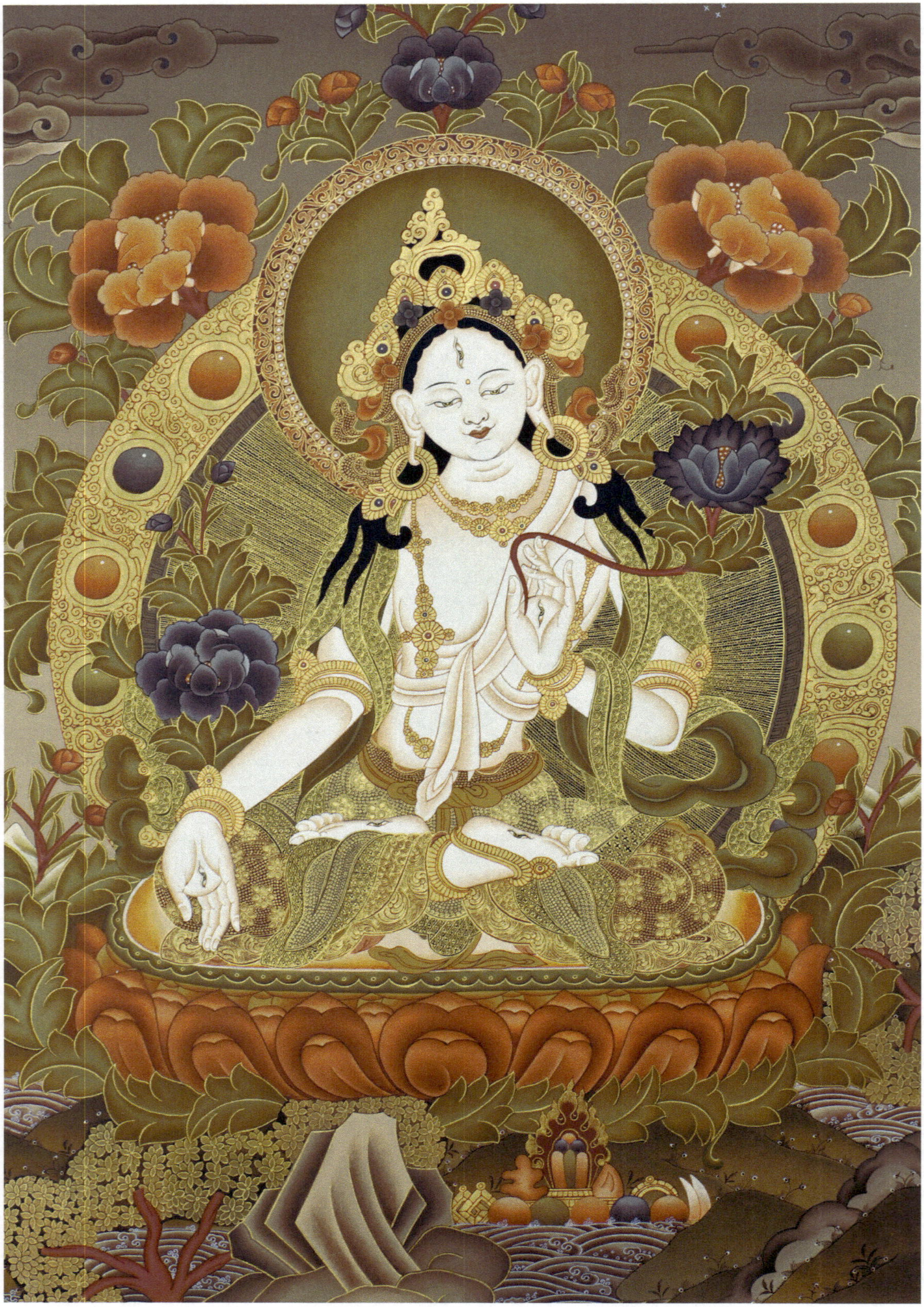

# Tara Speaks

Daughter, I am here for you. I am here with you. Lay down your troubles, your aches and pains. Let go of your tears. Give them to me, and in return I give to you my healing love, my compassion for all that you are enduring.

Look into the night sky and find a bright star. Make a wish upon it for healing and know that I see you. I hear you. I feel you. I will protect you. Your cries do not go unheard or unanswered.

In every challenge of life, in every hurt, there is the possibility of transformation, of redemption. While you are going through it—whatever it is—I am with you. Give to me your trust, and I will take your hand, dry your tears, and hold you to my bosom. I bring you inner peace. I am the one who soothes you when you are hurting, scared, or confused.

Say my mantra, Om Tare Tuttare Ture Soha, which means "I bow to the Great Mother and Liberator of all the Victorious Ones," in the morning and in the evening. I will hear your song and swiftly help you find freedom from what ails you.

Write down what it is you want to heal and your wish for good health, roll it up into a scroll, and tie it with a ribbon. Find or create an image of me in one of my colorful manifestations, whichever one calls to you. Place the scroll next to it and place it on your altar. I will be there.

Emma found that by first working with Akhilandeshwari to accept her condition of thyroid cancer, she was able to imagine herself as broken but capable of repair. Creating an image of herself by tearing it apart, reassembling it, and filling the cracks with gold, helped her see her own power to heal and be complete. She knew it would be a difficult journey that included surgery, but she also knew she could feel whole again by accepting her brokenness and participating in her own recovery. She found a beautiful statue of Tara and put it on her altar. Tara helped her love herself through all of the health challenges she faced, which enabled her to call in friends and family to care for her. Emma realized there was strength in asking for help and a deep sense of gratitude and love as she received it.

# Invocation to the Goddesses for Healing

Oh, Akhilandeshwari and Tara, hear my plea. I ask for your soothing strength, your calming influence, and your healing powers to be with me now as I place this issue before you: _____ (name the discomfort or illness).

Help me to find the wisdom of this dis-ease. Help me understand why it is manifesting in me at this time and what I need to know to heal. I am open to your answers and your healing power. I trust in your wisdom as I trust in my own ability to know what is right and true for me.

**Journal about any messages, answers, or wisdom that come to you and follow through.**

## Objects and Symbols to Consider for Your Altar to Tara

**Colors:** green, white, orange, or any color related to one of her 21 manifestations

**Objects:** image or figurine of Tara, star, white candle

**Gemstones:** quartz crystal (clear or rose), green tourmaline, white or black pearl

**Flowers:** lotus, star flower, amaryllis

**Element:** air

**Chakra:** crown (7th chakra) or heart (4th chakra)

# Journal Prompts

In which realm of your health (mental, emotional, physical, spiritual) are you feeling out of balance?

What are the roots of this imbalance? e.g., a recurring thought, overriding feeling, physical ailment, sense of purposelessness, unresolved trauma? Write about it and see if you can discover its roots.

Which of these goddesses do you think can best help you with your health imbalance—Akhilandeshwari (acceptance), Green Tara (action), White Tara (compassion)?

Write a loving letter to yourself from one of these mother goddesses.

What does she want you to know?

What is her healing message to you with respect to your specific health imbalance? What does she want you to do?

How does fear play into your current state of health and any condition you might be experiencing?

How might you remove or overcome your fear?

What might you need to release to achieve your desired healing?

How are you or your life right now like the beautiful lotus flower that grows from the mud?

Where do you see perfectionism playing out in your life? What messages did you receive as a child that may have led you to believe you needed to be perfect?

One of Tara's gifts is to bring about liberation. In what way(s) would you like to be liberated?

In what ways do you need protection, compassion, or soothing? Who can you ask to help care for you in this way? In what ways can you provide this to yourself?

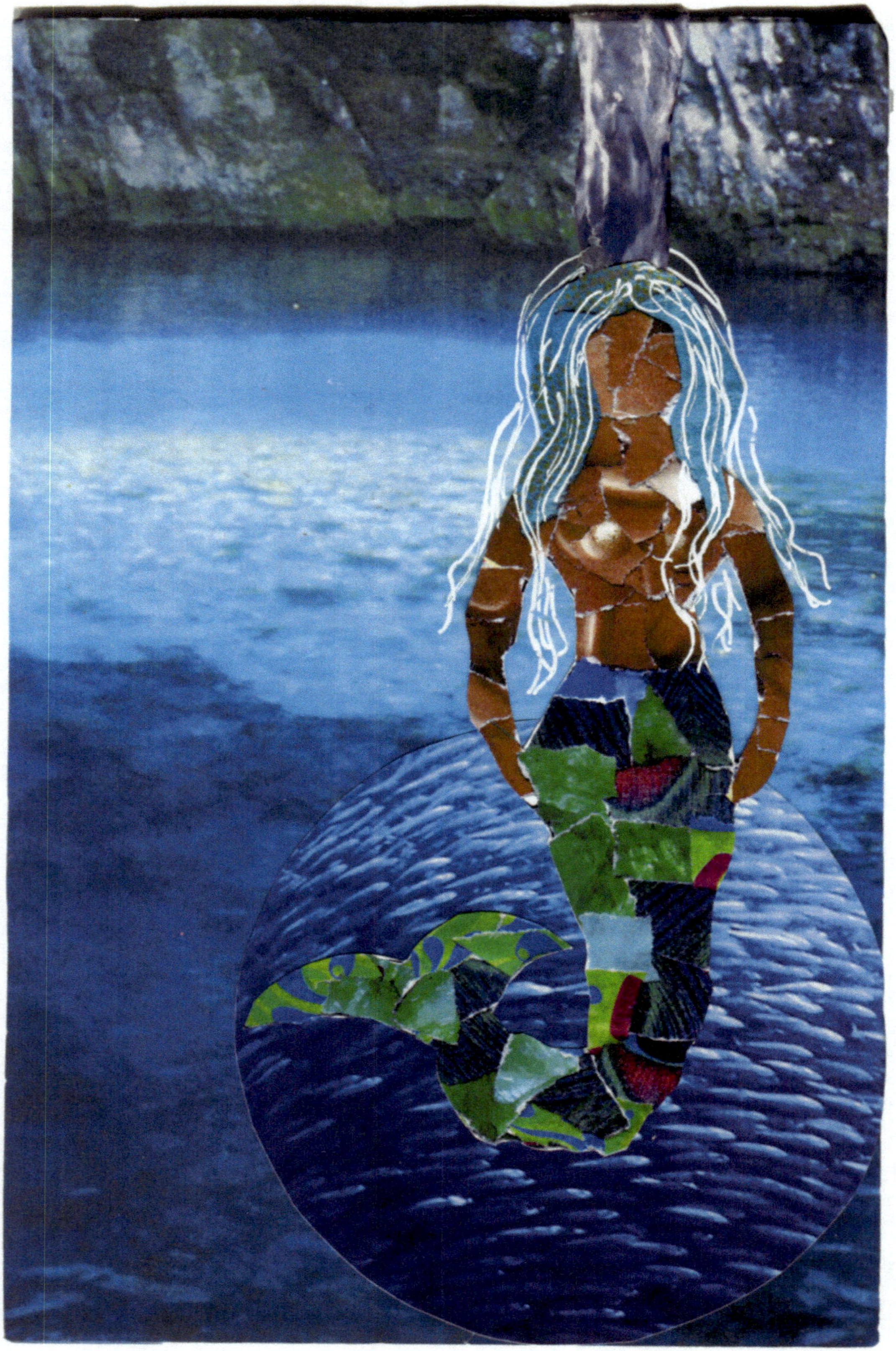

# Chapter Ten

# Anxiety and Fear

ANXIETY IS A SENSE OF DISCOMFORT, dread, and worry based on an imagined outcome or danger that is not currently present. It could be based on a very real fear of doing something new or different, but is often out of proportion. It is a product of the mind or mental processes, of how you think. You might imagine that it is impossible to change your thinking, but many times you are just practicing bad thinking habits or cognitive distortions (See Common Thinking Mistakes in CH. 8, page 178). You can change habits and learn to think differently with practice.

Anxious thoughts are a preoccupation with something that may or may not happen, and frequently include fear of the unknown. Sometimes anxiety is free-floating, with no apparent cause or threat (usually this means it is a learned behavior). Anxiety is often felt as nervousness, tension, agitation, uneasiness, and fear.

Anxiety has its place in life. It is a normal reaction to stressors, transitions, and challenges in the short-term. Anxiety based on an acutely stressful situation is normal and may even be beneficial in some situations, as it may help you mobilize your inner resources to handle an unexpected demand. Fear and anxiety have their place in everyday life, as humans are wired to feel angst when facing threats to safety and well-being. Sometimes you are wise to follow your fear and not do something you do not feel ready for, that you instinctively sense may be too dangerous or risky, or that you do not feel comfortable with. However, it may

## Amelia's Story

Amelia has experienced anxiety for most of her life. She describes it as a constant monologue in her head, questioning whether she is doing it right ("it" being everything from how she talks to a friend to living life as a single woman on her own), worrying about the future, and imagining the worst outcomes.

She lives in a near-constant state of alert with symptoms like panic attacks, when her heart feels like it is going to leap out of her chest, as well as an inability to catch her breath. Unforeseen events sometimes trigger her panic; at other times, it might be going into an uncomfortable situation like meeting new people. Often these panic attacks seem to come out of the blue for no apparent reason.

Amelia saw her mother react to many situations in life with anxiety and fear, shrinking back from social events and eventually avoiding them all together, and she does not want to follow in her footsteps.

become a serious problem if you are constantly racked with fear, dread, worry, and irrational thoughts, or if you find yourself avoiding or overreacting to everyday situations, living in a state of agitation or high alert.

Fear is an emotional component of anxiety. When confronted with a fearful situation, a signal is sent to the primitive region of your brain known as the amygdala. This is where you experience the fight, flight, or freeze response—essentially the same response any animal has when confronted with danger. The body releases stress hormones like cortisol, epinephrine, and adrenalin. These hormones help you in the moment, in very real situations where you must act instantly to prevent harm. However, when these hormones constantly flood the body, causing high-level reactions to low-level stressors, chronic stress and anxiety is the result. Studies show that continuous surges of cortisol actually harm you, leading to health effects like blood sugar imbalance, hypertension, heart disease, gastrointestinal problems, build-up of fat tissue, and weight gain.

While you may have some genetic predisposition to these stress responses, they are more often learned and set up early in life. You pick up these patterns from seeing how caregivers handled stress and anxiety or from being left to your own devices and without sufficient guidance and protection as a child. In addition, if you were faced with chaotic, stressful, or traumatic situations growing up, you are more prone to anxiety and fearful reactions as an adult. You can learn to override the primitive brain response of fight, flight, or freeze and the neurotoxic effect of too much cortisol by learning ways to calm and soothe yourself with your goddess guides showing you the way.

In this chapter you will meet two divine feminine deities who will help you counteract stress, soothe your worried mind, let go, and live more fully in the moment. They are Butterfly Maiden, a Native American goddess, and Yemaya, an Afro-Latin goddess of the sea. With their guidance, you learn to replace old, anxious habits with new ways of thinking and being.

It can be said that anxiety is living in the future—constantly wondering, "What if…?" You imagine the bad things that could happen rather than living in the present and noticing what really is happening. Butterfly Maiden, the peaceful goddess in Native American tradition, can help with this as one who allows change in and around her to take place with ease and grace. This maiden facilitates a different, more hopeful perspective.

Butterfly Maiden allows deep transformation to occur—learning to let go of worry so you are free to fly on wings of acceptance and joy. One of her many attributes is to bring you a sense of hope. To achieve contentment and ease, you need to feel a continuous renewal of hope for yourself, your loved ones, and the world. Butterfly Maiden instills hope for you to live more peacefully in the present.

The second goddess who helps you overcome fear and anxiety is Yemaya, the Afro-Latin Mother Goddess of the waters. She is known and loved in the regions of West Africa, the Caribbean, and Brazil. Yemaya helps you go with the ebb and flow of life, to let go of troubling thoughts and transform self-doubts that may be swirling beneath the surface. She teaches you to swim like the mermaid she is through turbulent waters to find the calm that cleanses and releases you from worry and fear.

Yemaya is a mother goddess of the Yoruba people of Nigeria who is believed to have accompanied enslaved people from Africa across the ocean to the Americas. As such, she is a protectoress. She provides shelter from the storm and shields you from danger and threats to your well-being, which may mean learning to swim away from the source of anxiety and fear or learning to face it and move past it.

Both of these goddesses are spirit beings. Butterfly Maiden is a kachina in the Hopi Indian tradition, who comes from the Underworld to dance with her people on the earth plane. Yemaya is an orisha, or water spirit, one of some 400 in the Yoruba tradition. Yemaya is the mother to 14 orisha water spirits, and she is also mother to the first man and woman in Yoruban tradition. It is believed that each person comes in with their own personal orisha who guides and protects them.

# Butterfly Maiden

Various Native American tribes, including the Shoshone, Blackfeet, and Hopi, honor Butterfly Maiden. She is associated with fertility, spring, and the pollination of flowers necessary for rebirth. A number of tribes have an annual Butterfly Dance as part of a coming-of-age initiation or harvest rite. Because of her cyclical nature, Butterfly Maiden is a symbol of transformation who abides with you through each season of life, death, and rebirth. As the butterfly is integral to flowers blooming, so is this goddess to your own budding and opening, no matter the season.

Butterfly Maiden helps you recognize when a thought or fear is irrational and may be stopping you from doing something you wish to do. She is associated with the element of air or the mental realm, and thus gives you the ability to understand your intrusive thoughts in a more rational way and overcome them with positive, realistic self-talk, offering you a different perspective than the one you started with. She also helps you understand the need for change and gives you hope that you can evolve and not remain stuck in fear and anxious thought patterns.

One common anxiety trigger is change. Fear of change is based on the illusion or false belief that things should stay the same, that once something is established it should not be expected to alter. It may be that a sense of safety and security comes when some aspect of your life is set in place—a job, relationship, home, baby, etc.—but you have to learn to live with the reality that nothing is permanent and *the only constant is change*. You, as a human being, are meant to learn, grow, and change.

Call in Butterfly Maiden as an ally to help you learn to accept fluctuations in life, make the needed alterations in your habits and thought patterns, and live in the moment.

# The Story of Butterfly Maiden

A Shoshone legend tells of a beautiful butterfly whose mate was killed in battle. In her sorrow, she wrapped herself in a chrysalis and refused to come out. After a while she emerged and went on a healing journey to find herself again. Still steeped in sorrow, she could only look down as she trod along the earth's floor as a caterpillar. One day she noticed that amongst the drab, dirt-covered stones, which looked the same day after day, one stood out in its stunning radiance. It sparkled and twinkled its many colors like a rainbow caught in a crystal. Was it truly dazzling, or was she seeing it differently on this day?

She realized that her old way of seeing the world had shifted, and with her newfound perception she was healed. She had grieved what was and now she was ready to live again. Liberated, she grew magnificent wings and began to flutter and dance on the air currents, her life force renewed and restored. She felt hope for the future as she learned to accept change and transform herself.

## Objects and Symbols to Consider for Your Altar to Butterfly Maiden

**Colors:** rainbow and iridescent colors

**Objects:** butterfly wings, butterfly figures and images, candle

**Gemstones:** opal, ammolite, agate, kyanite

**Flowers:** pansies, orchids, butterfly bush

**Element:** air

**Chakra:** third eye or brow (6th chakra)

Inherent in the life of the butterfly is the metamorphosis from egg to crawling caterpillar to chrysalis, from which she emerges as an adult butterfly—transformed with wings to fly. This process may be likened to these stages of creation:

- Beginning or creating something new: **the egg** holds all manner of potential and then hatches into a baby that has to learn to walk and feel her way in the world (this could also be an idea that is hatched). It is a time of learning and feeling your way in the world as a **caterpillar** does. This is the time of the Maiden.
- Then there is a period of dormancy or introspection/inner work while in **the chrysalis** stage, a reminder that change is an inside job. These early stages imply a time of gestation, growth, challenge, and struggle—facing yourself—before you fully come into Being. This is the time of the Mother.
- And finally, **transformation**, the emergence of the butterfly, project, or situation—now ready to take wing and have a life of its own. This is the time of the Crone.

Butterfly Maiden alleviates your anxiety by coaxing you through these life stages with the promise of hope and freedom—by overcoming your fears and becoming the person you want to be, the woman you were meant to be, and showing your true colors to the world.

## Butterfly Maiden Speaks

Dear Sister, what helps you feel like a carefree maiden? Do you remember a time when you were a little girl without worries? What helped you then? What did you enjoy doing that did not entail worry or fear that you may have forgotten or set aside? I encourage you to find it and reclaim it for yourself now.

If anxieties burdened you as a child or if you lived in fear growing up, know that you can find your way out and set yourself free. You need not be bound by the past. Your time in the chrysalis is over. Your wings are ready.

I invite you to write down all of your fears. See them for what they are: thoughts and feelings about what could happen but very likely will not happen. For each fear, write down a reason it does not serve you and why you no longer want to harbor it. Now write what you know to be true and what you hope will happen—a loving affirmation or intention that helps you feel better and carry on.

Imagine the metamorphosis taking place within you as that old, creepy-crawler fear turns into a positive thought—a truth—and see it emerge from the chrysalis and fly free. It no longer crawls around in your head. Anytime the old fearful thought or feeling rises in you, say the truth or affirmation to yourself as you picture yourself letting fear go on gossamer wings.

Know that I am with you through it all. I exist in all of your vulnerabilities and trembling boldness. Come fly with me!

# Yemaya

In the Yoruba language, her name, a contraction of Yeye Omo Eja, means "Mother Whose Children are the Fish." As such, you are her daughter, born from her watery womb, a little fish who swims in the great ocean of life under her protection. The ocean is where all life began, and the watery womb is where your life began. She represents the element of water, the place of emotions, where both fear and its antidote, love, reside, along with all the other feelings we can feel.

She is *Mother Courage*, who teaches that love conquers fear and shows you how to love yourself through your tremblings. You can diminish your fears with her comfort and discerning eye, helping you see your fearful thoughts and preoccupations for what they are—lies you tell yourself and have come to believe. With her help, you learn to tell yourself the truth and thus negate the fear so it is no longer an obstacle that stops you.

When you live primarily in fear mode and your thoughts tend to be more worried than calm, it is often because you were unmothered or under-nurtured as a child. You may have had a worried, anxious mother (or father), who knew no other way to parent or be in the world than to fidget and fret and project their worries onto you. Or you may have had an absent parent who was not there to comfort and protect you when you felt afraid, and therefore you have not learned to comfort yourself and feel secure in your own skin. When you experience fear and anxiety, Yemaya is a comforting presence, a Mother Goddess who offers security, protection, and acceptance.

Your mother may have abandoned you emotionally, if not physically. A lack of anchoring, of safe harbor that you feel in a mother's arms, sets you up to have an *anxious attachment* to your mother, and subsequently to significant others in adult life. You learned not to trust, to live in fear, without a sense of a safety net. To heal this emotional wound, you have to both grieve these losses and unlearn these outmoded, reactive patterns. You want to learn to replace fears and insecurities with new, healthy responses and habits. Forming a relationship with the mother goddess Yemaya teaches you to soothe and love yourself—and trust again.

## The Story of Yemaya

Yemaya and her male counterpart, Olokun, were once one deity, but split apart into feminine and masculine beings, although each contained the energy of the other. Olokun became a fierce and powerful god who ruled the lower depths of the ocean, while Yemaya was the protective, caregiving goddess who ruled the surface waters. This upper layer is the part that teems with life and where the waves break upon the shore. Thus, Yemaya is more readily accessible to humans who meet her in the liminal space where earth and sea meet.

She is the *Great Mami Watta*—Mother of the Waters. When she was pregnant with the world, her waters broke and created all the waterways of the world—rivers, lakes, streams, and oceans. She wears seven blue and white skirts to represent the seven seas. Water is the element that is synonymous with emotions, depth of feelings, and it is in this realm that she guides her children.

When her human children were put on slave ships during the African diaspora, she accompanied them to the Americas, swimming alongside the vessels. She became known as a potent guardian spirit to the African people brought to the Americas and Caribbean islands. While syncretized with the Virgin Mary in some places, Yemaya is still a beloved goddess in many countries.

One way people honor her is to make an offering of flowers into the ocean on her Feast Day, September 7. If you are not near the ocean, you can go to a stream, lake, or river, and do the same, saying a blessing or prayer asking for her help and guidance.

Envision Yemaya as an abiding presence, the one who nurtures you through difficulties, who shows you how to flow through problems and challenges without letting fear overwhelm or stop you. She is the blessed mother whispering in your ear that *You are enough, You are loved, You are safe* because *She is with you*. She shows you the way through the deep, murky waters of fear, gently coaxing you to trust she is there, leading you to the clear, calm waters of love and truth.

Eventually she steers you to the other side, to the shore, where you can walk peacefully and purposely to your destination.

Consider how Butterfly Maiden and Yemaya can help you quell and transform worry and fear in the following anxiety-provoking scenarios:

## Living in the Future and Catastrophizing

This is a habit of imagining the worst outcome that you really do not want to happen.

**Butterfly Maiden**, the Goddess of Metamorphosis, helps you see the anxious thought, examine your belief, and change it. Write down the persistent thought or fear and first ask yourself if it is true (e.g., "I am afraid to try this because I will fail"). As you examine this thought, you realize you do not know for sure if you will fail, so it is not true. Next, tell yourself a truth about the situation, perhaps writing it down. For example, you could say, "I might fail, but it is worth the risk as the good outweighs the bad, and it is an opportunity I do not want to miss. I will be okay even if it does not work out."

Remind yourself of this truth as often as needed. Write it down to carry with you, and read it as an affirmation. It may help to imagine what you would do in a worst-case scenario and have a plan of action, i.e., what you would say or do—how you would handle it if your worst fear was realized. When you have imagined yourself working through a challenge, yo u can more easily meet it.

Studies show that for people with anxiety disorders, over 90% of their worries and fears do not come true. Knowing this, you can decide whether to put your time and energy into using your imagination to create something you don't want and that you know is unlikely to happen, or to live in the present with what you know to be true. This way you use your precious time and energy by hoping for the best and making peace with what is, which means accepting reality.

Like the good mother she is, **Yemaya** helps you swim through imagined fears offering a sense of security and protection with whatever decision you make for your highest good. Picture her as the helpful, fearless mother offering a guiding hand as you move through a difficult situation. She reminds you of the truth that you are safe in your own being, that you are loved and cherished, and are deserving of the good that comes to you. It can help to write down these soothing words of wisdom and say them to yourself, as a mother would to a child, and keep them with you or place them on your altar.

## Panicking—Feeling a Sense of Intense Fear or Dread, Often for No Apparent Reason

When experiencing panicky feelings or panic attacks, it helps to pause and take deep breaths. Often when you go into panic mode, you unconsciously hold your breath or breathe shallowly, your heart beats faster, and you feel dizzy and disoriented. Stop and sit or lie down, and come back into your body by taking slow, deep, belly breaths.

Call in **Butterfly Maiden** and envision the butterfly landing on a flower, no longer fluttering. See this as a time to regroup, pause, and be in the moment with your breath—slowing it down, and drinking in the nectar of life. Imagine Butterfly Maiden alighting on a flower on the inhale, pausing to taste the nectar while you hold, and then flying to the next flower on the exhale.

When panicked, picture Mother Yemaya guiding you from turbulent or deep water to calm, surface waters. There you feel buoyed, at ease, your breathing calm. Practice the yogic *Ujjayi* or ocean breath: slow, deep, belly breaths of inhale and exhale, approximating the sounds of ocean waves moving in and out.

Imagine **Yemaya** holding you gently as a mother would a child learning to float. Feel yourself letting go of the fear—all you have to do is float while she supports you. Imagine the soothing words she might use: *"You're safe now. I've got you. You are loved. I am here to protect and guide you through this. You are okay."* Keep a talisman like a small, smooth stone or shell with you to hold onto during these times, grounding you and reminding you of her soothing presence.

## Social and Performance Anxiety

Fear of failing, being embarrassed, humiliated, looking stupid, feeling awkward, not knowing what to say, or freezing in the spotlight are fairly common forms of anxiety. These fears can lead to avoidance of social situations or career opportunities. They can get in the way of friendships and other relationships, which can lead to loneliness and isolation. Fear of public speaking or performing can potentially affect work or other activities you might enjoy doing but do not allow yourself because you're worried about looking foolish, making a mistake, or becoming paralyzed with stage fright.

**Butterfly Maiden** asks you to imagine being in the chrysalis where no one can see you, bound up, but wanting to come out. From here you can envision becoming the beautiful, free butterfly you are destined to be. She assures you that it will help to let out the shameful, secret fear you are hiding. Perhaps you are afraid of being laughed at for making a mistake. Write it down or whisper it to her. Or tell it to someone you trust, confiding your nervousness or worst fear. Having a safe someone to talk to makes it easier to bear, as so many others share this form of anxiety and can offer empathy, understanding, and encouragement.

Take classes or seek a reliable person—perhaps a coach, therapist, or mentor—to help you learn ways to express yourself and account for your progress as you take baby steps out of your comfort zone. Find someone trustworthy with whom you can practice, whether it is how to start a conversation or give a speech, what to say in a job interview, or how to perform in front of an audience without distress.

Know you are not alone. With Butterfly Maiden's gentle nudge, it is safe to emerge from hiding and allow your wings to unfold a little at a time as she helps you learn to fly. The more you do it, the easier it will become as you burn through the fear, leaving it in a pile of ashes.

**Yemaya** guides you through feelings of inadequacy and not being enough, the fear of being embarrassed or humiliated, by allowing yourself to feel these feelings, to name them, and then let them go into her hands.

She takes your fears and dissolves them like salt in water. She whispers words of encouragement. Yemaya provides a reflecting pool for you to see yourself as strong, courageous, and worthy. Look in a mirror and tell yourself heartening words of love and comfort as an adoring mother would her daughter. Think of her as the good mother who nudges you to try something new, even if it is scary, praising every step you take towards your own happiness and freedom from fear. Imagine this inner mother holding your hand and guiding you. Imagine her voice talking to your Inner Child, expressing confidence in you and your abilities.

Yemaya encourages you to reward yourself every time you make a little progress towards overcoming an old fear or habit. Healthy rewards might include a day off, a fun activity, a treat, pampering yourself, a mini-vacation, a flight of fancy.

## Changing Your Thoughts

Remember that when you change your thoughts, your feelings change as well. This leads you to take different actions than if you had continued to believe the original self-limiting thought, which is most often a lie you tell yourself. If you consider love as the antidote to fear, you can imagine transforming fear-based thoughts and uneasy feelings with truth, love, and confidence with the Goddesses' help.

## Make a Spirit Doll

You can create simple effigies of Butterfly Maiden and Yemaya by gathering shells, stones, sticks, seaweed, moss, and other objects from nature and putting them together to form a three-dimensional figure of a woman with butterfly wings or a mermaid tail. You can fasten or glue the pieces together or just leave them in the impermanent, feminine shape you have created somewhere in a garden, along the shore, or on your altar. You may want to tuck a little written prayer beneath or inside of her.

Amelia created spirit dolls of both Butterfly Maiden and Yemaya and put them on her altar to remind her of their soothing and transformative abilities. Anytime she felt anxious or panicked, Amelia stopped what she was doing, sat down in a cross-legged position, and took slow, deep breaths, imagining Butterfly Maiden fluttering about and then alighting on a flower. She found that water helped her feel safe, secure, and relaxed, so she took to having daily warm baths in which she put flower petals, salts, and bubbles. There she named her worries and fears and let them go while she soaked. She also walked on a trail that led by a woodland stream and found peace meditating there. Additionally, she worked with a coach to help her get over her fear of social situations and meeting new people, and found that her confidence grew as she practiced stepping into the unknown with less and less fear.

# Yemaya Speaks

Dear Daughter, come with me into the sea of cleansing salt waters. I invite you to make a bath with Epsom salts or other sea salts. Add flowers and essential oils. Perhaps you would like to try a seaweed mineral bath. Lower the lights and light a candle as you soak in the warm, healing waters.

Close your eyes and imagine old wounds and lingering fears you carry. Say out loud what it is that is causing you pain or worry. Feel where it is in your body. Put your hands there and caress it gently, seeing my hands along with yours take away the hurt, alleviate the distress.

I am ready to listen to what it is you need in order to heal, to finally let go. Say it out loud. This is a powerful declaration of longing and love for yourself. Now imagine yourself receiving this gift of whatever you desire for yourself from my hands.

As you luxuriate in the warm bath, see the old pain you have carried for so long, start to dissipate. Let yourself cry if you need to. Give me your fears and tears, Child, your worries and wails. Let them flow into the water that envelops you. Let go of all you have been holding. See the old wound grow smaller and smaller as it begins to heal.

Hear my soothing words as you let go of this wounded part of you. I remind you, "You are loved and worthy of love." Feel my gentle hands cup your face as I whisper, "There, there, My Child. I see you. I am with you. You are not alone. I will not abandon you, and you must not abandon yourself."

When it is time to get out of the bath, know that the hurt and fear have dissolved in the water, and watch them go down the drain. Know that you can now move forward in the flow of life. Rub oil onto your body and get a good night's sleep, My Child.

⇛ ⋯ ⇚

Note: When doing healing work on familial pain and patterns, it is important to not let guilt take over and prevent you from seeing and admitting the truth of how you were wounded (even if you now have a better relationship with your caregiver). You can only truly get to forgiveness when you have done the work of speaking your truth and releasing your anger and hurt at the original pain. This does not necessarily mean speaking it to your caregiver or the person who wounded you, but speaking for yourself. By taking back your power as a woman and loving yourself unconditionally, you can resolve old, familial, possibly even ancestral, pain—the original wound that keeps showing up in different guises and circumstances. By doing so, you heal back generations. (See also CH. 11, page 230, Reparenting: Learning to Mother Yourself.)

You may need help with healing these wounds, particularly if you have experienced abandonment, abuse, or trauma. In addition to calling in your goddess guides and attuning to your *Wise Mind*—your Higher Self that loves you, knows what is best for you, and wants to assist you—consider seeking help from a qualified professional.

## Objects and Symbols to Consider for Your Altar to Yemaya

**Colors:** blue, aqua, white

**Objects:** shells, coral, beach glass, dried seaweed, mermaid figures or images of Yemaya

**Gemstones:** pearl, mother of pearl, aquamarine

**Flowers:** anemones, white roses, larkspur, hydrangea, sea grasses

**Element:** water

**Chakra:** heart (4th chakra)

# Journal Prompts

How much of your thinking on an average day is filled with anxious worrying? How much time do you spend during an average day feeling fearful and uneasy?

What commitment/statement are you willing to make to reduce your anxious and fearful thoughts and feelings? Be specific about what you want to change.

What strategies outlined in this chapter are you willing to commit to on a daily basis to alleviate your anxiety and fear?

Where do you feel anxiety/fear in your body? What memories do you have related to these bodily sensations? What does this part of your body want to say to you?

What does your anxiety want you to know?

What are some anxious habits you learned from your mother or father?

What do you wish they would have said or done to help you with your fears and anxieties? How can you use these messages to help yourself now?

What has been your experience in overcoming a fear? What helped you succeed? What did you learn from this?

Which Goddess of Self-Care do you feel will be most helpful to you in dealing with your anxiety and fear? Butterfly Maiden, who helps you accept change, have a different perspective, and provide hope? Or Yemaya, who helps you feel mothered, soothed, fortified, and in the flow of life? Write a letter to one of these goddesses asking for the specific help you need, then write a letter from her answering you. Place it on your altar.

Make an altar to one or both of these goddesses as you work on changing your anxious thoughts, habits, and patterns. Place a container on it where you can drop the fears you have written on slips of paper and close the lid. Notice how often these fears are overblown and how often they are realized. You may want to burn them when you feel ready to finally let them go.

~230~

## Chapter Eleven

# Reparenting: Learning to Mother Yourself

NOTHING BRINGS THE INNER CHILD into your awareness more acutely than becoming a parent yourself. Ideally, you want to come to know the wants and needs of your Inner Child and how to mother her before you take on the role of being a parent. Holding your innocent, helpless baby and trying to figure out how best to nurture your child often brings up your own unmet—and often hidden—needs and desires. When you learn to mother yourself, you are able to be a better partner and parent, if and when you decide to take on that very important role. When you learn to mother yourself, you actively heal childhood wounds in the service of self-care.

A woman might ask herself: How can I care for a baby when I was not cared for adequately as a child? Beyond providing the basic survival needs of a child, such as food, clothing, and shelter, attending to the emotional needs of a child is the most crucial aspect of being a good parent—making sure your child grows up feeling loved, adored, wanted, and respected. A child has a much greater chance of a healthy emotional life and partnership when she grows up without experiencing neglect or abandonment. For example, being left to your own devices with little guidance or parental interaction is a form of neglect. Parents who showed little interest in your feelings or who rarely expressed emotion and affection leave you feeling unseen, empty. On the other hand, situations where a child is smothered and manipulated, or expected to caretake an

### Mariah's Story

It has been a year since her divorce was final, and Mariah is realizing how her troubled relationship with her mother played out in her marriage. Growing up, the roles were reversed—she was the mother, and her mother the child who needed constant love, attention, and reassurance. Mariah learned that to be seen and valued she had to repress her feelings and put her mother's needs first or her mother would ignore her, criticize her, and call her selfish.

Consequently, Mariah learned to put everyone's needs ahead of her own and become a people-pleaser in her friendships, workplace, and marriage. She knows now she married a man much like her mother, who expected her to cater to his wishes with little thought to her own. She assumed the mother role again, trying to meet the demands of a needy man-child. Mariah is beginning to see that putting herself first does not mean she is selfish, but empowered. She is determined to learn to be the good mother to herself that she never had.

emotionally immature parent, or made to feel she has to be perfect, always the "good girl," also lead to wounding. These are all forms of emotional abuse, which is often harder to acknowledge and identify than physical abuse.

If you experienced any of these kinds of emotional wounds growing up, it is important to acknowledge them and determine what needs healing in you. Learning to reparent yourself—to be your own best mother by looking to the example of the archetypal Great Mother—is a way to start healing the wounded Inner Child.

**What does a good mother do when her child is hurt, lonely, scared, angry, or sad?**

> She sees her.
> She listens to her.
> She allows her feelings.
> She soothes and comforts her.
> She reassures her.
> She expresses empathy and understanding.
> She holds her.
> She protects her.
> She helps make it all better.

# The Mother Wound

Chances are, if you had a mother who was usually there for you on a consistent basis—"the good-enough mother" (because there is no perfect parent)—you have developed an ability to comfort and care for yourself (even if that ability may need a little fine-tuning). If, however, you had a mother who was inconsistent in her love for you and left you unsure of when you would receive care and attention; or a mother who was emotionally unavailable and let you down more often than not; or a mother who expected you to support and care for her, to put her needs first; or a mother who was verbally or physically abusive, you have a *mother wound*.

This emotional wound sets up an unconscious pattern of self-destructive behaviors and limiting beliefs that may include self-sabotage, self-sacrifice, and people-pleasing, leading to overriding feelings of guilt, shame, and low self-esteem. Without help, guidance, and healing, you may repeat these patterns in adult relationships.

All children deserve unconditional love to see them through the difficulties and challenges of growing up. If you did not feel loved unconditionally as a child, it leaves you feeling that you either have to work hard to be loved and valued or that there is something wrong with you. Unconditional love means you are loved even when you make mistakes, when you misbehave, when you do not know any better. It does not mean you received no consequences, but it does mean your parents continued to love and guide you when you slipped.

The mother wound is intergenerational and gets passed down through the *motherline* until you decide to heal yourself and stop the pain lineage. Because the mother is generally in the role of the primary caregiver, the nurturing role tends to fall more heavily on the mother than the father, but a father who is abusive, absent, or under-nourishing can also cause wounding (see below). This wound extends back to the dawn of patriarchy, some 5,000 years ago, when women's generative power, autonomous sexuality, and role in society were devalued and depotentiated. This inherited wound is largely due to living under a patriarchal power structure in family, church, government, and culture.

In healing your mother wound, you need not vilify or hate your mother. You simply need to see the truth of your wounding, as well as her wounding, without trying to save her or put her needs before your own. Your job now is to save yourself and become the mother that you need and want. When you learn to set boundaries that allow you to be a separate person from your mother or father—to have your own feelings, to make your own way, to follow your own North Star—you recover your sense of Self. When you heal yourself you do your part to heal the world.

## What about a Father Wound?

You may have a father wound if you had an undeveloped relationship with your father or one in which he was absent or abusive, whether physically, sexually, verbally, or emotionally. Having a father who is loving, affirmative, and supportive helps you feel good about yourself as a female and develop confidence in your relationships.

A father who is not in good relationship with his own inner feminine feeling aspect may not be able to relate to his daughter in a healthy emotional way. A father who projects a fear, disregard, or hatred of women onto his daughter will also cause her to have a father wound.

## What is the Inner Child?

The term "Inner Child" refers to the part of you that still sees the world through the eyes of a child, that remembers feeling open, playful, joyful, spontaneous, and creative as well as hurt, angry, scared, and lonely based on your childhood experiences. In many ways, the Inner Child can be thought of as your *True Self*—how you came into the world, with your own special qualities, quirks, feelings, unique personality, and perspective. Of course, how you were parented affected your Inner Child and your childhood experiences, but on some level this is the part of you that sees through the cultural and familial overlay and stays true to her core identity. She knows what she wants and needs to thrive if she can just be supported and allowed to develop into her own person. As you heal childhood wounds and practice self-care, you become aware of an internal drive to protect and care for your Inner Child, and at the same time develop a willingness to allow her to be seen, to express her true nature.

You could look at helping and healing this part of yourself as removing the bindings of shame to get to your soul essence, as well as giving yourself permission to be all that you are. The degree to which you heal your childhood wounds and learn to mother yourself is the degree to which you will be a good parent—one who is present for your own children's feelings, thoughts, needs, and wants, including your own Inner Child's. Knowing how to nurture yourself helps you have healthier relationships. When you learn to meet your own needs and at the same time receive love and care from your partner, you live in balance.

Your tender, vulnerable Inner Child needs love and protection. Once you have left your parents' home, it is up to you to provide the care and compassion you craved by mothering yourself the way you always wanted to be mothered.

**You learn to:**
- listen to, not judge yourself
- accept and comfort, not criticize and punish yourself
- love and forgive, not hate and hold on
- nurture your passions and make time for what you love, not ignore them and talk yourself out of them
- encourage yourself, not denigrate yourself
- have faith in yourself, not stop believing in yourself
- see your strengths and build on them, not put yourself down
- acknowledge your flaws with empathy, understanding, and determination to do better, not criticize yourself
- ask for help when you need it, not try to be all-knowing and perfect
- give yourself pats on the back when you succeed at something, not treat yourself as undeserving or never enough
- forgive yourself for making mistakes and learn from them, not shame yourself and stop trying
- give yourself time to rest, relax, and recuperate, not push yourself to exhaustion
- give yourself the gift of play and fun, not all work and drudgery
- acknowledge your creativity and make time for it, not tell yourself you are not creative
- allow all your feelings, not repress them

- choose people in your life who love, respect, and support you, not people who put you down or hurt you
- be vulnerable and real, not closed and inauthentic

## The Great Mother

The Great Mother Goddess in her many forms—from the Virgin Mary, the Black Madonna, and the Virgin of Guadalupe, to Asherah, Isis, Kwan Yin, and Parvati—will help you be a good mother to yourself, and by extension to your own child. Mother goddesses dwell in all cultures, ethnicities, and skin colors. It is up to you to decide which of these archetypes you resonate with most and call upon her to guide and protect you.

The Great Mother has existed since the dawn of time, since humankind began imagining its origins. Early people noticed that as babies were born from a female's body, so plants and trees grew from the fertile soil of the Earth, which became synonymous with the Mother and Mother Earth, the life-giving vessel. The Mother is one of the most primal archetypes known to us. She exists in the collective unconscious, that vast storehouse of ancestral knowledge, memory, and imagery to which all human beings have access through dreams and the imagination.

In the beginning was the Mother. Early groups and cultures, before the establishment of civilizations and religions, were matriarchal, not patriarchal. Early people did not know the father's role in procreation. They only saw how the female body swelled with life and gave birth. They witnessed the awesome power of this life-giving ability and the mythological conception of *goddess* as fertile mother was born. A baby has a direct experience of the archetype of the all-giving, all-powerful, all-nourishing Great Mother upon whom he or she depends. The reality of the personal mother only begins to be understood through the formation of ego, consciousness, and separateness as the infant grows.

The icon of the mother holding her child can be seen in early images of the Egyptian goddess

Isis that morphed into the Black Madonna and then the white Virgin Mary as Christianity took hold. They all convey a sense of oneness between mother and child. Many of these images show her suckling her baby, a reminder of the nourishment you receive from the mother who births you. These figures symbolize both the initial birth of a newborn babe and rebirth as an adult who develops and changes over time with the sufficient loving care and tutelage of a caring mother.

It is the nurturing mother who helps you through transformative experiences—externally in early life, and internally as you move away from your personal mother and begin life as an adult. Holding to this image of the primordial symbiotic relationship helps you feel protected, safe, and connected to the source of life as an adult. That is why it is important to develop a sense of your Inner Mother to see you through life and help you feel lovable. The Inner Mother is the impetus for practicing self-love, self-compassion, and self-care.

The shadow of the Great Mother is the Terrible or Devouring Mother, an archetype that can be seen in myths and fairy tales, often as the jealous, vengeful goddess or the rejecting, wicked stepmother. It is important to come to terms with this shadow side of the mother and integrate this part so that it does not become an unconscious destructive force that acts against yourself or upon others. The archetype of the Great Mother contains both the light and the shadow, for she, like Mother Nature herself, is both a creative and destructive force. Work with her positive aspects that you relate to and feel comforted by, but be aware of the shadow, which will show itself as an unhealed mother wound.

In this chapter you will meet the Virgin Mary and one of her manifestations, the Virgin of Guadalupe, as well as Kwan Yin, the Chinese goddess of compassion and mercy. While Mary has her roots in Christianity and Kwan Yin in Buddhism, both are beloved Mother Goddesses who transcend their religious origins and are revered across faiths and cultures.

# Make a Mandala of the Great Mother

A good way to bring in the energy of the Great Mother is to visualize her multitude of forms by creating a collage. Begin by gathering various images of the Great Mother from cultures and countries around the world. This could include the ones mentioned above, as well as the mother goddesses you have met in this book such as Aphrodite, Demeter, Yemaya, Sophia, Tara, Kali, Isis, and assorted pictures of Madonna and Child.

Collage these images onto a poster or foam core board on which you have drawn a large circle or mandala. Or you may choose to make it on a circular poster board or in your art journal. Consider using pre-cut, round, cardboard cake bases you can find at craft and hobby stores as a canvas.

A mandala is a symbol of the Self—the circle represents the whole being comprised of the many parts within it. See the Great Mother as a round jewel containing the myriad goddesses that reflect her many facets. You may want to add paint, fabric, ribbon, washi tape, buttons, charms, beads, and other elements to your collaged mandala. Let it come to life in a way that mirrors you and your desire to love and mother yourself. Select images of the goddess that you find comforting and fill you with a sense of safety and security, protection and promise.

Mariah found that the process of gathering images of mother goddesses and gluing them into a circular form was healing in and of itself. It was as if she were putting back together pieces of herself—pieces broken by a deep, ancestral mother wound. Seeing pictures of loving mothers holding their child allowed Mariah to feel more compassion for herself, her mother, and her grandmother, whose stories of neglect and abandonment had been handed down to her. She knew that to be healed and whole, she needed to be that good mother to herself, and so she started giving herself the things she desired and longed for—time to be with herself, time to journal and create art, time with caring friends who understood and appreciated her. She placed her finished mandala above her altar, where she could see it every day and remember the capacity to love and nurture herself that her Inner Mother contained.

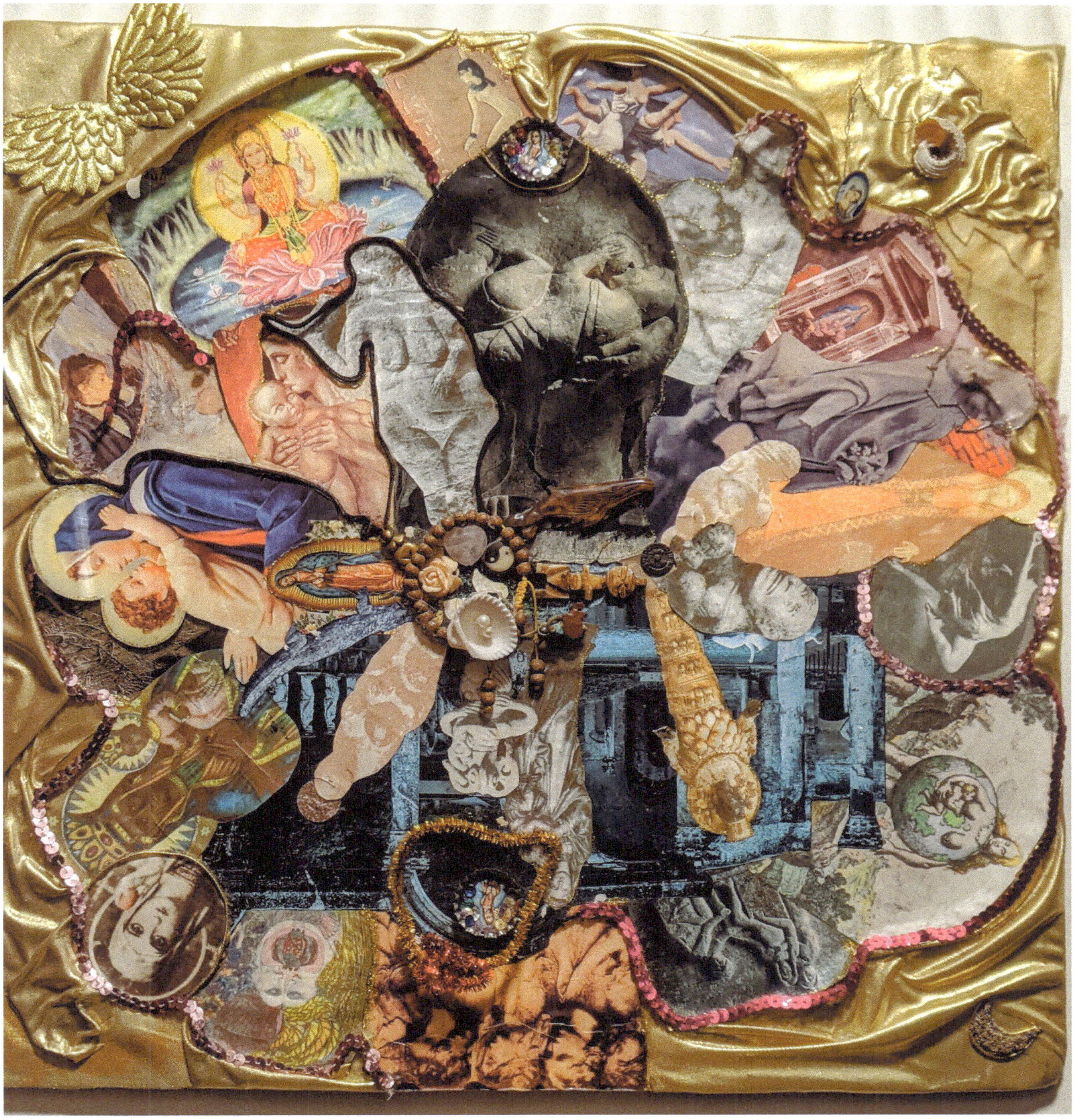

# The Story of the Virgin Mary

Mary was a young teenage girl betrothed to the older Joseph and living in Nazareth when she received a strange visitation. The angel Gabriel appeared and gave Mary the message that God had chosen her to bear his son.

After Jesus's birth in a manger in Bethlehem, Herod, the king of Judea, heard of the prophecies of a new king that would usurp him. Acting very much like the old jealous gods, Herod ordered that all male babies be killed. Fearing for their son's life, Mary and Joseph fled to Egypt where they lived for twelve years. Mary went on to marry Joseph and have other children, so she was in one sense a very real human woman and in another a woman raised to the status of goddess by virtue of being named the *Theotokos*—Mother of God, with its surrounding myths.

Mary and Joseph returned to Israel with their family and so began the story of Jesus Christ and the miracles he performed, ending with his death and resurrection. As a mortal mother, Mary stood by her son as he became "The Chosen One." She witnessed his compassion for *the least of these*—the paupers, the prostitutes, the lepers—and she was there when he was crucified. Like Demeter, she represents the abiding presence of a mother who never gives up on her child.

The cult of the Virgin Mary grew throughout the Christian world. Her motherly devotion and compassion provided comfort to those who prayed to her. She was seen as the soft counterpoint to a judgmental and punishing God.

She was the nurturing mother who was there for all, particularly the sick, the weak, the poor, the powerless. Yet the Church has kept her in her place, making her subservient to the patriarchy, doing their best to strip her—and by extension, women—of equal power. Yet she persists as a feminine icon of strength, abiding love, protection, and succor.

The Holy Mother or the Virgin Mary is the extant goddess who stands in for all of the ancient Mother Goddesses revered in times past. Although Christianity created a new story for this particular mother goddess, it borrows from earlier myths of mother and child in which there is a miracle birth or the child is taken away and sacrificed or becomes king or queen. Isis became pregnant and gave birth to Horus, the falcon god and king, after putting together the dismembered pieces of Osiris's body and fashioning a golden phallus. Demeter searched for her daughter, Persephone, lost to the Underworld until they were reunited when Persephone rose from the land of the dead in the spring and summer, but reigned there as goddess and queen the other half of the year.

As discussed in previous chapters, the virgin goddesses were not necessarily women who had not had sex, but women who had sovereignty over their own mind and body and did not need to be in relationship with men or gods to wield power. That is, until Mary's story became one of literal virginity to absolve her and her son of "original sin." Her power as a mother goddess was stripped away by the church fathers in the Christian story. It was men who decided which stories would survive and how they would be told.

By the 5th century, Christianity had spread over much of the ancient world. The texts and books of the Bible written by learned men were selected by those in power as a way to rule their subjects. Men now controlled the story. The many gods and goddesses previously revered were replaced with one God—a father, not a mother. However, people who were used to venerating a protective mother goddess were not satisfied with the one God the Father, and so over time elevated Mary to the status of a mother goddess through myth and art.

The name Mary comes from the Hebrew *Mariamne*, which means "lady" or "wise woman" and the Latin root *mare*, synonymous with the sea. Many of the Great Mother goddesses, from Aphrodite to Isis to Yemaya, come from the sea, the primordial womb of all life, the feeling waters of Mother Earth. She is known by many names, which connect her to the earth, sea, and stars, including Stella Maris (Star of the Sea), Queen of Heaven, Morning Star, and Queen of Life.

# Mary Speaks

Dear Daughter, I am the creative, life-giving force that exists within you. I am spirit transformed into matter, which comes from *mater* or mother. I am your body, soul, and spirit—wholly or holy yours—human and divine. What is mine is yours. I am but a reflection of your divinity.

I wear a blue mantle reflective of the earth and sea, from which we are born. The stars upon it are to remind you of your heavenly divinity. My red dress represents our shared blood. I stand on a crescent moon to remind you of your changing tides as a feminine being, of the cycle of birth, death, and rebirth, of which we are a part. I wear a golden crown, a symbol of our sovereignty, Daughter. The guardian angels that surround me serve as messengers between heaven and earth. I hear you. I see you. I am with you.

> I am here to help you heal your wounds, Daughter.
>
> If you were hurt as a child or your body betrayed, I am here to help you love yourself and know that you were innocent and good, then and now.
>
> If you were not adored and cherished, I am here to love you and help you know that you are always treasured.
>
> If you were not protected and pampered, I am here to offer you my lap and my arms to hold you.
>
> If you were neglected or abandoned, I am here, abiding with you always. You are not alone.
>
> If you were not seen for all of who you are, I am here to see you and witness your uniqueness and your wholeness.
>
> If you were not allowed to be yourself, I am here encouraging you to be all that you are.
>
> If you came to believe there is something wrong with you I am here to tell you that you are enough.
>
> I love you for who you are. Remember to love yourself in the same way, for you and I are one.

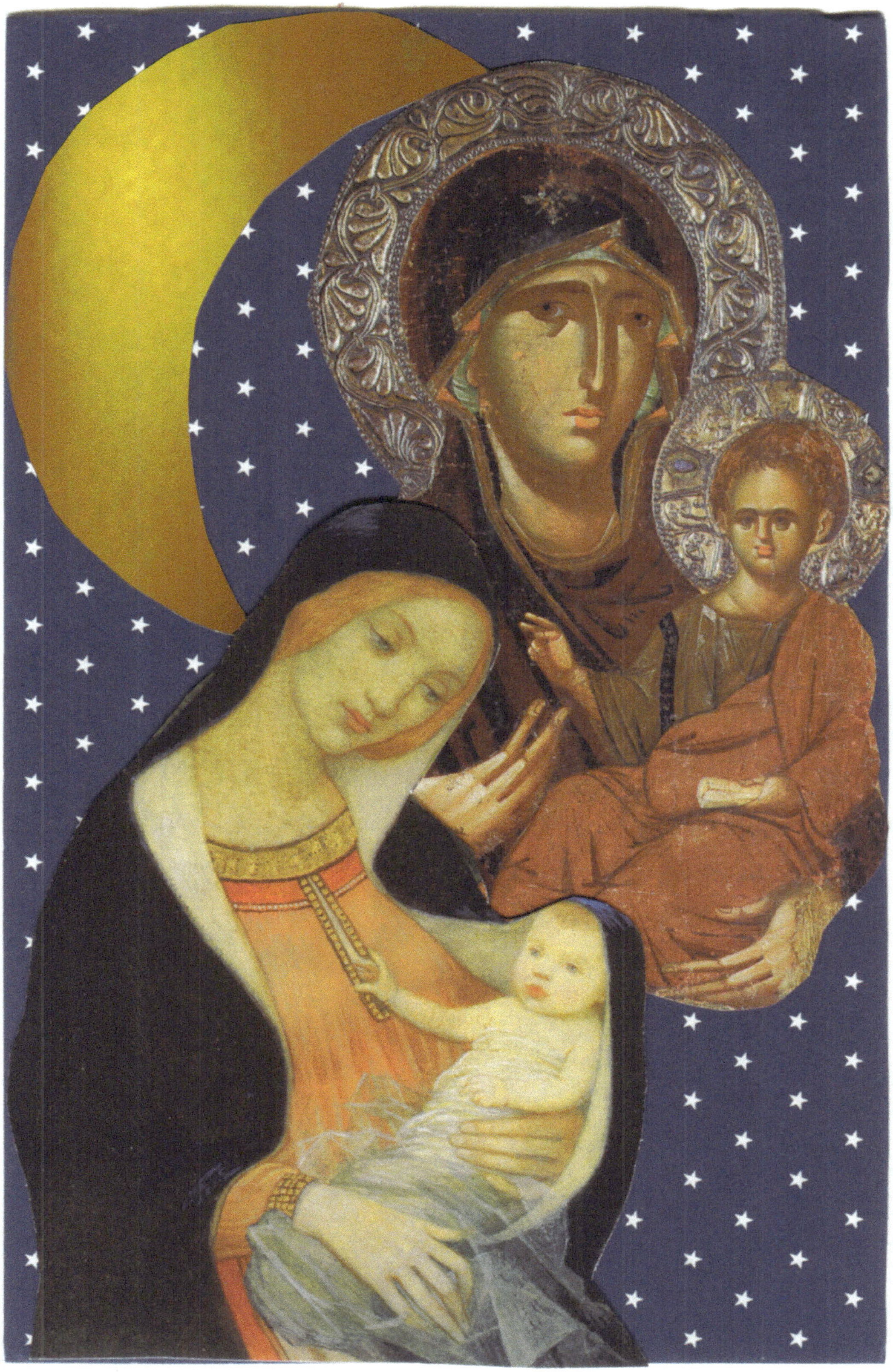

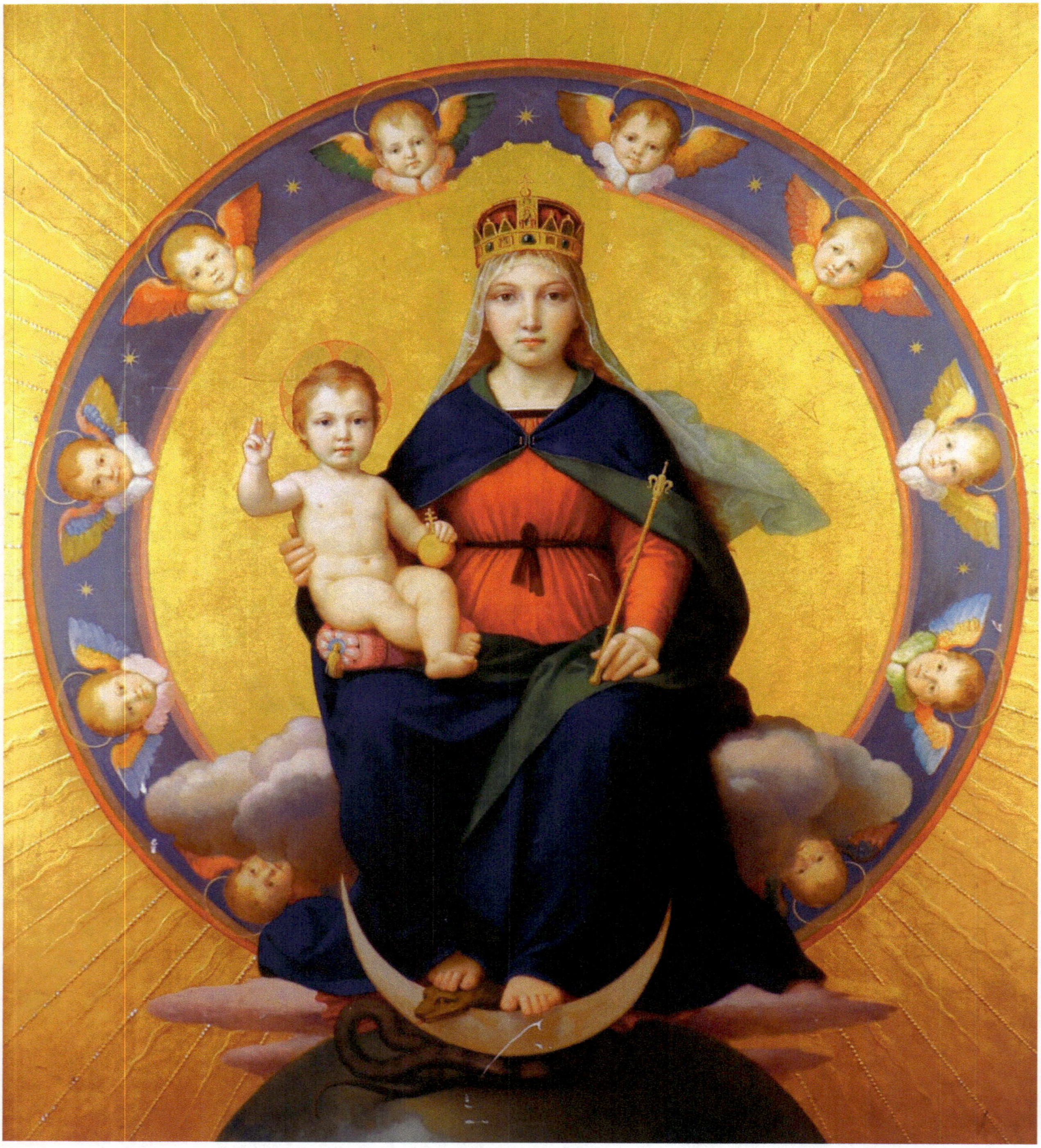

**A Prayer**

*Look to the Star, call upon Mary!*
*In danger, in difficulty or in doubt,*
*think of Mary, call upon Mary.*
*Keep her name on your lips,*
*never let it pass out of your heart.*
*Following in her footsteps, you will not go astray;*
*praying to her, you will not fall into despair;*
*thinking of her you will not err.*
*While she keeps hold of your hand,*
*you will not fall,*
*you will not grow weary,*
*you will have no fear.*
*Enjoying her protection,*
*you will reach the goal.*
*~ Saint Bernard*

# Objects and symbols to consider for your altar to the Great Mother or Mary

**Colors:** blue, red, white, pink

**Objects:** figurines and images of madonna and child, the Virgin Mary, red or white candle, seashell, rosary beads, a picture of you as a young child, a photo of your mother, grandmother, or a mother figure in your life

**Gemstones:** rose quartz, carnelian, pearl

**Flowers:** rose, lily

**Element:** water

**Chakra:** heart (4th chakra)

# The Story of our Lady of Guadalupe

One day in December 1531, Our Lady appeared before a peasant named Juan Diego on the hill of Tepeyac in Mexico, where once there stood a temple to an ancient Nahua (Aztec) goddess of love and fertility. Her name was Tonantzin, which means "Our Mother." When Our Lady appeared to Juan Diego, she instructed him to tell the bishop she wanted a church built for her on this hill. He took the message from the Blessed Mother to the bishop, but the bishop did not believe he had seen such an apparition and demanded proof.

Juan Diego reported back to the beautiful lady that he needed to provide evidence of her existence. She then told him to gather flowers to take back to the bishop. The flustered man could not imagine he could find flowers blooming in December, but as he descended the hill he saw that it was covered in blooms of every color and kind. He gathered as many as he could and put them inside his *tilma*, or cloak, and brought them to the bishop. As he opened his tilma, the flowers fell to the floor in a great profusion and the image of the Virgin was visible on the cloth. The Basilica of Guadalupe was built, and the tilma with Our Lady emblazoned upon it was put on display, where it can still be seen to this day.

The Virgin of Guadalupe, also known as Our Lady of Guadalupe, revered in Mexico and the Americas, is another form of Mary, though she is not shown with a child. Instead, she is pregnant, ensconced in an oval-shaped mandorla suggestive of an agave plant as well as the vulva.

The story of this Marian apparition was first told in the 1600s, some 100 years after most of the Nahua and other indigenous peoples of the land now known as Mexico had been converted to Christianity. It is significant that the date of the apparition was 1531, just ten years after Cortez conquered the Aztec people, as his mission was to convert the native people to Christianity.

The Virgin of Guadalupe's syncretism from indigenous goddess to Christian icon made her a beloved mother figure throughout the Americas and Spain. It was in Spain that she was originally honored as a Black Madonna before she appeared in Mexico as La Vírgen Morena (the Brown Virgin). When Mexico achieved independence from Spain in 1810, the Virgin of Guadalupe became the patroness of free Mexico. She is one of many manifestations of Mary associated with miracles. She is a goddess who brings strength, hope, love, and non-judgment to those who seek her favor. She also embodies the spirit of social justice for she is a warrior for the poor, the marginalized, the oppressed. She is an avatar of liberation, whether from internal strife or societal and racial injustice.

Both Marys—the Holy Mother and the Virgin of Guadalupe—are examples of currently revered goddesses born out of reverence for ancient mother goddesses like Isis and Tonantzin, who came before. The Virgin Mary has a number of feast days, including January 1, the day she is celebrated as the Holy Mother, and September 8, her birthday. December 12th is the day The Virgin of Guadalupe is celebrated.

# Our Lady of Guadalupe Speaks

Dear Daughter, There are many burdens that women, and particularly women of color, have been forced to carry—many forms of oppression we have had to bear, all while having guilt and shame for our womanhood, for our sexuality, heaped upon us. As the Brown Virgin Mary, I offer you a model of standing tall, standing firm, unafraid, unbowed, unbroken, asking for what you want and need, and seeing to it that your needs, and those of your children, are met.

It is time to throw off the shackles of the patriarchy and claim your wholeness, holiness, and equality with men and with people of all races. I stand with you in fighting the good fight, in righting wrongs, in treating all people with dignity and respect, and expecting to be treated likewise.

When I rose from the soil on Tepeyac Hill, I spoke up for what I wanted, and I implore you to as well. I am your strength, your courage, your steadfastness, your knowing. I encourage you to speak your truth, not stay silent. I support you to take a stand, not hold back in fear. I urge you to fight for yourself and others, not accept mistreatment, abuse, or injustice.

Am I not here? I, who am your Mother?

I am listening. I am watching. I am with you.

I have been with you since the beginning of time. I am of the earth. I go by many names. I have had many incarnations. I have your back. You can lean on me. Call on me and I will protect you.

## Objects and Symbols to Consider for Your Altar to the Virgin of Guadalupe

**Colors:** blue-green, white, red

**Objects:** figurines and images of Our Lady of Guadalupe, candle with her image, picture of you as a young child and mother figures who were there for you

**Gemstones:** amazonite, jasper, turquoise, abalone

**Flowers:** rose, agave plant, poinsettia

**Element:** earth

**Chakra:** root (1st chakra)

# Kwan Yin

In China and throughout many Asian countries, the most widely beloved mother goddess is Kwan Yin (also spelled Kuan Yin, Quan Yin, Guanyin, and Kannon in Japan). Her name means "she who hears the cries of the world." She is the Goddess of Mercy in the Buddhist tradition. Like the Himalayan Tara, she is a *bodhisattva*—one who is becoming Buddha but remains on Earth to alleviate suffering and bring enlightenment. Call upon her when you need protection, compassion, and rescue.

    She is typically shown holding a vase or jar in her left hand (the side of the receptive feminine) and a willow branch (sometimes a lotus flower) in her right (the side of the active masculine). The vase holds water—the nectar of life—as well as the compassion she pours out onto the world. (Kwan Yin is also considered a goddess of the sea, who watches over sailors and fisherfolk.) The willow is known as a tree that bends without breaking and is used to whisk water for energy clearing. In some likenesses, she holds a *mala*—prayer beads in Buddhist tradition similar to a rosary. Kwan Yin often wears a flowing white robe, symbolic of her purity and regenerative ability, and a crown with the Buddha, her teacher, upon it. She is shown sitting or standing on a lotus flower or riding a dragon. The lotus is a lovely flower, yet it grows out of the mud, a reminder of the ability to rise from darkness and bloom in the light. The dragon represents spiritual wisdom and transformation.

Kwan Yin may be seen as gender-fluid. It is believed the goddess originated in India as Avalokiteshvara, a masculine bodhisattva, who began to be revered in China in the first century CE, some 500 years after the Buddha lived. By 1000 CE he evolved into the feminine emanation of the bodhisattva known as Kwan Yin. She became a reminder that women hold up half the sky; that the divine feminine is as important and necessary as the divine masculine. Over time she became a treasured goddess and savior to people in need—from infertile women to fisherfolk in danger of drowning at sea—a divine mother to all.

## The Story of Kwan Yin

One story about Kwan Yin imagines her as Creator of the World and of all species—from man to monkey to praying mantis—10,000 in all. It was her job to teach the many different animals how to live together, how to find shelter and sustenance, and how to treat one another with respect. As long as Kwan Yin lived on Earth with them, they thrived and were happy. They loved being able to turn to their Mother Goddess for guidance and advice whenever there was trouble or misunderstanding between them. She always helped them sort it out, and they lived harmoniously for many eons. When she saw that her work was done, she ascended to the heavens, much to the dismay of the many creatures who had come to depend on her.

The animals tried their best to maintain harmony as if Kwan Yin were still with them, remembering what she would say and do to calm them and make peace. But before long, the animals began fighting each other for food, territory, and dominance. Eventually, some cried out for her help. Kwan Yin, of course, heard their cries and feeling compassion for her earthly children, returned to Earth.

She listened to their complaints, aided them in settling their disputes, and prepared to return to her mountaintop in the heavens. They implored her to remain with them, but she gently reminded them of their power to govern and care for themselves. A little rabbit who had been afraid during the turmoil when she was gone spoke up and begged her to stay and look after them.

Kwan Yin thought of a way to watch over her children with the help of a creature who lived among them. She chose a plain brown bird, and through her creative magic transformed it into a beautiful, multi-colored bird with spectacular iridescent tail feathers adorned with eyes at the end of each feather. This splendid peacock would be her eyes on the ground, and so the peacock struts proudly in its role as Kwan Yin's emissary.

Kwan Yin is the embodiment of motherly love, grace, and forgiveness. When you beseech her, she will come and alleviate your suffering with her open-hearted wisdom and compassion. Gazing upon her iconic figure, you will find she has a calming influence and the ability to soothe your soul, as all good mothers do.

Imagine her riding in on her dragon to rescue you whenever you are feeling unmothered, unloved, abandoned, or bereft—whenever you cry out to be heard. She arrives, holds you close, and pours her empathy and understanding onto you from her vessel of life. She takes her willow whisk and gently caresses your skin with it from your head to your toes, taking away the pain, drying your tears, comforting you with her gentle presence. See her as a part of you, your own Inner Mother. You may want to honor her on June 19, her feast day.

# Kwan Yin Speaks

I hear you, my daughter. Call upon me when you are sad, lonely, worried, perplexed, scared, hurt, or in danger. I am a miracle worker who hears your cries. I do not shy from suffering. I wrap my arms around you and hold you close so that you may cry on my shoulder.

Listen for my soothing voice, whispering…There, there, my child. I am with you. You are not alone. I am here to help you see that you can transform your old wounds by feeling all the feelings, by naming them, by telling me your story. I will protect you and help you by listening to you and loving you just as you are. I will remind you that you are enough.

You are loved, Child, you are loved. I am by your side, reflecting your goodness, your worthiness, your sweet soul essence. You must love yourself as I, your Great Mother, love you.

My miracles are not magical but work through understanding what is. You can shift your painful reality by making a change in the way you practice self-care, in the way you see yourself.

When you learn to see yourself the way I do—through the eyes of the loving mother—you will heal and grow from the darkness of fear, hurt, lack, trauma, and suffering into the beautiful lotus flower who rises from the mud and shines her love and light for all to behold.

## Objects and Symbols to Consider for Your Altar to Kwan Yin

**Colors:** white, pink, green

**Objects:** figurines and images of Kwan Yin, dragon, white or pink candle, vase, picture of you as a young child, peacock feather

**Gemstones:** jade, pearl, pink opal

**Flowers:** lotus, rose, chrysanthemum, willow branch

**Element:** air

**Chakra:** crown (7th chakra)

## Journal Prompts

What is your mother wound? In what ways was your mother not there for you?

What is your father wound? In what ways was your father not there for you?

How have these wounds affected your relationship with your parents?

What learned patterns and wounding from your childhood have you seen play out in adulthood?

How can the Great Mother archetype help you to better love and mother yourself?

How can the Great Mother archetype help you to better mother your child or children?

What mothering do you need now? Make a list of how you would like to feel mothered. How can you provide this needed mothering and nurturing for yourself?

In what ways could you be more compassionate with yourself? Create a prayer of love and compassion for yourself, put it on your mirror or altar, and say it daily.

How is it challenging for you (if at all) to see and accept God the Mother or the Goddess, given the patriarchal structure inherent in family, church, and culture?

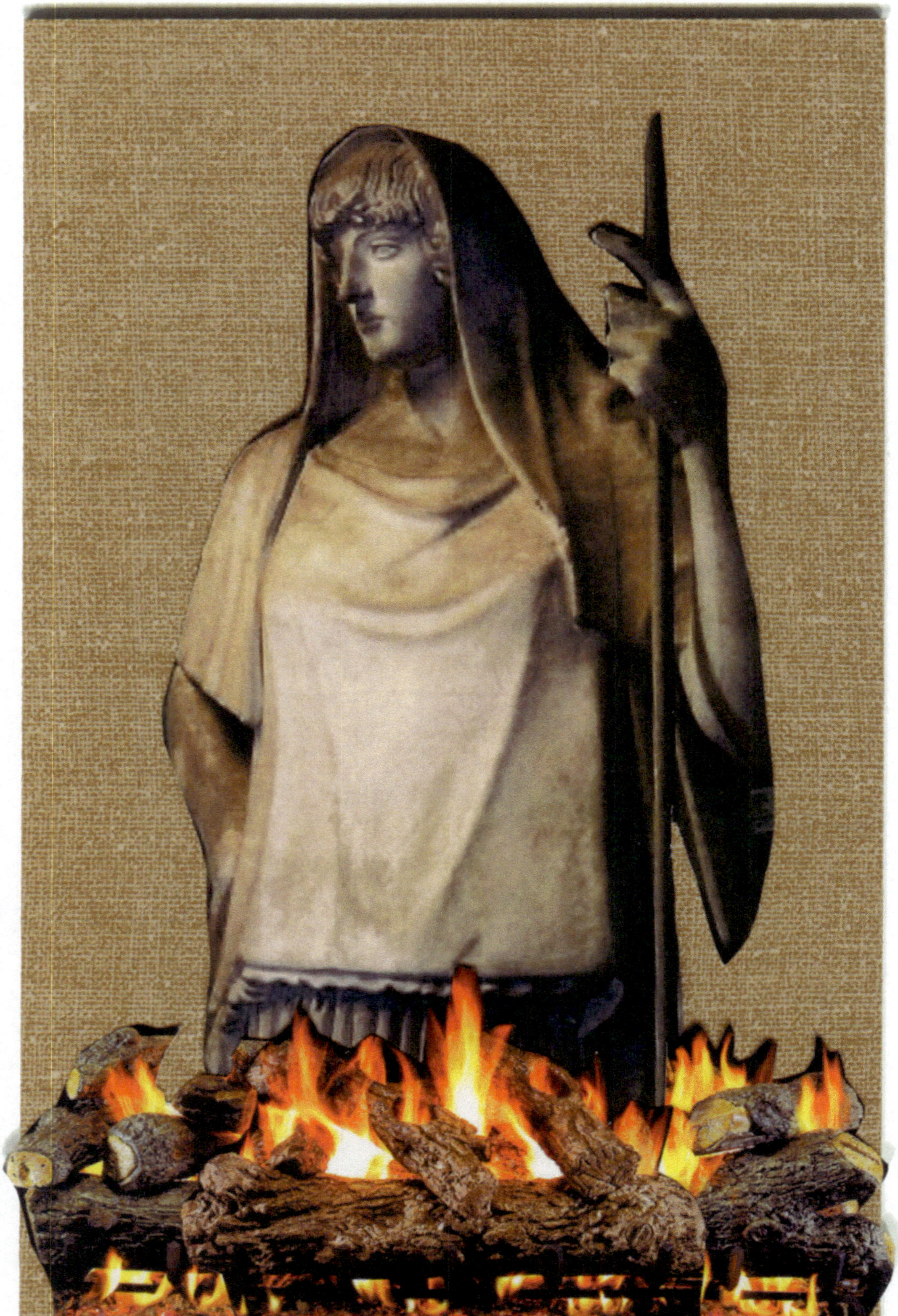

# Chapter Twelve

# Resting and Being Present

DO YOU LISTEN to your tired body and take time to rest? Do you know when your mind is overloaded, and it is time to take a sacred pause and empty out? Do you know when to burrow down and hibernate in rhythm with the waning moon or season? Do you listen to the wisdom of your body, mind, heart, soul, spirit? Do you know when it is time to put aside the to-do list, quiet the Inner Worrywart, release the frantic drive to accomplish and acquire more, to improve and impress, and *just Be*?

For women, learning to slow down, put the brakes on, stop, and breathe can feel like an impossible dream, always just out of reach. The problem is women too often do not give themselves permission to rest, stop, and say "no." Perhaps you fear your Inner Critic will admonish you for being lazy, useless, and unproductive, heaping guilt and shame upon your tired Self. That is how you end up feeling burnt out, depleted, irritable, and grumpy. Yet there is probably no more important tenet of self-care than making time to rest and be present. This includes developing better sleep habits, turning down requests and demands on your time and energy that you really do not want to do, and giving yourself the space to breathe and be with your Self.

To help you with this aspect of self-care look to Hestia, the Greek Goddess of the home and hearth and "Keeper of the Flame," and Sophia, the Judeo-Christian goddess of spiritual wisdom and inner knowing.

## Irene's Story

Irene is at a point in her life where she feels the need to learn to do less and be more. She has always prided herself on getting things done but realizes she has become a workaholic. She spends long hours at the office and seldom says no when her boss asks her to take on another project, although she resents it. She is not getting enough sleep and knows she is getting burnt out.

Irene moved into a new place a year ago but has had little time to fix it up and make it comfortable. Gardening gives her great joy and a sense of peace, but she has little energy for her favorite pastime. She feels like she is losing herself and knows something has to give. She longs for time to beautify her home and spend time there journaling, gardening, resting, and caring for herself. She knows that only when she decides she is worth it and deserves time to herself will she change this lifelong habit of overdoing it.

Hestia is an ally in your need for rest and relaxation by teaching you the importance of tending your inner fire as well as your home environment. She supports you in creating sanctuary—a place to rest and recoup.

Sophia, the Greek word for Wisdom, is mentioned in the Bible and thought to be part of the trinity in the form of the Holy Spirit. This feminine aspect of the tripart Father, Son, and Holy Ghost has been hidden and remains a phantom presence from the patriarchal perspective. Sophia reminds you of your own well-earned wisdom and deep sense of peace, which keeps you connected to spirit and your soul's yearnings.

# Hestia

Hestia is the Greek goddess of the flame (known as Vesta in Roman mythology). Even though revered and well-known in ancient times, very few artistic portrayals of her exist. Because she resided in the eternal flame of the hearthfire, it was believed that Hestia could not be adequately captured by iconography. In her few depictions, she usually wears a veil to obscure her face.

# Hestia's Story

Hestia was the oldest daughter of the Titan couple, Cronus, the sky god, and Rhea, the earth mother. You may remember from Hera's story that Cronus swallowed his children so none would usurp him. Hestia was the oldest child and the first one he consumed. Rhea was able to spare Zeus, the youngest child, by tricking Cronus into swallowing a stone instead. Zeus was given unto the care of woodland nymphs on Crete, then returned as an adult to free his siblings from his father's belly, and take his father's place. Devotees called her "Hestia First and Last," because she was the firstborn and thus first swallowed and the last to emerge from Cronus's stomach. All six siblings became Olympian gods and goddesses when they overthrew the old Titan gods.

Hestia, as the eldest Olympian, was venerated throughout the ancient Greek and Roman worlds. She received the first offering of food and the last libation of wine at every household meal and temple feast. She is a virgin goddess, meaning, as you have learned, that she is psychologically free to be herself, and is not beholden to any man. In fact, unusual for goddesses, she had no children or male consorts, though Poseidon and Apollo tried to win her heart. She was the antithesis of Aphrodite, goddess of love and beauty, who had many consorts—gods and mortals. Hestia was the quiet, passive one, most content tending to domestic duties of home and hearth on her own, albeit with a rich inner life.

Hearth fires were important in ancient times, not only in the home, but also in the temples, the places of community worship and ritual. The ancients considered the hearth a holy altar and kept the flame burning as a symbol of life, warmth, sustenance, and plenty. Hestia means "fireplace" or "altar." Priestesses who tended the temple fires in Greece were also called *hestia*. They were known as *vestal* virgins in the Roman world.

When you pay attention to the stirrings of your soul, Hestia is with you. She guides you in self-care by reminding you when it is time to tend the hearth of your own Being. It may be time to put your house in order, quiet down, and rest. She is an archetypal homebody who teaches you how to hibernate for the winter by cozying up to a fire, settling in with a blanket and a good book. You may enjoy puttering around the house cooking delicious food, creating and crafting as you feel moved, or simply doing nothing. If your soul is the hearth of your being, then Hestia teaches you to tend it.

- When you quiet down, stop moving, listen to the sound of your own breath, and feel it moving through you, you are in touch with Hestia.
- When you set aside your agenda and allow yourself enough time and space to relax and do nothing, you are in touch with Hestia.
- When you give yourself a day or week off, a staycation, you are in touch with Hestia.
- When you find yourself contentedly creating art or crafting, gardening, cooking, or tidying up, you are in touch with Hestia.
- When you crave silence and need to be alone for a time, you are in touch with Hestia.
- When you feather your nest and create a comfy, cozy home or inner sanctuary within your home, you are in touch with Hestia.
- When you make a fire or light a candle to provide warmth, light, mood, and comfort, you are in touch with Hestia.
- When you choose your own company in place of distractions and people who want more from you than you can give, you are in touch with Hestia.
- When you choose solitude or singlehood, you are in touch with Hestia.

For some, especially introverts, Hestia may come more easily; but for those who are more extroverted and who place a high value on being busy, productive, and surrounded by people, it may be more challenging to align with Hestia. She guides you to learn to be alone and find meaning without being lonely or bored. She teaches you the value of solitude and what it means to be at home with yourself.

This means finding sustenance in *Being, not Doing*, as well as *Being Enough* without needing someone else to fill the void, take care of you, or validate you. Being in touch with Hestia does not mean you cannot be in partnership or lovingly raise children; she just asks you to fill your own vessel first and to know when you need refilling before giving more to others. Hestia reminds you to be present with your partner and your children and find time to *just be with them* without distractions and constant busy-ness.

While she is a goddess of home and hearth, she is also a goddess who enjoys being in her own backyard, for there she can be with herself in nature, close to home. This is an important way to fill herself up—finding comfort in and around her home and garden. She has much in common with the Hermit archetype, though she may enjoy being with others at times, especially those who come to visit her in her sanctuary.

Hestia teaches you self-care in the form of being comfortable with your *Self*—slowing down; creating and inhabiting a comfy home; nurturing yourself with good food, rest, and sleep. She encourages you to create beauty and enjoy solitude without feeling lonely, because you are enough.

## Goddess Rituals to Help You Get Blessed Sleep

Rest and relaxation include a good night's sleep, which helps you have energy throughout the day, increased productivity, a better mood, and the ability to handle stress and other day-to-day challenges more easily. Call in the goddess to help you change habits that are not working for you and try these instead.

**Yoga Nidra**

*Nidra* means sleep in Hindi and refers to a Hindu *deva* or divine being of sleep as well as the yogic practice of deep relaxation. If you have tried yoga, you are probably familiar with the deep, meditative state, usually reserved for the end of a yoga class, called *savasana* or corpse pose.

To practice this yourself, dim the lights and lie flat on your back with your arms at your side, palms up, legs outstretched, and jaw soft, in a relaxed position with eyes closed. You are doing your best to approximate a corpse—lying very still—while you breathe slowly and deeply. It is helpful to bring your attention to your third eye as you do this and imagine closing it off to the world. The third eye chakra, above and between your eyebrows, is where the pineal gland, which releases melatonin, the sleep hormone, is located.

The idea in yoga nidra is to withdraw from your senses, except for hearing if listening to music, a guided meditation, or your yoga teacher's voice. This pose helps you achieve delta wave sleep—a deep, restorative relaxation with subtle awareness, similar to what you would experience during hypnosis. Studies show that relaxing like this with no distractions for 10-30 minutes helps with anxiety, trauma, depression, insomnia, menstrual problems, and general improvement of health and well-being. Thirty minutes of yoga nidra is equivalent to a two-hour nap. You will find that sleep is often the best meditation.

**Progressive Muscle Relaxation**

Here is a way to relax your body and prepare for sleep. Practice it when lying in corpse pose or in bed at night to release tension in each body part. Start at your feet, first tensing and then consciously relaxing this body part, imagining sending your breath to it. Then move up to your ankles, wiggling them and releasing them as you breathe. Move up to your legs, tightening and letting go, then up to your hips, pelvis, tummy, chest, arms, hands, neck, and face, in turn clenching and then releasing. You often do not realize you are holding tension in various body parts until you check in and allow each part to soften and relax as you breathe slowly through this progression.

**Good Sleep Hygiene**

If you have trouble falling asleep, make sure you are preparing yourself for the sacred time of sleeping and dreaming. This means creating a sleep ritual that works for you. Once you decide *when* you want to be in bed, begin to prepare an hour before by sipping a cup of hot herbal tea or golden milk, dimming lights, and turning off computers, phones, and other screens. Stop doing any sort of busy work, although before your hour of slow-down starts, you might want to tidy your room or write in your journal, jotting down any troubling thoughts or things to do tomorrow. This way it is off your mind as you start the hour to decelerate and give your brain and body a needed break.

If music helps you unwind, play soothing music during this hour. Take a hot bath by candlelight or with a night light (all bright lights off). Soak in Epsom salts, a CBD bath bomb, or relaxing essential oils like lavender. Burn incense or use a diffuser to perfume the air. Meditate at your altar, asking for sound sleep and peaceful dreams. Put a moonstone or other sleep-enhancing crystal (e.g., amethyst, calcite, selenite) by your bed or under your pillow. Consider an eye pillow, sleep mask, or noise-canceling earbuds. Listen to a guided meditation. Try Progressive Muscle Relaxation again if you wake up in the middle of the night. Sweet dreams!

*Note: Drinking alcohol before bedtime does not help with restful sleep. You are more likely to wake up in the middle of the night or have restless sleep rather than a peaceful slumber. Likewise eating or snacking before bed is not conducive to a good night's rest. It is best to stop eating two to three hours before bedtime.*

# Hestia Speaks

Dear Daughter, I am with you, ever-present in the flame, in the heart of your home. Anytime you want to call me in, light a candle or make a fire and invite me to come. I will gladly come and sit beside you. I will happily dream with you, rest with you, and help you feather your nest.

I love living a simple life, free of worry and extra things to do and buy. Take inventory of the things you truly need in your life, ones important to your daily rituals and well-being. Then ask yourself if there are things you are doing and acquiring that you could live without. Take note of how you are spending your time and money, and ask if there are excesses or energy drains you can begin to eliminate. See what it feels like to let some things go and say no to what does not serve your highest good. Appreciate the beauty of the old, familiar, and known objects and surroundings in your home. Notice how you feel when you live more simply, more mindfully.

My vestal virgins tend my temples. They keep the place clean and tidy. They make it comfortable, beautiful, and sacred. They stoke the fire and light candles. They serve delicious food and drink. Call in your Inner Vestal Virgin to do the same for you in your temple. Ask yourself what your home needs and does not need, and make it a shrine to your True Self.

## Objects and Symbols to Consider for Your Altar to Hestia

**Colors:** red, yellow, white, black

**Objects:** candle, incense burner, scarf or veil, chalice

**Gemstones:** dolomite, obsidian, garnet

**Flowers:** poppy, gloriosa (fire or flame lily), red or yellow sunflowers

**Element:** fire

**Chakra:** root (1st chakra)

If you share a space with someone, find one room or area to call your own. Create sanctuary there. Create an altar there. Create art there. Create your life there. Welcome to my world, Daughter.

Irene found that she had much in common with Hestia once she gave herself permission to set boundaries and put herself first. She realized that when she was on her deathbed, it would not be her boss by her side, but her family and friends, whom she had neglected. She was determined to give herself more time with them and to herself.

Irene negotiated shorter work hours and took some accumulated vacation time so she could rest and reset. She went to bed earlier and gave herself a break from the internet and worldly distractions. She took time to putter in her garden, beautify her new home, and invite friends over for dinner. She learned to be more present by practicing yoga, meditation, and breathing exercises. She made an altar to Hestia on her fireplace mantel, where she could look for Hestia in the flame and be reminded of her own inner temple, which she was now committed to tending whole-heartedly.

# Sophia

The goddess Sophia personifies wisdom and peaceful presence. Her ancient Hebrew name was *Chokhmah,* who became the Goddess Asherah, once worshipped as the Goddess alongside Yahweh, the Hebrew name for God.

She became widely known as Sophia, which means *Inner Knowing* in Gnosticism. The Gnostics were an early Christian sect born out of Jewish mysticism who believed in a direct, personal connection to God without need of intercession. The Kabbalah, which provides an esoteric interpretation of the Bible in the Jewish tradition, sees Sophia as the female expression of God and co-creator. Sophia symbolizes God's deeper, hidden, meaning—his feminine soul. She is the wise mediator between God and humanity, resolving the dualism of masculine and feminine, logos and eros (head and heart), spirit and matter.

From these beginnings in the Judeo-Christian tradition, Sophia can be seen as the feminine face of God. She is the divine feminine counterpart, the creative vessel, known as Goddess, to the divine masculine counterpart, the activating force, known as God. In this understanding, God is androgynous and contains both of these energies, as do all humans regardless of their gender identification.

Sophia is closely aligned with Isis, the ancient Egyptian goddess of wisdom and a divine feminine avatar for thousands of years throughout the Mideast, Africa, and Europe. When Christianity took hold, there was concern among the patriarchal powers that Isis, whose temples abounded throughout the ancient world, might now be venerated and called Sophia. So the Roman church pushed her underground and began to speak of God only as a He. They didn't even speak of her as part of the trinity, although logically the third aspect with father and son would be mother. But as the Holy Spirit she is still here if you are willing to see and accept her presence.

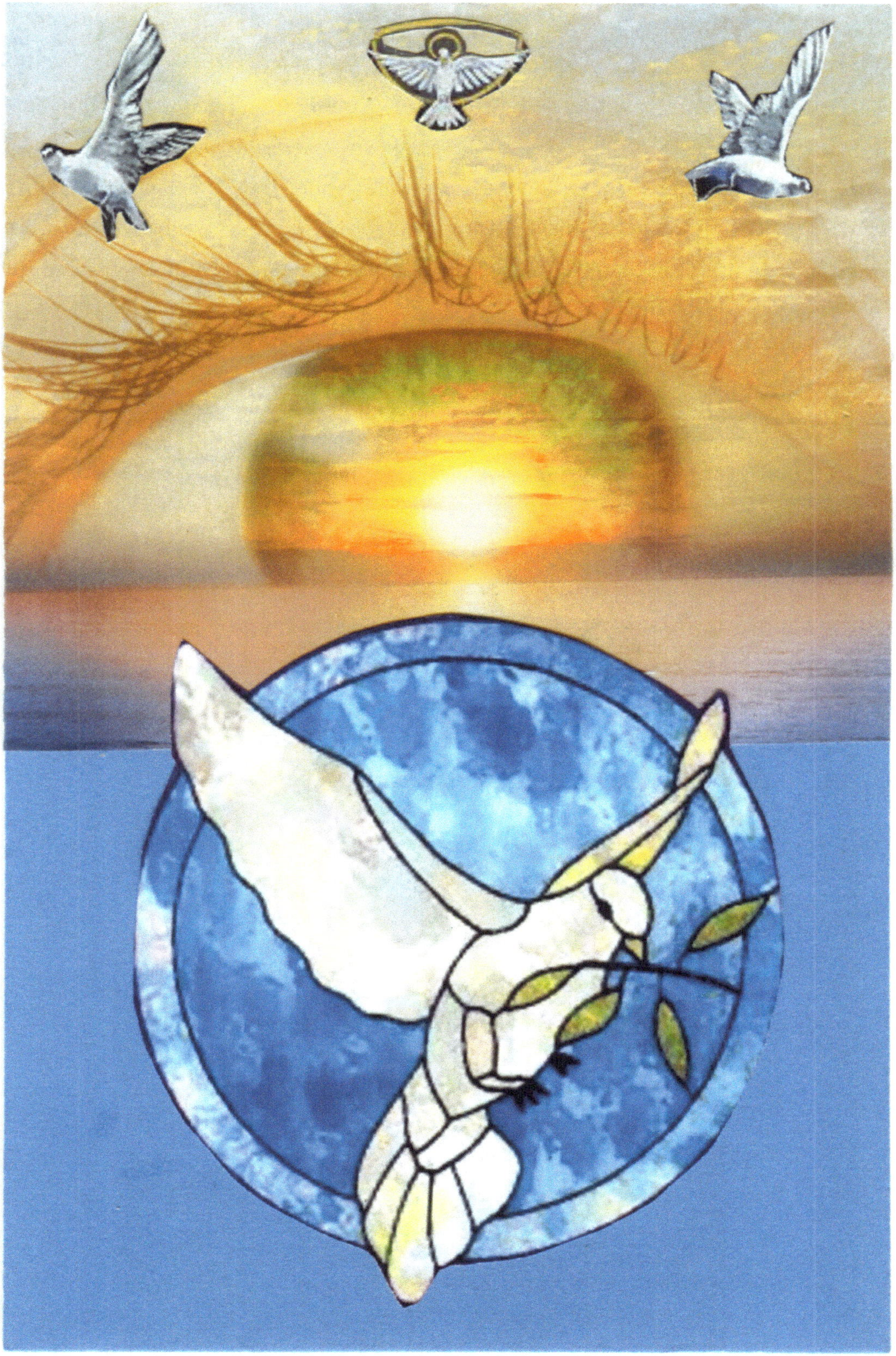

# The Story of Sophia

Sophia was born of silence and became the Mother of All. She is the *world soul*, the *divine spark* within each human being. In Gnosticism she is the *syzygy* or twin flame of Christ, and is sometimes conflated with Mary Magdalene. One of the lost Gnostic Gospels, the *Pistis Sophia* (101:15-18) says of Jesus, "His consort is the Great Sophia who from the first was destined in him for union." She was responsible for creating the material world and human beings, containing both feminine and masculine energies, equal in value.

One of Sophia's progeny, according to the Gnostics, was the serpent who tempted Eve in the Garden of Eden. When Eve ate the apple from the Tree of Knowledge of Good and Evil, humans were initiated into the material world, where ignorance was no longer bliss. Humans were now conscious of the world, including suffering, learning, growing, and aspiring to the spiritual realms of God and Goddess from whence they originated. They now had to learn to distinguish between good and evil—the knowledge that one doesn't have in infancy (innocence) and only gains through maturity (experience).

Sophia is a being that is one with the Tree of Life, another tree in the Garden of Eden alongside the Tree of Knowledge. Like the branches of the trees that extend heavenward, she serves as a bridge to the spiritual realm of existence, guiding her children to aspire to their own higher power.

*"All Her paths are peace. She is a tree of life." (Proverbs 3:17-18)*

She is a Tree of Life

The wisdom books of the Bible and other religious writings refer to her as "Hagia Sophia," meaning *Holy Wisdom*, and as such, she forms half of God's light. She is another way of naming the divine. In Michelangelo's famous painting on the ceiling of the Sistine Chapel, *The Creation of Adam*, the golden-haired woman whom God has one arm around is thought to be Sophia—the Mother God to his Father God.

The Hagia Sophia, the Eighth Wonder of the World, is a monument in the center of Istanbul (once Constantinople). It was built by the Roman Emperor Constantine, and for a thousand years it was an Orthodox Christian cathedral. (Constantine was the first to legalize Christianity and codify the New Testament to consolidate power between the church and state.) The church then

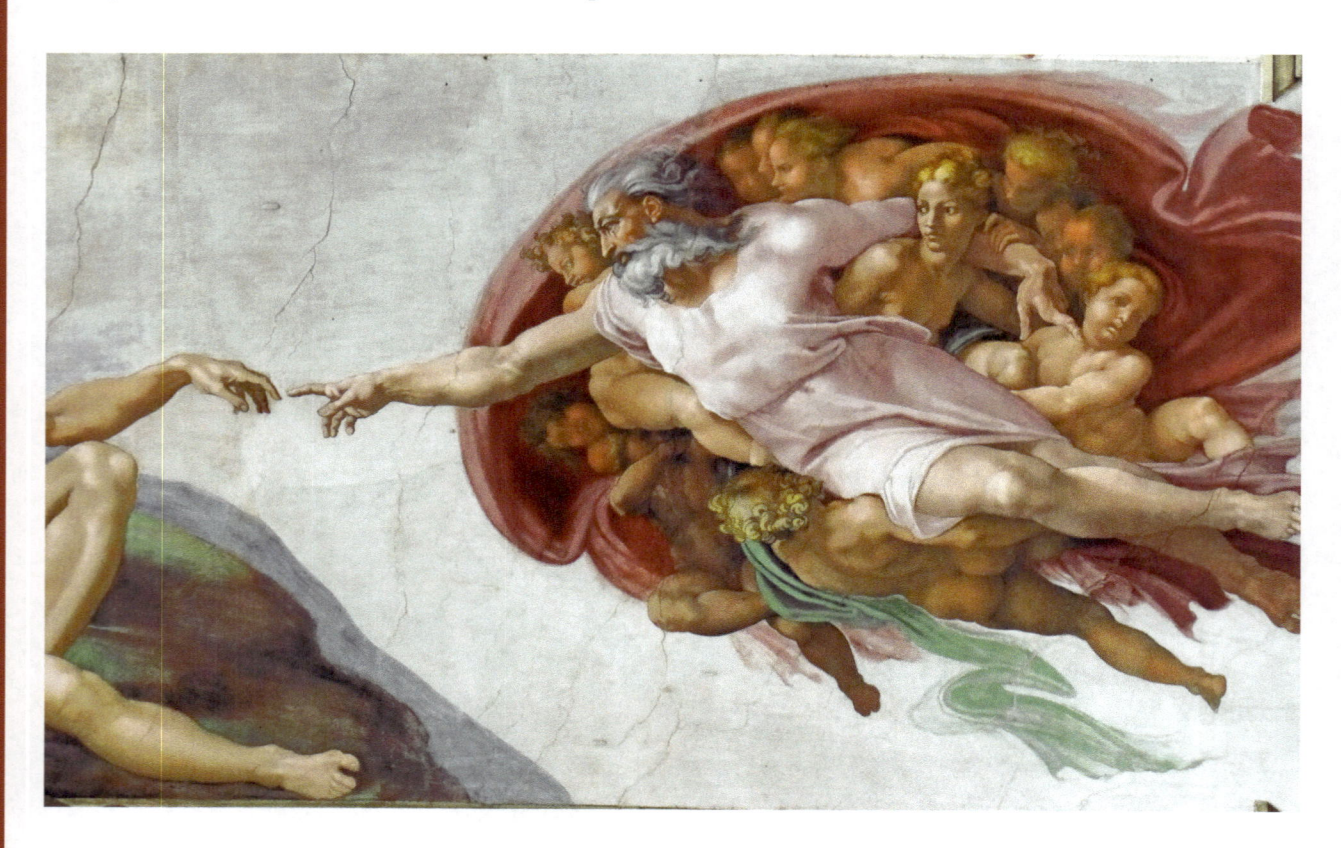

became a Muslim mosque for seven hundred years and later a museum and world heritage site. Built and named for the goddess, this shrine to Holy Wisdom stands as a symbol of harmony and peace as well as religious tolerance. Today it is once again a mosque.

The patriarchal religions marginalized the Goddess Sophia and all but lost sight of her, yet *She* is here and always has been. When you seek her, you will find her. She is ever-present. She is described as a mother, teacher, tree of life, counselor, "more precious than jewels," the light, and the law.

Christian feminists reclaim Sophia as part of the Trinity—the feminine Holy Spirit, the source of God's true power. Sophia carries the archetypal energy of an independent woman who is able to support herself, to be empowered in the world, to use her mind—to be both knowledgeable and wise, holding her own alongside men. She guides you to *know what you know* and not hide your knowledge or shrink from it. She gives you the gift of a greater perspective, seeing the bigger picture. She helps you to not sweat the small stuff.

Sophia is often depicted as the winged dove. The dove is a symbol of the Holy Spirit and of the goddesses Inanna, Aphrodite (Venus), and the two Marys (the Virgin Mother and Mary Magdalene). The ancient symbol of the dove is a reminder of her long-abiding divine presence—spirit come to earth through this sacred feminine totem.

When you wish to be present in mind, body, and spirit, and not distracted by worldly matters, call on Sophia to remind you to be in the moment, to remind you of your connection to the feminine divine. Use her help to live in the here and now—not in the past, where depression holds you hostage, and not in the future, where anxieties reign about what may come.

Invite her in; feel the beating wings of the dove of inner peace and breathe a sigh of relief. Stop striving and know that you are enough. See Sophia as the culmination of all your self-care practice. The more you love and take care of yourself, the more you embody your wisdom—the collective wisdom of all you have learned and gained through your lived experience on this earth.

## Make a Timeline

One way to take stock of your experience and accumulated wisdom is to make a timeline of your life, decade by decade. Outline the major milestones and turning points, relationship beginnings and endings, births and deaths, triumphs and mistakes. Then sum up the wisdom you gained in a sentence or two for each decade. See how you have learned from setbacks, overcome obstacles, created beauty, grown stronger, and transformed from Innocence and Naivete to Wisdom and Knowing—all that Sophia embodies. It is important to give yourself credit for all that you have accomplished, for all that you know, for all that you are, and own your power.

# Meditative Practices For Being Present and Quieting Your Mind

- Whatever you do today, do one thing at a time and allow yourself to be fully present with the task or activity, taking your time to do it mindfully. This includes making the bed, washing dishes, raking leaves, taking a walk in nature, making a meal, wrapping presents, dressing for work, driving your car, putting your kids to bed, etc.
- Take a day or weekend off from technology. Turn off the television, radio, phone, computer, and other devices. Notice how it feels to live and breathe without constant distraction.
- Enjoy uninterrupted silence while you eat a meal, make art, or just sit by a window looking out at the world.
- Sit quietly outside and feel the sun on you, noticing sights, sounds, smells, colors, and textures in nature, without making any value judgments. Just take in the life around you.
- Declutter a room mindfully, getting rid of any and all things that do not bring you a sense of joy or peace. Sit and breathe in the emptied space.
- As you sit, practice breathing while you count: deep breath in for a count of eight, hold for a count of four, and release for a count of eight. Do this until you feel a deep sense of peace.
- Try the 5-4-3-2-1 exercise of slowing down and using your senses. Notice 5 things that you can see; 4 things you can hear; 3 things you can touch; 2 things you can taste; 1 thing you can smell.
- Make an altar, light a candle, and meditate on Hestia in the flame. See her in the fire and intuit what she wants you to know.
- Meditate on Sophia. Invite her to be with you. How do you envision her? Where does she reside in you? Allow an image or symbol to come to you that represents your inner wisdom, a gift from Sophia. Make a SoulCollage® card, art journal page, or other piece of art for this aspect of your being.
- Find something to love about your job/work/situation today, even if it has come to feel routine or uninteresting. Look for new inspiration, another way of doing things, a different perspective.
- Give yourself a day off from your usual routine and choose something to do with your time and energy that feels inspiring, interesting, different. Go at it with Beginner's Mind, the mindset that allows you to start fresh, without preconceptions, setting aside what you know to see what you do not know.

- Do nothing all day and just be with yourself. Take a nap. Notice what gives you comfort. Stay out of past and future thinking and just be quiet and present with yourself today. Time does not always need to be filled.

# Sophia Speaks

Dear Daughter, Wise Soul.

Know that it is never too late.

It is never too late to try something new.

It is never too late to leave a bad relationship.

It is never too late to start a new relationship.

It is never too late to change a habit.

It is never too late to leave a bad situation or job.

It is never too late to move in a different direction.

It is never too late to claim your life and make it what you want it to be.

It is never too late to speak up and take a stand.

It is never too late to be present.

It is never too late to embody your Wisdom.

It is important to see the Wise Woman within and to honor her.

It is I who am you, and it is you who are me.

And wherever you are, I am there.

For I am sown in all, and you collect me from wherever you wish.

And when you collect me, it is your own Self that you collect.

# Objects and symbols to consider for your altar to Sophia

**Colors:** white, blue, purple, gold

**Objects:** image of Sophia, figure of a dove or tree, white feather, candle

**Gemstones:** amethyst, calcite, clear quartz, dendrite agate

**Flowers:** lily, lotus, white rose

**Element:** air

**Chakra:** crown (7th chakra)

# Journal Prompts

What, if anything, makes it difficult to be alone or in solitude? What would it take to find more comfort being with just yourself?

What, if anything, makes it difficult for you to slow down and rest or take time for yourself? How could Hestia or Sophia help you?

Is there anything about your living environment that you would like to change or make more comfortable? How can Hestia help you make a room a sanctuary or your house a home?

What helps you have a good night's sleep? What hinders you? What steps are you willing to take to change your sleep habits?

What archetypal qualities do you share with Hestia, goddess of the hearth?

What archetypal qualities do you relate to with the goddess Sophia? What is her gift to you?

What does your inner Wise Woman or Goddess Self want you to know at this point in your life?

How does the idea of the feminine face of God sit with you? How do you imagine the feminine aspect of God might differ from the masculine aspect?

What would be an ideal day off for you? How would you spend it? How could you give yourself this gift?

What mindfulness practice would you like to make a daily habit? How can Hestia or Sophia help you with that?

# Resources

The following is a list of resources to help you find your creative mojo and bring the divine feminine to life through collaging, painting, journaling, writing. Many of the artists and teachers listed have written books and offer online and in-person workshops and retreats to help you get started. You are encouraged to find local teachers, classes, and communities to explore the creative path your passion leads you to.

**Art Journaling**

    Everything Art: everything-art.com
    Artful Haven: artfulhaven.com/how-to-start-an-art-journal/#what-is-an-art-journal
    Your Visual Journal: yourvisualjournal.com/art-journal

**Painting**

    Fresh Paint - Flora Bowley: florabowley.com
    Art Becomes You - Alena Hennessy: alenahennessy.com
    Tracy Verdugo: tracyverdugo.com

**SoulCollage®**

    Learn more about the creative process of making collaged cards with found images that combine psychological and spiritual insights into the Self at: SoulCollage.com

**Writing**

    Find Your Voice/Tell Your Stories - Jennifer Louden: jenniferlouden.com
    Learn to write from published authors who teach you about their craft: Masterclass.com
    Become a Writer Today (with resources for journal writing): becomeawritertoday.com
    Katie Wolf, writer, editor, coach - thekatiewolf.com

# Acknowledgments

Thank you to the many guides and helpers, both human and divine, who helped me bring this book to fruition.

As for the humans, I am ever grateful to Karen Regina, Henry Cordes, and Chloe Ladd for their thoughtful editing.

Many thanks to Heather Dakota for designing a beautiful book in keeping with my vision.

Thank you to my friend and soul sister, Pixie Lighthorse, for inspiring and encouraging me to take creative leaps.

I could not have done this without the technical and emotional support of Rob Ladd, my loving and steadfast partner in life.

# About the Author

Stephanie Anderson Ladd is a psychotherapist, feminist, and archetypal explorer. Her practice focuses on the psychological and spiritual means to better understand the Self. She teaches classes, leads workshops, and speaks on the divine feminine and various goddesses, as well as on myths, fairy tales, tarot, and SoulCollage®.

Learn more at **stephanieandersonladd.com**

Printed in Poland
by Amazon Fulfillment
Poland Sp. z o.o., Wrocław